MYSTERIOUS
CELTIC
MYTHOLOGY
IN
AMERICAN
FOLKLORE

MYSTERIOUS
CELTIC
MYTHOLOGY
IN
AMERICAN
FOLKLORE

BOB CURRAN

PELICAN PUBLISHING COMPANY
GRETNA 2010

To my wife, Mary, for all her help and support while writing this book and to Michael and Jennifer for their faith in their father

The word "Pelican" and the depiction of a pelican are trademarks of Pelican Publishing Company, Inc., and are registered in the U.S. Patent and Trademark Office.

Library of Congress Cataloging-in-Publication Data

Curran, Bob.
  Mysterious Celtic mythology in American folklore / Bob Curran.
    p. cm.
  Includes bibliographical references and index.
  ISBN 978-1-58980-743-3 (hardcover : alk. paper) 1. Folklore—United States. 2. Celts—Folklore. 3. Mythology, Celtic—United States. I. Title.
  GR105.C87 2010
  398.20973—dc22
                                        2010008649

Printed in the United States of America

Published by Pelican Publishing Company, Inc.
1000 Burmaster Street, Gretna, Louisiana 70053

Contents

Introduction

There have always been strong connections between the western Celtic world and America. In earliest history, tales of Celtic monks who are said to have traveled to the shores of the New World are plentiful and varied. Other ancient travelers allegedly found their way to "strange lands" which, from the descriptions, were most probably the eastern shores of the American continent, where, according to legend, they set up small settlements and colonies.

During the seventeenth and eighteenth centuries, Celtic religious dissidents—Catholic Irish, Presbyterian Scots, Breton spinners and weavers, and many others—fled to American shores to avoid religious intolerance in their homelands. They set up communities in the nearly inaccessible mountains, remote hollows, and deep swamps of the country where their beliefs and traditions could flourish in a vast new land. In their wake came those fleeing hardship and disease—linen slumps in the North of Ireland, typhoid and cholera in the south, the Irish Potato Famine and bad harvests in the West of Scotland and in Wales. All of these became absorbed into the rich social mix that was to form early and developing America.

And, besides their physical possessions, each one of these migrant peoples brought with them their own culture, tradition, and perspective. These were deeply imbedded in the songs they sang, the stories they told, the beliefs they held; in essence, they were a part of the people themselves. And it was these traditions, these perspectives and interpretations, that helped the migrants settle in an unfamiliar place and overcome the hardships they were to face there. Therefore, it was this rich cultural mix that helped to shape the developing American nation. Although the continent now boasts a "modern" cultural identity, many of these early visions still underpin the way in which Americans view themselves, touching on their deepest fears and thoughts. All across the land, the idea of darkness drawing in around some small rural community or of unseen spirits among the woods or mountains or along the rivers is not really all that far away.

It is not surprising then that many of the oldest tales seem to have a supernatural aspect. Many of them have their basis in old Celtic wonder stories; they are tales of spirits—which the Celts believed lived in the rocks, trees, and streams all around them—but they also reflect the awe and mystery of the country they now called their own. The ideas they brought with them from the Celtic lands were now transposed onto the American countryside. The ghosts and demons that had frightened them back in Western Europe also frightened them in America, albeit in different guises. The spirits which lurked in the European forests now lurked just beyond the outskirts of their settlements and on the edges of their towns. Areas similar to those they had considered sacred or terrifying in Europe were to be found in America as well. This ancient consciousness has been molded and adapted throughout American history, lying just below the surface of American society, surfacing from time to time in local folktales and in rural cultural perspectives. It merged with older and indigenous tales told by the early Spanish and the Native Americans, together with the legends of other immigrants, to develop a curious hybrid lore which is, arguably, found nowhere else in the world.

This book is both an examination and a celebration of the folkloric and cultural connections between America and Celtic Western Europe. It explores the underpinning motifs and traditions that have created the rich corpus of tales, stories, and legends that are still common throughout America today. Here are tales of ghosts, spirits, dark people, and evil places that have been brought from the Celtic world and grafted onto the traditions of the New World. These are the legends of American nightmare that can trace their origins back into the mists of Celtic folklore. For all our so-called modern culture, the ancient mysteries and enigmas are still amongst us.

MYSTERIOUS
CELTIC
MYTHOLOGY
IN
AMERICAN
FOLKLORE

Part 1
Lost and Fabulous Kingdoms

Alabama

The Legend of Prince Madoc

Almost from the earliest times when our forebears began to travel, there have been legends of mysterious kingdoms ruled by extraordinary individuals. Giants, ogres, witches, and dwarves were all believed to control lands that lay beyond the horizon, beyond the ocean, beyond the sky, or just out of normal vision. Travelers returned with tales of mythical countries where immortal queens presided over affairs of state (the basis of Henry Rider Haggard's classic novel *She*) or where men with supernatural powers held sway. With the dawn of the medieval period and wider travel and trade, such tales only increased. Many descriptions of these fabulous realms reflected the hopes and aspirations of the people themselves. In a world riven by war, disease, famine, and poverty, the thought of a marvelous kingdom somewhere beyond the seas must have seemed incredibly appealing. For people who were hard-pressed by tyrannical politics and religious intolerance, stories of a country where peace and freedom reigned was the embodiment of all their dreams.

One of the most prevalent of such stories throughout the West during the twelfth and thirteenth centuries was that of the exotic paradise ruled by the mythical Christian monarch Prester John. This beneficent king who reputedly ruled somewhere in the Far East exercised a persistent and powerful fascination in the minds of many medieval writers. References to him are first found in the reports of Otto of Freising around 1145. This report is most certainly a secondhand account and may be based upon a garbled report of an actual battle near Samarkand near the Quatvan Steppe in 1141. Otto himself claimed to have heard it from the lips of Bishop Hugh of Jabala while traveling in Lebanon. Near Samarkand, the forces of the Seljuk Sultan Sanjar were defeated by a Christian army sent by the mysterious "Presbyter Johannes," a "Priest King from the East." It was from this source that the story grew, drawing upon certain Biblical sources and Hebrew legends, embroidered by fanciful travelers' romances. Then, in approximately 1165, a letter purporting to be from "John, Priest by the Almighty power of God . . . King of Kings and Lord of Lords" was sent to various Western kings; to the Byzantine emperor, Manuel I Comnensus; and to Pope Alexander III. This letter, which was strongly Biblical in tone and written in a number of languages, including Latin and Teutonic, described a wonderful country of peace and tranquility so far away in the East as to be almost inaccessible. Interpretations as to the location of this country abounded. Some scholars claimed that this could be the court of the Khans on the borders of China; others claimed that it might be India while still others claimed that Prester John's kingdom lay somewhere in what is now present-day Ethiopia in Africa. The idea of a wonderful country ruled over by a strange king caught the medieval mind and percolated down through the ages as an ideal of something weird and exotic. It has certainly retained its fascination to the present day.

As the settlement of the American continent continued, tales of mysterious kingdoms began to surface there too. Many of these realms were connected with ancient travelers who reputedly came to the new lands and founded communities there. Some of the tales concern monks—for example, St. Brendan, who allegedly journeyed from Ireland to settle on the American east coast, leaving behind certain of his Brothers when he returned home again. And there may be some shred of truth in this since Celtic monks often traveled unimaginable distances to carry the word of God.

The most persistent tale, however, relates to a kingdom in the American southern states, which was ruled over by a Welsh prince, Madoc. Like Prester John, Madoc was a Christian king and his realm was an incredibly tranquil region even though it was surrounded by pagan Indians, with whom many of Madoc's followers intermarried. The story lingers even today, but is there any truth in it? Could medieval travelers have indeed come from Wales and settled somewhere in the American south? What evidence do we have for such a claim?

In a letter to Maj. Amos Stoddard, written in 1810, John Sevier, first governor of Tennessee and an authority on American Indians, recounted a fascinating tale. He had met with a Frenchman (whose name is not given) who had been captured by the Cherokee and lived amongst them for some considerable time. During his captivity, the Frenchman told Sevier, the Cherokee had traded with a tribe of Indians living on the Missouri River who had spoken a strange dialect, which he had later identified as a form of Welsh. The females of this tribe were exceptionally fair skinned and his Cherokee captors told the Frenchman that they had sprung from a group of white people who had come along the river in a distant time. Later, the explorers Lewis and Clark would hear the same stories concerning a tribe of Indians who adopted a superior— almost "European"—manner with regard to their neighbors. Their lifestyle was also said to have been more "cultured" than any of the tribes around them. They were known as the Mandans and William Clark, who was subsequently in charge of Indian Affairs between 1822 and 1838, believed that Mandan women were amongst the most beautiful in the world. Their features, he declared, were more like those of European women than of Native American Indians. There was also an old legend amongst the Mandans that they had come across water in wooden canoes and, using the river systems, had found their way into Missouri.

The painter George Catlin, who lived among the Mandans in the 1830s, also believed that they had European (specifically Welsh) origins. He pointed out that they constructed permanent homes, laid out very much in the style of a medieval town—with streets and squares and surrounded with a picket fence or a trench. They sailed up the rivers in small, round, tublike boats made from rawhide and stretched over frames of willow—just like Celtic coracles. Catlin also noted that their jewelry bore certain motifs that closely resembled Celtic design and was made using closely guarded secrets unknown to other Indian tribes. Lastly, he observed that there were "many complexions" amongst them, including various colors of hair and that some of the women had eyes that were almost blue or hazel.

No real verification of Catlin's assessment can be made today. The Mandans were virtually wiped out in a smallpox epidemic in 1837, dwindling from a nation of 15,000 to a handful of 125 survivors. Those who did survive were rapidly absorbed into the surrounding indigenous tribes. Today, while some vestiges of the tribe remain, they constitute only about 300 individuals of mixed blood and all traces of their original language have vanished.

The most astonishing story linguistically and physically linking Indians to Welsh settlers, however, was recounted by Francis Lewis, one of the signatories of the Declaration of Independence. During the War of Independence, following the fall of Oswego, he was captured near Albany, New York, by a group of unidentified Indians. Struck by their physical similarity to Europeans (one is said to have had traces of a beard; another, blue eyes) Lewis paid attention to their language, which sounded similar to an imperfect dialect of Welsh. Speaking the language himself, Lewis spoke to them in the Welsh tongue and asked for his freedom. The Indian chief replied in halting Welsh and ordered him to be set free. A similar tale is told by a Welsh minister who, captured by some Indians along the Missouri and seemingly condemned to death, fell to his knees and in his native tongue asked God to spare his life. He was astonished to find that the Indians understood what he said and immediately freed him. Whether these stories are true is another matter, but legends of a "European-looking" Welsh-speaking Indian tribe are so persistent that they cannot be completely ignored. However, with the general demise and disappearance of the Mandan nation (which appeared to be the commonly agreed tribe in this respect), such tales are unverifiable.

If the Mandans are now gone, what other suggestions are there for supposing that Welshmen settled in America in medieval times? Perhaps the most compelling remains are the stone fortifications along several small creeks near Chattanooga. They bear striking similarities to the defensive forts of ancient Wales. According to Judge John Haywood, writing in 1823 in his book *The Civil and Political History of Tennessee,* there were originally five such forts, designed in a circle around present-day Chattanooga, that, according to legend, had been built by white people long before the Indians came to the land. Now under Chickamauga Lake, a large defensive position was situated at the mouth of the Chickamauga Creek, near a settlement called Dallas. According to Irene Parker in her book *The Welsh Connection,* written in 1970, a second fort lay roughly twenty miles from Chickamauga Creek and yet another at a place named Pumpkinville on the Hiwassee River, now the site of Athens, Tennessee. The major fortification, however, was situated on the Duck River near Manchester, Tennessee, and this was locally referred to as the Old Stone Fort. The walls of this stronghold were alleged to be some twenty feet thick. The fifth fort was situated at Fort Mountain in Georgia. There appears to have been, however, a sixth fort and it is this one that is of particular interest. It was situated at DeSoto Falls, near Mentone, Alabama, and it was noted by an early Kentucky surveyor that it bore remarkable similarities to Dolwyddelan Castle in Gwynedd, Wales (the presumed birthplace of Madoc). He also noted that it had been built in quite a unique style, a style that was common in medieval Europe. This was confirmed by members of the local Echota Cherokee who stated that none of the Cherokee or any other Indians of the southeast area had ever built such complex defensive structures. They had simply thrown up circular earthen ramparts to protect their settlements. The fort at DeSoto Falls was built as long, horseshoe-shaped walls slightly crenellated for added cover. Further, they were constructed as double walls so that if one was breached, invaders were confronted by another. In addition there were moats and ditches that surrounded the outer walls for greater defense. Such architecture was unknown to the Indians but was a feature of many European castles and walled towns and cities. Old Stone Fort and Fort Mountain were both situated on high and dangerous bluffs and had small entrances very much in the style of Celtic fortifications. Over the years, the moats were filled in with dirt and shrubs and the walls fell under the weight of creepers. Ruins of the DeSoto Falls fortification stood until the early 1920s when locals began to use the stone in the construction of roads and dams. Some of it was even used for the building of summerhouses and for repairing existing dwellings in the vicinity. Worked stone was a valuable commodity and those who carried away the remnants of the DeSoto fort claimed that it had been properly cut and had been "stacked" without mortar and must have been expertly chiseled to hold it together—something the indigenous Indian population could not have done.

In addition to the fort, there is a series of small caves at the back of the site where the structure stood, looking down onto the Little River, just below the falls themselves. Although several of these are natural, there is ample evidence that they have been enlarged by cutting tools and that some have been artificially made by the same method. They seem to have been created to guard a narrow path that leads up from the river to the fortification site and it is possible that a handful of men could have created a line of defense against invaders by positioning themselves in these caves and hurling the attackers into the water, some 325 feet below. Again this is more a "European" defensive strategy than an Indian one. Indeed, Indian lore tells that the caves were built by white men who came along the river and wore clothes and beards and carried long metal "sticks" (swords?). Assuming that the Indians were speaking of the Spaniards, who were known to have passed through certain areas of Alabama and Tennessee, Americans named the falls after Hernando de Soto, who was said to have partly explored the region. There is no evidence that de Soto even knew of the existence of the falls, let alone visited them. However, there may be some evidence that de Soto himself had heard of Madoc, because an ancient map purportedly showing the area and allegedly used by the explorer— still extant in Seville—bears the word "Madoc," together with an arrow pointing to the mouth of the Mobile River.

Apart from de Soto's map, there is other evidence that the legendary prince might well have existed and that he may have made the journey to America. Such evidence comes from Wales itself and more specifically from ancient Welsh texts. Around 1590, the eminent seventeenth-century historian and geographer Richard Hakluyt published three folio volumes of early English voyages entitled *Principall Navigations*. Included in this history was an account of Prince Madoc's journey, which Hakluyt had taken from an earlier work by Dr. David Powel (*The Historie of Cambria,* published in 1584) and from Humphry Lloyd's manuscript *Translations and Continuations of Caradoc of Llancarvan,* which itself was based on a manuscript written by an earlier scribe, Gutyn Owen, a renowned Welsh historian and genealogist. According to this history, Prince Madoc was one of the seventeen sons of Owain Gwyneth, king of Gwynedd, a region of northern Cymru (Wales). While a great multiplicity of children may well have been proof of a monarch's virility and prowess, it often led to problems upon his death. This was certainly the case when Owain died in 1169 and a number of these sons disputed the throne. Many of these claimants were considered illegitimate by the church, which denounced their increasingly bloody struggles. The eldest legitimate heir was Jarwarth (Edward), but he suffered from an important disqualification to the succession. Brehon Law—the law system under which many

Celtic lands operated and codified in Wales as the laws of Hywll Dda—decreed that no king with a blemish might rule. This was because the monarch was the personification of both his land and his people and any personal physical imperfection that he or she might have would be translated into the realm. Thus, the great Irish high king Conn of the Hundred Battles was forced to vacate the throne when he lost an eye in conflict. Jarwarth had some form of "facial disfigurement." This may have been nothing more than a birthmark or it may have been something more serious, but it debarred him from the kingship. Another brother named Howell or Hywll came forward to seize the throne of Gwynedd. Howell was older than Jarwarth but was illegitimate. This would not necessarily have barred him from the monarchy (in these times illegitimacy did not carry the same stigma as it would later); however, Howell's mother was Irish and had been only one of Owain's wives. She may even have been a captive. Howell was therefore considered basely born and not fit to assume the kingship. Nevertheless, Howell seized the throne by force and continued to rule until his mother's death shortly after, when he became involved in a campaign in Ireland against his mother's kinsmen. While he was across the sea, yet another brother—Daffyd—grabbed power and killed Howell on his return from Ireland. Daffyd continued to rule by the sword, largely uncontested, until Jarwarth's son Llewellyn came of age and attempted to wrest the throne from him.

In the middle of all this confusion, murder, and mayhem, another brother turned tail and fled for his life. His name was Madoc, and he was also probably illegitimate. Tradition says that he fled to an island of the Culdees. The Culdees were monks of Irish origin whose rule had been established by St. Maelruan of Tallaght (near Dublin). Fiercely austere, their house was cloistered although later they became slightly more worldly. They had a reputation for mysticism and "secret knowledge" and were later denounced as heretics by the more established orders. By the twelfth century, however, though avarice and neglect had taken over from piety and zeal, the Culdees still retained their mystical perceptions and were said to harbor occult secrets. They had spread out through Scotland but there was only one recorded Culdee house in Wales— on Bardsey Island (Ynys Enlli), off the tip of the Lleyn Peninsula on the North Wales coast. It was allegedly from the Culdees that Madoc first heard of a strange paradise far to the west beyond the raging Atlantic Ocean, a place the Celtic monks called the "otherworld." How they themselves had come to know about it is unclear but it may have been from other monks who had possibly made the voyage. Alternatively, it may have been an old Viking tale that the Culdees had picked up.

Returning from Bardsey, Madoc found Gwynedd in utter turmoil. In order to protect his claim to the throne, Daffyd had had three other brothers murdered and his reign was rapidly becoming more and more bloody. But there was also another menace. The reign of Owain Gwyneth, his father, had been characterized by bloody struggles against the English Normans who were expanding their influence from beyond Offa's Dyke. The Normans had now firmly established themselves in the kingdom of Powys and were already making inroads into Gwynedd. There was little for Madoc in his own country except possible death at the hands of his brother or captivity by the Normans. With very little to lose, early in 1170 he sailed a ship into the west with a number of trusted companions to search for the otherworld.

According to legend, the voyage was an arduous one and Madoc is supposed to have landed in the West Indies and in Mexico. However, late in the year, he allegedly sailed his ship into the Gulf of Mexico and dropped anchor in Mobile Bay. The choice of landfall seems to reinforce the idea of the trans-Atlantic journey. The writer Richard Deacon in his *Madoc and the Discovery of America* suggests that the prevailing ocean currents and tides would have naturally carried his ship to the Gulf of Mexico. Once there and seeking a landing site, the prince would have been attracted to the harbor offered by Mobile Bay. The place was a landing for later explorers such as Ponce de Leon, Alonzo de Pineda, Hernando de Soto, and the Portuguese Amerigo Vespucci, after whom the continent is named.

The land to which the voyagers came was lush and green with plenty of fruit and flowers. The climate was warm and pleasant. For hard-pressed Welshmen after a long sea journey, it must indeed have seemed like the otherworld paradise of which the Culdees had spoken. Madoc and his followers reputedly established a small coastal settlement on the shores of the bay then, leaving most of the adventurers behind, he set sail back to Gwynedd, together with a handful of crewmen. His aim was to bring back more colonists to populate this wonderful new land.

When he returned to his native soil, things were no better. Gwynedd was engaged in a bloody struggle against the Normans in Powys, and he seems to have had no difficulty in recruiting Welshmen to return with him to the otherworld. In the year 1171, he set sail once again in the vessel *Gwennon Gorn* on a return journey to the new paradise. This time he did not go alone; he was accompanied by his brother Rhyrd in the ship *St. Peter* as well as a number of women (legend says that at least two of his sisters went with them). The query of course is that if Madoc stumbled into the New World by accident, how did he find his way back to the colony in Mobile Bay? There may be an answer. Centuries before Madoc's voyage, Vikings guided their ships by an ingenious compass. This was a needle, magnetized by a lodestone, which floated in a bowl of water and continually pointed due north. From this, seafarers could work out their positions. It was said that Madoc had received one of these from the Culdees although he may have already possessed one. No more than a few years after the prince set out, a fleet of several ships assembled in support of the English King Richard I's Third Crusade, each carrying the same navigational device. The name of the boat in which he sailed gives slightly further credence to this theory: *Gwennon Gorn* means "Horn of Guenon" or "Staghorn" and legend states that Madoc designed and constructed a ship using nails made from the antlers of a stag so that iron nails would not interfere with his lodestone. Whether or not the compass worked is unknown as tradition tells us that Madoc and his companions sailed west from Gwynedd and were never heard of again.

What happened to the second expedition remains a mystery. According to Irene Parker in *The Welsh Connection,* Madoc may have known the northeasterly trade winds would carry a ship down past Spain to North Africa and across the Atlantic to the Gulf of Mexico. It is her opinion that a gale blew up, driving the expedition off course and into the Caribbean. No one, however, is certain. There is even a (admittedly rather fanciful) tale that Madoc and his followers beached their ships in Mexico where the prince himself was dubbed Quetzalcoatl by the ancient Aztecs. The plumed dragon of Wales, which they carried on their flags, became the plumed serpent that was the embodiment of the god.

Back on the Gulf Coast, the remnants of Madoc's first expedition waited, probably in great terror. The Gulf of Mexico was a paradise, but it also contained strange, wild, and savage men—the forerunners of the Indian peoples—who were utterly hostile to the new settlers. Frequent attacks along the coast forced the Welshmen to move further inland. Because of their seafaring background, they used the waterways which led to the interior, the Alabama and Coosa Rivers as far as DeSoto Falls. Here they began a series of wars against the precursors of the Cherokee, who themselves were pressed by the neighboring group who would become the Sioux. Gradually, the Welsh were forced to retreat even farther inland along the Missouri River. A number of treaties and peace deals followed in which the Welsh soldiers married amongst the nearby tribes—perhaps as part of various alliances—slowly becoming more and more like Indians themselves. These could have been the ancestors of the Mandan nation.

The Mandan villages were visited in 1738 by the French explorer Pierre Gaultier, Sieur de la Verendrye, who was following ancient fables of bearded Indians who spoke a tongue unknown amongst other Indian nations. Visiting this people at the height of their power, the Sieur records in detailed diaries how a Mandan chief explained to him that the ancestors of the tribe had lived farther to the south but had been driven north and west by "many enemies." The explorer described the Mandans as essentially "white men with forts and towns" and recounted an old Mandan legend that these ancestors had originally come from beyond "a great lake" (the Atlantic Ocean?).

The Sieur de la Verendrye was not the only European traveler intrigued by tales of the "Welsh Indians." In 1492 a group of Europeans led by a Genoese adventurer dropped anchor somewhere off the Bahamas. The expedition of Christopher Columbus had been financed by the king and queen of Spain, and Columbus himself believed that he had found a new trade route to the Indies, where he had been promised a governorship. Although that promise was never realized (Columbus died in 1506, neglected by and embittered against his former Spanish masters), the land at which he had accidentally arrived, America, would soon become one of the centers of European politics.

In 1500, it mattered little who had originally "discovered"

America, but as European trade routes developed and European political relationships descended into competition, the notion of first claim became increasingly important. As relations between Catholic Spain and Protestant England threatened to slide into outright warfare, both sides looked towards the New World as a source of revenue to finance their respective war machines. Both sought to establish colonies there. Naturally, the notion of a group of British descent already living in the American interior cast question upon Spain's claim to large areas of the land. Throughout the sixteenth century, the idea of a Welsh kingdom along the Missouri worried the Spanish monarchy so much that they decided to mount an investigation into the rumor. In 1557, Parda de Luna was sent up the Mobile and Coosa Rivers to look for the *"gente blanco"* who had dominated ancient American legends. He found nothing. Even as late as 1624, Spanish expeditions were still being mounted to search for Madoc's kingdom and had penetrated as far as the Alabama-Georgia line near Chattanooga. Although all of them found many stories regarding the Welsh, none found the white Indians with beards. In 1710, Spain sent Pierre le Moyne, Sieur d'Iberville, to America to select the site for a new colonial town on the Gulf Coast; he founded (in 1711) Mobile on a river that the local Mobilia Indians called the Mad Dog River (known simply as the Dog River today). It is not inconceivable that this was a corruption of "Madoc" and the river was one of the waterways that had been used by the Welsh explorers. Using Mobile as a base, further expeditions were launched and soon the ruined fortress at DeSoto Falls was discovered, seeming to suggest a medieval English presence in America centuries before the Spanish had arrived. However, it made virtually no political difference. In an agreement symbolizing the new friendship between the English king James I and the Spanish in 1604, even the English now recognized Christopher Columbus as the discoverer of America. By 1607, the settlement of Jamestown (named for the English king)—the first permanent true English colony—had been established.

Not that Madoc was forgotten. He already appeared in a number of ancient Welsh texts, the most impressive being Gutyn Owen's *Brut Y Twysogion,* which had been written during the reign of the English king Edward IV (1451-1483). Owen detailed Madoc's journey from Afon Ganol in Penrhyn Bay to the shores of an unknown country.

For many years, this was dismissed as mere fantasy for Penrhyn Bay had no harbor from which the prince could have sailed. Then in the mid-1950s workmen found the remains of a thousand-year-old quay (it stands in the garden of a home called "Odstone") on the sea front between Penrhyn and Rhos-on-Sea. Parts of another manuscript known as "The Romance of Prince Madoc 1255" were discovered in Poitiers, France, during the seventeenth century. This romance, seemingly written by a thirteenth-century Flemish writer named William the Minstrel, tells the historical story of the prince and of his discovery of a paradise under the sea. There are other manuscripts that, while not directly connecting Madoc and America, add credibility to the legend. One of these, dated 1477, presently stored in the British Museum in London, identifies the kings of Gwynedd and gives their lineage. It notes that the son of Owain Gwynedd was an explorer of "unknown lands."

Apart from the ancient texts there were other references to Madoc naming him as the discoverer of the American continent. The story of his epic voyage was related in *A Brief Description of the Whole World* (1620) and a version was recounted by Sir Thomas Herbert in the last section of his *Relation of Some Years Travaile* (1626) using source material that Sir Thomas said were records of "200 years agoe and more." The Dutch writer Hornius also tells of Madoc in *De Originibus Americanis* (1652), suggesting that he was amongst the first people to found a colony in America. Despite Columbus's claim, the memory of the Welsh prince was still to the fore.

And there were many Indian legends too. When Governor Sevier visited the Cherokee in 1782, he met with an old chieftain named Oconostota, who had been the ruling chieftain of the Cherokee for well over sixty years. Sevier asked the chief about the people who had built the forts along the Alabama River. The chief allegedly told him, "It is handed down by the Forefathers that the works had been made by the White people who had formerly inhabited this country." He also added that he had heard his grandfather say that "they were a people called Welsh and that they had crossed a Great Water and landed first near the mouth of the Alabama River near Mobile." Other legends stated that the Welsh pioneers had ventured as far as the Ohio River where they fought a series of bloody wars against and were eventually defeated by the Iroquois. These, of course, were only tales.

Although the evidence for Madoc's arrival in America in 1170 seems strong, there are those who dispute it. In July 1797, a Welsh explorer named John Evans wrote a detailed letter relating his long search for "Welsh Indians" along the Missouri. He was in fact the first to map the Missouri from its confluence with the Mississippi to nearly two thousand miles above this point. He had negotiated with various Indian tribes all through this area, including the Omaha and the Sioux, and in his capacity he had met and lived amongst the Mandan. Evans claims that he spoke to them in his native Welsh and that they gave him no indication that they understood. He also suggests that, apart from a few relatively insignificant cultural differences, they were similar to most other indigenous tribes of the region. Consequently, he concluded there was no basis for the Welsh claim and that the legend of Madoc was only a myth.

Against this, there is the suggestion that Evans may have been a Spanish agent. In 1793, he set out from Baltimore, walking west to reach St. Louis, where he was arrested and imprisoned by the Spanish authorities. He was released and by 1795 was working for the Spanish Missouri Company, which planned to clear a way to the Pacific Ocean—hence his mapping of the Missouri territory. Many conclude that Evans's refutal of the Welsh claim owed more to the politics of his paymasters than to any personal belief. Nevertheless, Evans died in 1797, aged twenty-nine, in New Orleans, still denying that Madoc's arrival in America was anything more than a fanciful tale. Others such as Samuel Eliot Morison have used his letter to debunk the idea of the Welsh. Morison posits that the ancient forts along various rivers owe their existence to early Indian cultures and not to the survivors of Madoc's expedition at all. The legend of Madoc and the American kingdom he founded, Morison deduces, is nothing more than Celtic folklore.

Not everyone in America shares Morison's view, however. In November 1953, a memorial tablet to the Welsh prince was erected at Fort Morgan, Mobile Bay, Alabama, by the Virginia Cavalier Chapter of the Daughters of the American Revolution. It reads: "In memory of Prince Madoc, a Welsh explorer, who landed on the shores of Mobile Bay in 1170 and left behind, with the Indians, the Welsh language."

J.C. Brown and the
Lost World

For centuries, legends and tales of lost kingdoms somewhere near at hand have both fascinated and intrigued travelers throughout the world. Many of these were situated on the tops of mountains—Shangri-la—or beneath the sea, near the coast—Atlantis, Lemuria. Always they were near enough to influence folklore but remote enough to be beyond reach. For the Celts, these places were the embodiment of the otherworld in which they strongly believed—totally unseen yet close to our own world. Many of their folktales reflect the proximity of a realm separate from that which they knew and experienced daily. Hence stories of Kilstaveen, the drowned city that lay off the Clare coastline in Ireland and whose bells could be heard still ringing on clear summer evenings, or the mysterious island of Eynhallow in the Orkneys which only appeared to the human eye on rare occasions (usually every seven years). The notions of nearness and inaccessibility held sway over the Celtic mind like nothing else. But what better place for an invisible world, it might be argued, than beneath the ground?

Certainly the notion of subterranean kingdoms captivated many other cultures in the ancient world. For the Romans, the terrible god Pluto was the lord of the underworld, driving the unshriven Latin dead through rivers of eternal fire. The Greeks believed in an underworld as Orpheus ventured there to seek his dead love; the ancient Semites believed in Sheol where the listless spirits of the dead wandered and muttered to themselves endlessly. Such underground places were usually associated with evil and death. For the Semites, Sheol transformed into Gehenna—actually a valley housing a town dump outside Jerusalem—where dark and malevolent demons tormented the human "rubbish" who did not worship Jehovah. This fit in well with the Celtic concept of the otherworld, a region from which the dead watched (and sometimes protected or cursed) the living and where the veil between it and the everyday world was sometimes very thin. Gradually, the concept of a parallel otherworld gave way to the idea of a world of spirits, the dead and fairies, lying beneath our feet. After all, were the dead not buried in the earth below? The notion of evil, however, did not diminish and when Christianity began to spread across the Celtic west, it too took the notion of an underground realm, transforming it into a place of great wickedness and endless torment. This was the realm to which the spirits of evil persons migrated when they died. In addition, it became the abode of the Devil himself—or at least so the church taught—and where the souls of those who served him languished in eternal damnation. It became hell.

The Celtic west was also full of caves, many of which had been occupied in prehistoric times. Into the medieval period, such places often became equated with the entrances to underground realms— to hell, the fairy kingdom, or the country of the dead. Many of the caverns were dark and mysterious; some held cave paintings, some held bones and other remains of previous occupancy. All were treated with a sense of awe. In much of the early Celtic folklore (remnants of which have been retained in the twenty-first century), dark spirits and sinister fairies loitered in these places, seeking to seize or lure away the pure of heart, the true Christian. All true believers were well advised to stay away from them lest they be drawn into a dark and supernatural realm.

However, throughout the medieval period there was also a strand of thought that sought to view the notion of an otherworld— a parallel existence under the earth—from a more scientific viewpoint. There was talk of lost Celtic tribes who had set up home beneath the surface of the world. Although such ideas were purely speculation, they nevertheless found their way into folklore. A good example is the celebrated tale of the green children who were said to have emerged from a great hole in the ground near the village of St. Mary's-by-the-Wolfpits (near Bury St. Edmunds, Suffolk) in England. According to the medieval English writer Roger of Coggeshall, who was famous for his rather tall and unsubstantiated stories, they appeared during the reign of King Stephen (1135-54) and were taken in by a local Norman knight, Sir Richard de Colne, who was a noted traveler in far and exotic lands. Roger goes on to state that there were two of them, a boy and a girl, both with bright green skin and extremely strange airs and manners about them. They babbled in some "queer, foreign tongue" and refused to eat meat, preferring only green beans. When they were eventually understood (having learned Norman English with some rapidity), they stated that they came from an underground kingdom known as St. Martin's Land, which had been founded by ancient Celtic peoples; they complained of a "great weight" (gravity?) upon their shoulders and they found the manners and customs of the "surface people" incredibly strange. The boy became moody and ill and soon died but the girl lived on for a number of years—becoming wild and flirty in her ways and eventually marrying one of Sir Richard's squires—before inexplicably vanishing. Perhaps she had found her way back to St. Martin's Land.

The time against which this folktale is set is one of warfare and turbulence. It was a period of civil war in England between King Stephen and the forces of Matilda—Henry I's daughter, known as the Empress Maud—for the English throne (an era described by one commentator as "19 years when Christ and his saints slept"). It was also an unsettling time when visions and signs were supposed to portend the end of the world, and in the scrambling, warlike years, there were few who disagreed that the end of all things was imminent or that God would give some sort of sign of its approach. Whether the green children actually did exist or whether they were simply a story emerging out of the conflict is unclear, but several quite plausible theories have been put forward. One thing they do demonstrate is that a belief in a mysterious underground otherworld still existed in the medieval Celtic mind.

This belief did not completely disappear as the generations passed. As late as the nineteenth century, there was still an interest in many West European countries in the possibility of some sort of underground country deep in the earth, below the human world. Tales like Jules Verne's *Journey to the Center of the Earth* even posited the theory that whole worlds might lie beneath the terrestrial crust. The "pulp" fantasy magazines of the 1930s, '40s, and '50s rekindled much of this interest. With the continuing threat of total atomic devastation of the surface world during this era, the idea of some form of subterranean existence appealed to many people. Stories about the remnants of ancient civilizations—Celtic, Roman, Greek, and Egyptian—living in pockets far beneath the ground flooded the pages of many fantastic journals and magazines. Some more imaginative souls even portrayed advanced, futuristic cultures that had developed far in advance of our own, living almost cheek-by-jowl with us, in the depths of the world.

In 1964, a book was published entitled *The Hollow Earth*, allegedly written by one Dr. Raymond Bernard. In it Bernard claimed that Earth was in fact hollow and that its core was inhabited by an advanced superrace. The so-called flying saucers that attracted much interest in the early 1960s did not come from outer space at all, as was speculated, but from this interior culture, emerging from holes at both the North and South Poles. The book had its origins in earlier tales, most notably Richard Shaver's "Shaver Mysteries" published, as fact, in *Amazing Stories*, beginning December 1943. Shaver spoke of a truly fantastic civilization ruled by Kut-Humi, the King of the World (thus reflecting many old Celtic folktales regarding a similar entity), who had aurally contacted him via welding equipment he was using at the Ford assembly plant in Michigan. While this may sound laughable, over the following months and years (the series in *Amazing Stories* ended in 1947), Shaver constructed a complex and quite believable account of an underground world populated by amazing beings. If the "Shaver Mysteries" and Bernard's description of a hollow Earth were nothing more than fiction, then they were in the tradition of the old Celtic storytellers relating stories of the otherworld.

During the Second World War, the idea of a hollow Earth was enthusiastically adopted by the Nazis. So strong was this belief that the Nazi admiralty sent a naval expedition to the island of Reugen in the Baltic in April 1942 for the purpose of taking pictures of the British fleet by aiming their cameras through the earth. There was also a great deal of Nazi literature, much of it speculative, that dealt with the subject.

Even today, the notion of a subterranean kingdom appears in both films and comic books. The veteran actor Doug McClure has traveled to fantastic underground (and undersea) kingdoms more times than can be counted while magazines such as Paul Chadwick's *World Below* series deal with the exploration of a fantastic underground world in an exciting, pictorial form. All these, however, have their roots in otherworld mythologies of the Celtic world. So how did such mythologies come to America?

Like Western Europe, the American continent boasts large numbers of vast and mysterious caverns, many of which have also been the sites of previous habitation (both human and animal). As in the European caves, the detritus of former occupancy—bones, rubbish, and bits of ornamentation—was to be found around the entrances. Indians had tales of monsters and bizarre people who emerged from these places—ogres, giants, witches—and gradually these became intermingled with the memories of underground realms that settlers brought with them from Celtic Europe. Old legends of an evil kingdom beneath the ground suddenly came into play once more. Such stories were amplified and extended. Creatures lived down there in the dark, said commentators; they were cannibalistic, they worshipped strange gods, they were huge and monstrous. Given this resurrection of the idea of the evil underground, it is no surprise that many of the more fantastic tales deal with invasion from below or with people who were carried away by troll-like beings for some malicious purpose. In the H.G. Wells classic *The Time Machine,* the deformed cannibal Morlocks of the far future live underground, only venturing out in darkness or when the light is poor. In some cases, given the vastness of some of the caverns that early American explorers encountered, it was imagined that the subterranean world was inhabited by giants who fiercely protected their domain from outsiders. Places like the Mammoth Cave in Kentucky were considered to be entrances to some sort of giant underworld into which the unwary might stray.

However, Kentucky may not have been the only entrance to the suspected subterranean kingdom. Another way in may exist in California and it might have connections with the world of ancient Celtic giants. Arguably, no tale of the hollow Earth is more mysterious than that of J.C. Brown, who appears to have stumbled into such a strange place during the early part of the twentieth century. The tale begins late in 1904 near Stockton in California when the Lord Cowdray Mining Company—an English syndicate—engaged a man to prospect for them in the gold-bearing hills of California. The man so involved gave his name as J.C. Brown although it is likely that this was not his real name. He claimed to have had a great deal of experience at prospecting and had panned for gold, or so he claimed, all over California, getting to know the state like the back of his hand. This claim is also questionable but it was grand enough to impress the officials of the Lord Cowdray Mining Company, who hired him almost on the spot.

From the outset, Brown was an odd choice as a mining scout. He was extremely secretive and furtive in his ways and kept to himself, sharing little information about his comings and goings with others. He would seldom talk about his past beyond boasting that he had uncovered several big claims along the West Coast and that he might know the location of some hidden treasure that had been abandoned by the notorious pirate Captain Kidd and which was said to be hidden somewhere on the Californian seaboard. This was taken as simple boasting; if Brown knew the whereabouts of such treasure, why did he not simply go and collect it, thereby making himself rich? Nevertheless, the mining company had faith in him and financed him with some mules, sending him off to search for new veins of gold in the California wilds.

Trekking across the known gold country to the northeast of Sacramento, Brown pushed into the Cascade Mountains until he reached a wild and remote region well away from civilization. Here the trails twisted back on themselves and the tumbled landscape was crisscrossed by deep and gloomy canyons, some culminating in shadowy valleys and river bottoms. According to his own tale, he was climbing through some twisting canyons one day when he came upon an old rock fall that almost blocked the trail he was following. He paused to examine the rock in case it bore any traces of gold. As he examined further, Brown realized that the fall actually concealed what appeared to be an old tunnel or deep cave, which stretched far back into the rock face by the side of the trail. What was curious about it was that the entrance seemed to be man-made. He began to explore further and thought that he found carvings on the rock face nearby. These showed what seemed to be giant figures interspersed with crude Celtic-like designs. Curious, Brown climbed past the fall and into the tunnel, which seemed to lead farther and farther back into the cliff. At a number of places he had to duck underneath some overhang from the roof above. Then suddenly, the cave (if cave it was) emerged into an even greater and larger tunnel that seemed to slant downwards towards the depths of the earth. Still intrigued, Brown began to follow it down, his boots slipping and sliding on the loose gravel and dry earth. He was now almost in total darkness.

As his eyes became accustomed to the poor light, he became vaguely aware that the walls of this tunnel were covered in a fine, tempered metal which seemed to resemble fine copper and which rang hollowly when he struck it. The walls also seemed to be hung here and there with decorations of gold and bronze. Further, he noticed that the shaft he was following was cut precisely through the rock as if with some form of machinery and was obviously not a naturally formed phenomenon. The ground beneath him grew steeper and he had to keep close to the wall to prevent himself from sliding down and falling. The sides of the tunnel were smooth and gave him no purchase, so he had to move very carefully in the underground blackness.

At last the descent terminated and J.C. Brown emerged in a great subterranean room. Here there was a little light although he could not see the farthest limits of the place or the ceiling high above him. The roof simply seemed to arch up into even deeper darkness. The light in the chamber came from great tongues of fire that leapt out of holes in the ground set at various distances around the floor. At first Brown thought the area might be volcanic and that these fires might be a manifestation of that, but on closer investigation, he wasn't so sure. The fire-gushers seemed to have been artificially created specifically for the purpose of giving some light to the great chamber and they made a hissing sound as if powered by some sort of artificially circulated gas. Brown began to explore the chamber further.

Stacked against the walls of the cavern were a number of plates of a thin, unidentifiable hammered metal. Lifting one of these, Brown took it over to the light from one of the fire-geysers and studied it. The plate was practically covered in a sort of ancient hieroglyphic script, parts of which (although Brown did not know it at the time) held a similarity to the Celtic Ogham writing. The others more closely resembled Egyptian hieroglyphs. He examined all the plates and found that they were covered with remarkably similar writing. They were much larger than any plates he had seen before—some were so big that he could barely hold them—and although he had seen metals of most kinds, the material of which they were made was beyond his experience. Setting them aside, he stepped beyond the glow of the flaring torches. In the shadows lay great heaps of ornaments made out of gold and bronze. They were presumably carved in the likeness of birds and beasts although they bore a resemblance to no animal or fowl that Brown had ever seen before. He noticed, too, on the floor of the chamber, some traces of foliage that he could not identify. It was no more than a few strands but the texture and color of it were like nothing that grew in the sane, wholesome world above.

As he circled the greater part of the chamber, Brown noticed a number of smaller tunnels radiating from it. He followed one of these into a smaller room, which seemed to be lit by only one of the queer fire-fountains. This cavern seemed to be man-made and was lined with the same strange coppery material that had lined the tunnel on his way down. Here and there, great heaps lay in the shadows and when Brown investigated these, he had a shock. They were nothing less than the skeletons of gigantic warriors, each clad in a rough, oddly forged armor, and some of them still held very ancient weapons in their bony hands. Some wore helmets but there was a trace of long reddish hair around many of the skulls, which seemed to have been thrown into one of the corners. Some of the long-dead warriors appeared to be carrying medals of some kind, all embossed with the same strange writing he had seen on the plates in the main chamber. Around the neck of each skeleton was an ornament of gold, as if denoting some sort of status to its owner.

Returning to the main chamber, Brown explored the walls of the place and found another main passageway, which seemed to plunge almost vertically down into an all-encompassing darkness. He did not fancy exploring this shaft any further. Although he was still curious, there was something about this drop that unnerved him and besides, since he had entered the main chamber, he had experienced the distinct feeling of being watched. He walked farther through the main chamber but could see nobody and yet the sensation that someone—or something—was observing him only strengthened. The hairs on the nape of his neck began to prickle and sweat stood on his forehead in beads. He drew back from the dark shaft and, taking a gold circlet from the arm of a great skeleton, he made his way back to the surface once again. The sun caught his face as he stumbled from the cavern and, following the canyon beyond the rock fall, he found himself in a dried-up river wash which he walked along for a couple of miles until he found a trail that he knew. Before he left, however, according to his own account, he drew a crude map of the region. Then he made his way back to civilization.

It would have been reasonable to suppose that the average prospector would have made all possible speed to record his find and stake a claim to it in the nearest town, but J.C. Brown was no ordinary prospector. He was extremely cautious. Besides, there were legal implications. When he had found the cave, he was in the employ of the Lord Cowdray Mining Company and this might influence his entitlement to the claim. It appears that relations between Brown and the mining syndicate were not good and he may have been afraid that his employers would try to lay claim to what was undoubtedly an important scientific find and exclude him from it. Whatever his motives, he decided to keep quiet about it; he had the crude map showing the cave's position and he had resealed the entrance to the underground world. He continued a preliminary mining survey of the Cascades and returned to Stockton saying nothing about the find. He would not disclose the nature of his discovery for several more years.

Towns like Stockton, where prospectors and miners tended to gather, were often awash with tall tales. One of the most often told was that related by two half-Indian prospectors, Jacob Cahee and his partner Henry Chee. While prospecting in the Cascades, they had stumbled into an underground cavern system and, trying to find a way out, had encountered what they had first thought was a great monster but which turned out to be the dragon-prow of an ancient Viking ship lodged in the rock far beneath the surface of the earth. However, neither prospector had kept any record of where the cave might have been and subsequent searches to locate its whereabouts proved fruitless. It was simply dismissed as another tall tale from the Cascades. Yet the mountains had a somewhat mysterious and awesome reputation. Old Indian legends spoke of a race of giant red-haired men who had lived amongst the highest peaks. They had spoken a guttural, unintelligible language and the Indians were very afraid of them. Some white settlers connected them with either Vikings or ancient Irish, but most wisdom simply dismissed them as fanciful Indian stories.

If Brown knew about these stories, he kept that knowledge to himself. For the next couple of years he continued to journey through the Cascades on behalf of the mining syndicate, but his relationship with them was growing steadily worse. Finally, he either resigned his post or else was fired and suddenly left California.

Over the next three decades, Brown's activities are largely unknown but it is suspected that he spent a fair amount of time back east and that he may have consulted both public and university libraries on the subject of prehistoric races. Sometimes, he used the name J.C. Brown and at other times he may have used a different name. It is thought, however, that he immersed himself in the study of early America. In particular, he seemed extremely interested in early migrations from both Ireland and Scotland, but he never seemed to give an explanation for such an interest. It is also thought that he made at least two further visits to the cave. He was seen in Sacramento by a former associate around the mid-1920s, frequenting several bars in the town and spending money as though it were of no consequence. When in his cups, Brown was said to babble about ancient elder races that had colonized the land and once ruled North America from sea to sea and which themselves had come out of the east (relatively speaking). Much of what he said when drunk made very little sense. Then he would disappear again for a time.

On June 1, 1934, Brown turned up again in Stockton. He was now around seventy-nine years old and in poor health. He related his fantastic story to several prominent townspeople and showed them a torn, badly stained, and faded pencil map, together with a large golden circlet that he claimed to have found. His main purpose in approaching the townsmen was to encourage them to finance an expedition into the Cascades and help bring the bulk of the prehistoric treasure from the cavern. Much of his talk was extremely wild and concerned an "Elder race of giants" who had "come across the Atlantic from another land to make themselves the masters of America." Moreover, he claimed that some of these great beings were still alive and that they knew of his movements and were watching him. He had been hiding in the east to avoid them, he claimed. Although he must have sounded like an utter madman, a couple of Stockton businessmen were prepared to put up a small expedition and supply digging materials in return for a share of the alleged cache. News of the bizarre find and of the subsequent treasure hunt swept like wildfire through the town and on the morning of June 19, almost eighty people gathered to accompany the aged prospector into the Cascades. Brown, who had been lodging in a local hotel, never showed up. Although he had retired to his room the previous night, he had been uneasy, complaining to the hotel clerk that the feeling of being watched was very strong. During the night, he had simply disappeared again. Suspecting a confidence trick, the business backers called in detectives to investigate but their involvement ceased when it was disclosed that the old man had taken no money on the venture.

The hotel room, however, was in a great state of disarray. The door of a heavy oaken wardrobe had been broken from its hinges and a large chest had been overturned. Bedclothes were scattered everywhere, several hanging from a mirror in the corner of the room. Even more mysteriously, in the soft ground at the back of the hotel and below the window of Brown's second-floor room was the mark of a shoeless human footprint. Although its outlines were hazy in the mud, it was far bigger than any human foot and had been sunk well into the ground as if it had supported a mighty weight. Although investigators were called and several people saw the print, a sudden rainstorm obliterated all traces of it, leaving only a deep pool in its place. Had some member of an ancient giant race followed him down from that strange, underground chamber and carried away the man who had threatened to reveal their secrets? A hunt was initiated for the pencil map that Brown had shown but it was never found. Nor was Brown himself ever seen again, although certain travelers in remote areas of the Cascades claimed to have heard his voice calling for help. Where was that mysterious entrance that he found and where did it lead to? An underground lost world maybe? One that was populated by ancient Celtic giants who had somehow crossed the Atlantic Ocean? Who can say? Like all good mysteries, it remains within the realm of the lost.

Brown's wild stories of a subterranean lost world are not unique in California. Accounts of the entrance to a fantastic underground kingdom near Big Sur were widespread in the 1930s. The circulation of many of these tales was undoubtedly due to two men—prospector Alfred K. Clark (known locally as "Uncle Al") and Dr. Clarence

H. Pearce of San Francisco, who was Clark's financial backer—
who looked for the "lost land" back around 1910-1920. Clark was
a veteran of the Civil War, having fought as a boy for the Union.
After its end, he headed west, fascinated by old Spanish and Indian
legends of lost treasures. One such tale told of how Indians living
near the Little Sur River (a stream five miles north of the Big Sur
River) would regularly, and at the request of the Spanish settlers,
lead their burros into the Pico Blanco (White Peak) region around
the Little Sur and return the next day weighed down with silver
ore. There was talk of a lost kingdom somewhere near the stream
where silver was plentiful. This land, according to the Indians, had
been originally settled by a tribe of giants who had mined silver ore
for themselves and had left much of what they unearthed behind.
Clark befriended the Little Sur Indians and was eventually taken,
in confidence, to the entrance of an underground world. However,
the tunnel that led down to this realm had been blocked by several
rock falls and was impassable. Equipment would be needed to
clear it and this is where Dr. Pearce came in. He provided men and
equipment so that the tunnel could be cleared, but after months
of back-breaking labor, nothing was found. There had been further
falls along the tunnel, which also needed to be cleared away.
Disillusioned and seeing no obvious return for his money, Pearce
pulled out of the partnership. Uncle Al continued to dig on in the
Little Sur area and became something of a colorful hermit, often
talked about but seldom seen. In 1930 he turned up at the house of
one of his friends, Al Greer, in a very disheveled state and obviously
near to death. By this time, Uncle Al was over ninety years old.
Greer and his wife took him in and cared for him until he died a
little while after from pneumonia. In the course of nursing him,
Greer heard an astounding story.

The old man admitted that he had never found the silver lode
he sought, but he had found something else. While he was digging
in the wall of an underground shaft of an old Spanish mine,
Clark's pick had broken through into a mysterious underground
chamber. Peering through the darkened aperture the prospector
was staggered at the size of the cavern he had blundered into.
It seemed, he told Greer, to stretch away into infinity so that he
could not accurately determine either its scale or height. He began
to explore this strange underground world, treading carefully

because he had very little light to guide him. What illumination he had showed great glassy icicles hanging down from overhangs and rising up conelike from the floor close to his feet. However, he doubted that these were composed of frozen water. Eerie stone flowers seemed to grow from the walls around him and some of these appeared to crumble at his touch. Farther across the cavern, he came upon a bubbling stream in which swam peculiar pale-hued fish—so pale that they were almost white. They also appeared to be blind. Throughout his time in this underground realm, Uncle Al was convinced that he was not alone. Some sixth sense told him that he was being watched as he made his way across the vast cavern. What struck him most was the dry stone floor beneath his feet, which seemed to have been worked and pitted by Indian mortars and the queer drawings on the walls that he passed. These showed crude sketches of "elephants with long shaggy hair and curly teeth" and "cats with long, sharp teeth." However, there was more. Other drawings showed medium-sized men armed with spears fighting against armored giants. Scattered around the base of the walls were a number of shiny objects that Clark's light picked out. Before the prospector could examine these, there was a noise from somewhere else in the cavern, which made him turn. It might only have been a rock falling or earth sliding a little but it unnerved Uncle Al and made him hurry back towards the sunlight.

This was the story that the delirious old man told his astonished listener and there might be some rational explanation for his "lost world." Pico Blanco is said to boast the highest concentrations of dolomite limestone anywhere on the central coast. This is a highly porous limestone that lends itself to the carvings of subterranean rivers. The cavern could have been created by prehistoric floods in the area, leading to a kind of underground confluence of several small streams and the South Fork of the Little Sur River, which disappears underground at several locations and reemerges several miles farther on each time. The albino fish that Clark described could well be troglobites, blind fish that lose their pigmentation due to the amount of time they spend in the dark. The "stone blooms" might be what geologists refer to as gypsum flowers, petal-like discharges of a substance known as selenite from the chamber walls, while the "icicles" might be stalactites and stalagmites, formations of mineralized water which are a well-known feature of underground cave systems. The shiny objects Clark's light picked out might have been a number of things—lumps of rocks containing flecks of silver ore, for example. Although woolly mammoths (the "shaggy elephants") and sabre-tooth tigers were supposed to have roamed California before becoming extinct, no explanation is given for the drawings of the giant men, although these would tie in with the ancient Indian legends regarding the Big Sur River country. Certainly, the tool marks on the cavern floor showed evidence of a forgotten culture.

After his discovery, Uncle Al spent the rest of his life keeping inquisitive strangers away from the entrance to his hidden world, and he died before he could bequeath its exact location to Al Greer. The latter searched the area looking for a way into "the land beneath" for several years afterward but without much success. He did find what he thought might be the entrance of which Uncle Al had spoken but it had caved in and all attempts to reopen it proved fruitless. Since the 1930s, there have been many attempts to locate the "inner world," but all have come to nothing except the discovery of some Indian artifacts. Several axes have been found which seem to be too large to be held by any normal human hand and the legends of ancient red-haired giants often reemerge. The hills around the area of the Little Sur ring hollow, suggesting some sort of mammoth cave system in the locality—or the entrance to a lost kingdom.

The mysterious giants appear in yet another story, this time concerning the notorious Pacific pirate Hippolyte de Bouchard, who attacked and burned the Alta Californian capital city of Monterey in November 1818. During his years of piracy, Bouchard was constantly harassed by both Spanish and American warships and desired a hiding place for his men and booty. Another version of the tale states that he was in fact looking for a way overland in order to attack the fortress of El Castillo and the isolated inland missions of San Juan Bautista and San Antonio. An account, allegedly given by one of Bouchard's men known simply as "La Roque," states that the pirates came upon the entrance to a vast underground cavern system in a set of low hills near the coast. On entering the caverns, Bouchard discovered that they sloped downwards, through a series of connecting tunnels, towards the core of the earth. The walls of the outer caverns (the only ones the pirates explored) were covered in queer drawings depicting armored giants fighting with normal-sized men. However, many of the tunnels were choked with rubble and Bouchard's men had no time to clear them. The pirates moved on and left the strange entrance behind them. The experience unsettled them for their captain knew about old Indian legends concerning a kingdom of giants somewhere in the Monterey area and there had been rumors that several Franciscan monks had been carried away by these ogres while allegedly searching for silver north of Monterey Bay. "Even the great Bouchard," said La Roque, "was terrified when he saw the drawings of mighty men on the stone and it troubled him for many days afterward."

The story is quite possibly no more than fiction and is sometimes attributed to another sea rover who was said to have visited Alta California—Francis Drake. Even the location of the alleged kingdom shifts: sometimes it is said to have been located somewhere near the jagged and beautiful "Point of the Sea Wolves" (which was frequented by both Bouchard and Drake), while other versions of the tale locate it far across the Monterey Peninsula in the Carmel Valley, near Carmel Bay. Nevertheless, the story serves as a reminder that ideas of a lost underground kingdom of (Celtic?) giants is still foremost in the American mind.

Is there a strange subterranean world somewhere beneath California, populated by giant beings and did J.C. Brown accidentally stray into it, following in the steps of others? Or is it just a suggestion of the ancient Celtic otherworld, hidden somewhere in the deep recesses of the American mind? Maybe there truly are forgotten lands and mysterious races somewhere far under the ground, beneath our feet.

The Land of the Lost

Although mystical spirit countries were often central to Celtic lore, they usually remained mysterious and ill-defined, even though it was believed that they lay extremely close to our own physical world. They lay, it was thought, in cloudbanks, in the air high above the ground, or just across the horizon or in the far distance. These countries were beyond the reach of ordinary mortals and humans could only approach them if the beings, spirits, or gods that dwelt there allowed it.

It is, of course, easy to see how the belief in spirit lands might have come about. Towering cloud formations rising high into the sky are often suggestive of castles or strongholds and may have represented the same to the early Celtic mind. They may also have seen horses and men in the movements of such clouds, as well as trees and mountains, all suggestive of another, unknown country. In addition, when the Celts came to the lands they were to colonize, they often found great stones and tumbled features left by the Ice Age which hinted at the handiwork of giants, monsters, and primal gods, none of which, they thought, had really gone away but lived somewhere close by, perhaps in the mighty cloud citadels they saw above them. This was, in the ancient mind, evidence of a strange country beyond human reach where awesome and powerful beings dwelt.

Not only cloud formations might have beguiled our ancestors but changes in the very quality of the light might have played tricks on their eyes and stirred their imaginings. In the evening, as the light began to fail, the landscape the early Celts inhabited, which was littered and studded with the earthen fortifications of earlier, aboriginal peoples as well as boulders and various rock formations, could change in its aspect. Shadows might mislead the senses, perhaps creating features which were not there at all. In the evening murk, the tumbled stones took on the shape of a castle or a fortress; a narrow, dry valley might suggest a river. When the light changed again such things were revealed for what they were—ordinary geographical features—and the suggestion would be gone. To the Celtic mind, however, the half-glimpsed otherworld had simply melted away. This is probably why most visions of the otherworld, or the fairy realm, were to be seen at twilight or "between the lights," as the Celtic peoples put it.

With the climatic changes at the end of the great Ice Age, certain other phenomena might have occurred—phenomena that are no longer common in Western lands. For instance, mirages may have been more common in Celtic lands than they are at present. We normally associate such things with the desert or with barren lands, but such optical illusions may have once formed a distinct part of the Celtic experience. Distantly glimpsed lakes may have vanished upon approach; strange towns and cities may have come and gone in the very blink of an eye, leaving nothing but emptiness. Again this gave the impression that another more supernatural country lay very close to the mortal world.

Evidence in support of this theory comes from relatively modern times. On July 7, 1878, the inhabitants of the Irish seaside town of Ballycotton in County Cork were both surprised and astounded by the sudden appearance of an island that had not been seen in the ocean before. Sightseers gathering on the strand were able to see the new island quite plainly and were able to make out its coastline, woodlands, fields, and deep valleys. A number of County Cork fishermen set out in boats to investigate but as they approached, the entire island winked out of existence, leaving them amazed and wondering.

Similar islands have been seen from time to time off the coast of Kerry at Ballyheigue Strand, at Carrigaholt in Clare, and at Ballyinalearne Bay in Galway. Off the Mull of Kintyre in Scotland, mysterious islands were seen to come and go at certain times of the year. One such phantom island appeared off Portstewart Strand in County Derry in the North of Ireland and was recorded by the local paper. The vision appeared off the Derry coast on July 12, 1866, and was witnessed by a good number of people. Its notoriety stems from the fact that its appearance provoked much learned discussion and drew academics from as far away as Magee College in Derry City itself. One of the main academics who discussed it at length was the Reverend Prof. Thomas Witherow, then a senior lecturer at Magee and a correspondent for the *Derry Standard*, one of the main newspapers in the area. He describes the occurrence as "an optical illusion, arising from unequal light refraction."

It was a local paper, however, the *Coleraine Chronicle* (July 21, 1866), that gave the clearest and most descriptive account of the phenomenon. It also served to demonstrate how a mirage could be turned into a glimpse of another country or reality in the popular mind.

> At eleven o'clock this forenoon, the grandest optical illusion that we ever witnessed appeared on the coast of Ennishowen between Greencastle and the Lighthouse at the north-east point of the peninsula. When our attention was first drawn to it, the place where the Lighthouse stands was, as seen from Portstewart, occupied by a magnificent castle of gigantic proportions with two towers in the wings. In a few moments it was a villa of much humbler dimensions, surrounded by a lawn elegantly laid out and carriageways and footpaths clearly visible. Then, in a few moments, another castle of still grander proportions with three towers appeared, distinctly visible along the coast at Greencastle, encircled as it seemed by a dense forest. Magilligan Strand seen from this point at ordinary times, is little better than a golden thread hemming in the dark blue waters but on this day, one end of it, next to Donegal, seemed to rise up and stand as a perpendicular cliff—a grand precipice, enclosing the sea on that side like a mighty wall. In a few minutes all had changed. The precipice at Magilligan had faded away. The grand castle at the mouth of the Foyle had disappeared. Then the whole shore from Greencastle down to the Lighthouse seemed a continuous plantation, showing many openings, villas, stately mansions and, in one instance, a great square church tower, that was distinctly visible for upwards of thirty minutes. For two hours, up until one o'clock, the mirage continued, and was seen and admired by great numbers in the town. Shortly after one o'clock it had entirely vanished. We observed that, during the time it continued, there seemed a thin, hazy stripe of atmosphere accurately defined, along the margin of the water. Above this, the Ennishowen hills presented the same appearance as they do every day; on this side of it, the water glancing in the sunlight, presented the same appearance as it usually does. But

through the thin, hazy atmosphere appeared the strange landscape, ever varying in its forms, which we have described. Cliffs and cottages, forests, castles, churches, all successively appeared and vanished and at last the vapor set down on the peninsula for the afternoon, all minor objects became lost to view and nothing appeared by the long dark barrier of the Donegal mountains standing between us and the west.

Few who witnessed this beautiful illusion for two hours this forenoon are ever likely to forget that they have enjoyed a privilege that is of no common kind and which, for many years at the seacoast, they might never have again

Although the changing "island" was known to be little more than an optical phenomenon caused by atmospheric conditions, many people appear to have believed they had seen some other part of the world or some strange land which did not really exist. The impression on local minds created by the mirage was certainly a powerful one. The notion of "phantom islands," of course, was not a new one but one that was deeply ingrained into the Celtic psyche.

Lost islands were also common amongst many ancient peoples. Almost everyone is familiar with the legend of Atlantis, a paradise continent that lay, according to Plato, "to the west of the Pillars of Hercules" (the Straits of Gibraltar). It was regarded as the epitome of contentment, culture, and civilization but was completely overwhelmed by the sea following a violent seismic disturbance so that today no trace of it exists. And yet, the legend is just as potent today as it was in ancient times. And there were parallels of this essentially Mediterranean legend in Celtic folklore. The most famous of these was the legend of Hy Breasal, which was reputedly the physical embodiment of the fabulous otherworld. It was an island upon which Breasal, the mythical High King of the World, held his court every seven years. Consequently the island of Hy Breasal was visible only for a short period every seventh year. It became a Celtic version of the Mediterranean Atlantis myth and was usually depicted as a place of eternal happiness where everyone was immortal. It also had the ability to rise from and sink beneath the waves as its ruler saw fit, hence the infrequency of its sightings. Hy Breasal appears in records and on maps as an actual place and the Genoese cartographer Daloroto (circa 1325) shows it as a large landmass to the southwest of Ireland. It appeared sporadically, in that same location, on maps and charts until the late seventeenth century. For the Celts, the Country O'Breasal lay roughly where the sun touched the horizon or immediately on its other side—usually close enough to see but too far away to visit. It has, indeed, given its name to the South American nation of Brazil as early explorers in that particular country thought they had finally reached the mythical land.

A similar "fairy island" is said to lie just off the North Antrim coast in Northern Ireland, between the town of Ballycastle and Rathlin Island and was shown on sea charts as Green Island or Shamrock Island until the twentieth century—even though, like Hy Breasal, it was supposed to appear only every seven years. Gradually, the mythology concerning fabulous islands widened to include other themes and other places: Tir na nOg (the Land of Youth), Caer Sidhe (the mysterious city-island where, according to the Scottish folklorist Lewis Spence, the emperor of the fairies held court), and the Welsh Annwn (which sometimes lay far beneath the ground and sometimes far out at sea).

There were, too, remote islands where the mysterious otherworld touched with our own mortal world and which were dangerous for humans to visit. The island of Eilean Mor—Great Island—in the remote, bleak Flannan Isles (seventeen miles west of the Outer Hebrides) was always referred to by shepherds from Lewis who wintered their sheep there as "the other country" and was truly considered to be not of our world. Few men would stay there after dark and prescribed rituals—such as circling the ruins of the ancient St. Flannan's church upon one's knees—were performed when visiting the site. In 1900, three men—James Ducat, Donald McArthur, and Thomas Marshall, all lighthouse keepers—vanished from the Flannan Light (situated on the island), a mystery that has never been solved. For many local people there was little doubt that they had been spirited into the otherworld.

In later Celtic society, there was a strong belief that these mysterious landmasses were, in fact, the abode of the dead. Inherent was a strong tradition amongst many ancient peoples that spirits could not cross water, and on places like Rathlin Island (off the coast of Antrim) and Inishmurray (off the coast of Sligo) traces of extremely ancient burial sites can still be found. Around the time of the Roman Empire, the Celts strongly believed in the transmigration of souls, the journey of the dead from this world into the otherworld or the afterlife. Julius Caesar, in his *Gallic Wars (IV)* wrote: "The druids attach particular importance to the belief that the soul (or spirit) does not perish but passes from one body into another." There was a strong suggestion too—for example in the Roman writer Lucan—that the soul passed into another body in another world. In *Pharsalia I,* Lucan stated that the Celts simply considered death as an interruption of life in which the spirit passed between bodies and between worlds. What better place to journey than some mysterious island where the souls of the dead could gather without returning to annoy the living?

Some fathers of the early Celtic Christian church took up this theme and turned some of these strange mirages, particularly the oceanic ones, into some sort of embodiment of heaven, lying just beyond the grasp of every man but to be enjoyed by the blessed (those who died in the faith). The early Celtic Christianity was one of missionary work and proselytizing in far-flung places. Irish, Scottish, and Welsh monks traveled all over the Western world, large areas of which were unknown to them, seeking out converts and followers. Some of them certainly made extraordinary journeys, encountering strange lands and unfamiliar peoples. Many had remarkable adventures.

The most notable of all these wanders was St. Brendan the Navigator whose travels are recorded in the *Navigatio Sancti Brendani Abbatis.* Brendan is credited with having sailed from Ireland and landing on the coast of North America around the late fifth and early sixth centuries (nearly one thousand years before Columbus). Although some of the account may have been loosely based on the Celtic/Irish epic the *Immram Curaig Maile Duin,* which recounts the wanderings of the Irish chieftain Mael Druin in search of his father's murderer, there is no doubt that the account contains much detail regarding Arctic travel that Brendan could not have known about in his abbey at Clonfert. For example, there are descriptions of a "sea of glass" (ice flows) and of the birth of an island in volcanic fire which the saint claims to have witnessed. He also describes "moving islands," which were probably great whales or mighty icebergs. His description of the coastline of America (if such it was) may be fairly recognizable, and in 1976, the adventurer Tim Severin successfully re-created Brendan's alleged voyage and showed that it was indeed possible. Did an Irish saint visit American shores in the dim past, encountering many wonders and mysterious lands and islands on the way there? The answer is probably lost to history and is doomed to remain the stuff of legend.

When the early settlers put down their own roots in American soil, they perhaps experienced the same sense of awe and mystery as had beset the Celts when they established themselves in a new territory. The must have experienced the same brooding presences and the nearness of unseen things as they began to build their towns and settlements. Climatic conditions were also probably very different from those they had experienced back home and this may have contributed to their sense of unease and notions of invisible entities. Such feelings may have coalesced (as they did for the Celts) into ideas of an eerie and half-glimpsed world impinging upon their own. Those who dwelt by the sea or along lakes, with queer reflections in the air and on the water, may have particularly felt this sense of awe and mystery. Arguably, no place in America is more suited to have given rise to such sensations as the area of the Great Lakes.

The lakes—Superior, Michigan, Erie, Huron, and Ontario—together with their connecting channels, form the largest freshwater system on the surface of the earth. They are also one of the ecosystems that can be seen and recognized from the lunar surface. These freshwater "seas" are estimated to contain over six quadrillion gallons of water and cover an area of more than 94,000 square miles. They are truly an awe-inspiring phenomenon and have left their mark on the collective consciousness of the American people. Added to this, the history of the region has been a violent and bloody one. A number of Indian nations competed for power there, as did the British and the French, coupled with the Revolutionary War, the War of 1812 (which included a celebrated battle on Lake Erie), and the Upper Canada Rebellion of 1837. As some of the lakes straddle the U.S.-Canada border, conflicts between the two nations have added to the folklore of the area.

Scattered across the five Great Lakes lie thousands of small islands ranging from unnamed rocky shoals to the largest freshwater island in the world, Manitoulin. Many of these were initially uninhabited but, as the lakes were used to transport people, goods, and materials between inland settlements from the 1600s to the 1800s (being superseded by the railroads in the mid-nineteenth century), many islands began to boast lighthouses, way stations, and even the occasional township. All the islands are remarkably diverse—some have been formed in different ways from others—and the trade between them and across the lakes themselves has created a corpus of folktale and legend throughout the region.

Human endeavor and tragedy have left an indelible imprint on many of these landmasses. The bizarre histories of some of the islands of the Great Lakes—such as the mad Mormon "king" James Jesse Strang I, who established his realm together with a holy city which he called "Voree" on Little Beaver Island in Lake Michigan in the mid-nineteenth century—have also contributed to the air of mystery and enchantment, which is sometimes dismissed by skeptics. But not all of the stories can be easily explained away. There are tales, for example, of phantom islands that have been seen by a good number of people and therefore cannot be simply consigned to the imagination of a few individuals. Perhaps one of the most mysterious relates to an island sometimes known as "the Land of the Lost," which is said to lie near South Manitou Island, between Chicago and the Straits of Mackinac.

The Manitou Islands—North and South Manitou—have an almost spiritual association in their own right. The name "Manitou" is an Ojibwe Indian word that encompasses the spiritual in all its aspects. The father of all gods, the Kitchi Manitou (Great Spirit), had made these islands his home and was supposed to influence the world from that site. It is not surprising, therefore, that strange and mysterious things are said to happen in this vicinity.

As the shipping lanes across Lake Michigan developed, South Manitou became an important refuelling stop for the ships coming out of Chicago and heading on towards Mackinac. There they could take on more timber to feed their ravenous wood furnaces and also fresh water for those who traveled on them. And by the 1830s the numbers of travelers had increased. Lured west with the promise of new lands and rich pickings, thousands of Germans, Irish, and Scots caught the boats across the lake, seeing to escape the poverty, filth, and disease that was starting to characterize early nineteenth-century Chicago. In the century's early years steamers, many of them badly overladen, plowed across Lake Michigan stopping at or sailing close to the Manitou Isles. One of these was the *James Fitzmaurice,* owned by an Irish consortium in Chicago and originally used for carrying timber and ore but which was later used for transporting passengers.

In the 1830s, Chicago was visited by a new nightmare, cholera. The poorer areas of the city were soon experiencing a minor epidemic of the awful scourge, coupled with a wave of dysentery that left it reeling. In an attempt to escape the disease, desperate immigrants—Poles, Germans, Irish, and Scots—climbed aboard filthy and unseaworthy boats in order to begin a new life on the other side of the Great Lakes. As the 1830s progressed, the badly overcrowded *James Fitzmaurice* plied a lucrative trade back and forth across Lake Michigan, often stopping at South Manitou Island for refuelling. Neither lake storm nor fog kept the boat in port so lucrative was the trade.

One evening with a heavy fog hanging over Lake Michigan like a shroud, the *James Fitzmaurice* set sail from Chicago with her usual cargo of wretched passengers. Somewhere off South Manitou, she almost collided with another ship that came out of the mist towards her. The vessel seemed to be an old-style sailing ship with a tall mast and ragged-looking sails. She emerged wreathed in fog directly in front of the *James Fitzmaurice* moving extremely slowly and seemingly with some difficulty. A number of anguished passengers crowded the ship's rail to see what was going on but as they did so, the other vessel disappeared into the mist once more and it seemed to some who witnessed her that she was partly powered by oar. The crew thought nothing more of it but continued to steer their ship through the fog, hoping to make South Manitou before too long. The expected landfall did not emerge out of the fog; rather, the crew of the *James Fitzmaurice* found themselves sailing close to the coast of an unknown island where sheer cliffs rose up above grasping, water-pounded rocks. Her captain, Robert Townsend, had no idea where he was except that he was somewhere on Lake Michigan. He consulted what charts he had but could see no island at that particular spot. The nearest landfall was the Manitou Islands, still some way off by his reckoning. Nevertheless, he kept his vessel close to the unknown coast, noting its narrow bays and mighty cliffs. All the crew had the distinct impression that they were in some other reality than the familiar, sane world they knew. The currents seemed to grow more and more fierce and threatened to draw the ship onto the rocks. Townsend was frightened that there were hidden shoals somewhere nearby which would send the *Fitzmaurice* to the bottom of Lake Michigan. Then, as the mist seemed to thin a little, one of the crewmen saw what appeared to be the twinkling lights of a small settlement in a tiny bay. It could not have been more than a few cabins but there were small fishing boats in the bay and there looked to be a reasonably safe anchorage there. Townsend took a chance and ordered his crew to drop anchor beside the settlement until the fog lifted.

As the *Fitzmaurice* anchored in the fog, she was suddenly hailed from the shore. Several small boats put out and Townsend and his crew prepared to receive visitors. They were unprepared, however, for the visitors who arrived. A stiff, old man clad in the dark frock clothes of another era was the first on board and he was followed by several younger men in ragged, hand-dyed homespuns. A couple of the younger men carried what looked like ancient muskets and one seemed to wear the clothes of a military man.

The old man greeted them quite civilly but in a thick, arcane tongue—full of catches and quavers—which neither Townsend nor many of his men could follow. One of the crew declared that it was a form of English dialect long out of fashion but that the old man spoke it like a language. And all the time that he spoke, the young men kept their old-fashioned muskets trained on the crew and several of the passengers who had come up to see. It gradually emerged that they thought that this was a pirate ship carrying the poor wretches into slavery.

As his tongue became more understandable, it became apparent that the old man called himself Obediah Newton and that he was a minister or religious leader of some kind. He was certainly the chief figure in the settlement on the edge of the bay. The group he led had come all the way from England seeking religious tolerance; they were an obscure sect known as the Brethren of the Seven Testaments. Settling in Puritan New England, they had found little tolerance for their beliefs. Newton mentioned such towns as Boston and Concord from which they had been driven out. Their beliefs, which were heavily Christian fundamentalist, also included the notion of "spiritual brides," a form of polygamy, which did not accord with Christian teaching. Consequently they were hounded and harried out of most of the areas of New England in which they settled. Newton had heard of new and unexplored lands beyond a great inland sea (the Great Lakes) and one night, he received a vision from God that he should go there. Gathering his followers together, they purchased an old sailing boat in which they set out across Lake Michigan for new lands on the other side.

They had made good headway across the lake when, unexpectedly, a strange fog came down. In the mist, their old boat had run aground on an island; there they came ashore and formed a small settlement. Obediah Newton subsequently had another dream which gave fresh directions from God. This was their new home and it was to be the site of a new holy city from which missionaries would go out to proselytize in this strange country. There appeared to be timber aplenty on the island from which they could make cabins and fishing boats and there was game for food. However, the Devil was also at work on Lake Michigan for the eerie fog which had driven their boat ashore never seemed to lift and their newly constructed vessels could only venture a little way from the island's shore. They were effectively trapped in their new country.

Newton went on to say that they had been there for about a year and in that time they had made tentative explorations of the island but they had not as yet visited every part of it. It seemed to be far bigger than they had first imagined and its upper end was covered in thick woodland, which seemed almost impenetrable. But there were other people there. At one stage some of his followers had glimpsed what they thought to be the turrets of a castle "built in the Spanish style" rising above the woods. And there seemed to be Indians there too, whom the settlers declared were the agents of the Devil. Late at night, fires were glimpsed in the woodlands and drums and chanting were sometimes heard. In general, the settlers gave them a wide berth.

One evening a Scotsman had blundered into their camp raging with some sort of fever, claiming that he had been wrecked off the coast of the island. He was lodged with one of the families, where he spoke of many strange things: carriages that ran on rails with no horse to pull them, guns which men could carry on their hips. It was all very strange. The Scotsman was their only visitor for in all the time they had been on the island, no ship had come near them, nor had they seen anyone from beyond Lake Michigan. Townsend and the crew and passengers of the *James Fitzmaurice* were the first they had seen.

Eagerly and with an almost childlike curiosity, Newton asked the captain for news of England, from whence they had come. Who was king? Townsend said that he did not know and Newton told him that when they had fled, James II had been on the throne but that his hold on power had been a precarious one. Puzzled, Townsend asked him as to when they had set sail across the lake. The old man's answer startled him. Newton and his companions had come to America in 1686 and had set sail on Lake Michigan the following year. They must have foundered on the shores of the strange island in 1687—almost two hundred years before. And in this strange land, the time had passed as if it were only a year.

Suddenly Townsend was very afraid. He told Newton that he would go back to Chicago and send help. This seemed to satisfy the old man, who wished him God's speed and returned to the settlement. Townsend immediately weighed anchor and set sail into the fog, badly shaken by what he considered to be a supernatural encounter. He set course back towards Chicago but the fog was still very thick and the crew had the impression that vessels came and went unseen in its murky depths. Several times they saw shapes through the mist and tried to hail them, receiving no answer.

At length the mist cleared and the *James Fitzmaurice* found herself on the untroubled waters of Lake Michigan. She made good headway back to Chicago where another odd surprise awaited Townsend and his crew. Almost three weeks had passed since they had set sail and the ship's owners were becoming concerned for their boat. It was assumed that the *Fitzmaurice* had run aground on a shoal somewhere out on the lake during a peculiar fog which had suddenly come down. And yet, the ship had only been anchored at the strange island for a few hours before turning back. Time, thought Townsend, must have operated very differently around that eerie settlement.

For the remainder of his life, Townsend was a changed man. He gave up his captaincy and spent his time in the area of the Great Lakes, mostly engaged in religious pursuits such as preaching and copying out long portions from the Bible. He also listened to old myths and folktales of the region. It was in the course of this research that he came across an old Indian tale about a strange island out on Lake Michigan. It was considered to be a separate realm where the spirits lived and was known as the Land of the Lost. Those who ventured to it were never heard from again, mainly because they could not find a way back. The tale had almost disappeared from memory but it certainly struck a chord with Townsend. He was convinced that he had visited the mysterious place. No one believed his story, least of all his employers, who thought there had been some sort of conspiracy to cheat them out of the passage money paid by the wretches who had set out on the voyage. They threatened to hound their former captain through the courts, but in the end, the threats came to nothing. Those who had sailed with Townsend were unsure what had happened; some could not even remember visiting the curious place, let alone what had transpired there.

Although enquiries were made regarding a lost ship of Lake Michigan in 1687, no trace of Obediah Newton's ill-fated expedition was ever found. Nor was there any trace, even in England, of a sect known as the Brethren of the Seven Testaments, nor of any of their teachings. Many people thought that Townsend had dreamed up the old man and his followers. No trace of the cult or of the mysterious island upon which they lived was heard of again and the matter drifted into local folklore.

Townsend died in 1862, a year after the commencement of the American Civil War, still insisting that his story was true. Several of those who had been with him had been questioned in an attempt to verify the tale, but they had given conflicting accounts regarding the landing in the bay and the meeting with the settlers and some had even denied the incident altogether. Although several ships mysteriously vanished on the lake, their disappearance was simply put down to covert military activity or to pirates. As the war progressed, the story was quickly forgotten and today remains no more than a seldom-told legend of the Great Lakes.

And yet, there are other disquieting accounts of mysterious landmasses being seen on Lake Michigan. And there are more stories of strange ships of antique design seen at a distance or through a fog plying their way across the waters of the Great Lakes. On South Fox Island, for example, loggers working in a timber camp spotted what appeared to be a pilgrim ship under full sail passing by the coast of the island during a rainstorm. The vessel vanished into the driving rain and was lost to view. It was never seen again and no explanation as to what it was has ever been given. A small island is reputed to appear from time to time near Lake Huron's Bowes Island. There, a small cabin with smoke rising from its chimney is occasionally seen. Some witnesses have even claimed to have seen a wild-looking individual come down from the cabin to the shoreline and watch passing ships with a hostile stare. At other times, there is no island there at all, just a stretch of empty lake punctuated by tiny shoals. This story may, of course, stem from a time when there actually was an insane hermit on Bowes Island, which has also been nicknamed "Madman's Island" or "Wildman's Island." He constructed a little cabin out of driftwood and wreckage, the ruins of which survived long after his death, and lived in splendid isolation, subsisting on fish and mollusks that he caught along the island shore and filling the rest of his time in making strange noises—roars, catcalls, howls, and singing—as ships went past his domain. No one knew who he was or why he had become an exile on the island but it was believed that he was someone who had been crossed in love or who had suffered some great grief which had unhinged his mind. One day his primitive canoe was found drifting upside down on Lake Huron and it was assumed he had drowned. However, his ghost was said to haunt a phantom island that appeared every once in a while to passing ships and was sometimes seen paddling his spectral canoe in the direction of Georgian Bay.

The madman of Bowes Island may even have belonged to a number of religious hermits who retreated to the islands of the Great Lakes to pursue their beliefs and meditations. This was again in the manner of the Celtic monks who withdrew from the world into remote and inaccessible places such as mountains and islands in order to experience God and to see visions. Many of these isolationists claimed to have seen paradise, hell, or other realities and to have seen beings coming and going from these places. These may have included other islands or continents inhabited by angelic, demonic, or supernatural creatures. Throughout the Great Lakes there were many of these *religieux* who either lived alone or ruled over small communities of followers—as Obediah Newton was supposed to do.

On Lake Erie, too, a mysterious light, as if from a lighthouse, is sometimes seen near Kelleys Island. There are several minor shoals in the area—none big enough to be called an "island"—amongst which a ghostly warning beacon is said to appear. What this beacon might be or what its purpose is are unknown but many lake-going mariners claim that they have been thankful for it as a guide. Perhaps it comes from yet another mysterious island that takes a benign interest in the affairs of our own. Maybe it is a gift from the otherworld to the travelers of this one.

Phantom lands, lost civilizations, and forgotten countries are the stuff of Celtic legend and mythology, a corpus of belief and folklore which has been transported to the New World. Even on the brightest, most peaceful day, the Great Lakes often have an awe-inspiring, mysterious, and sometimes sinister aspect to them that readily blends with the ancient tales of the Celtic peoples concerning the otherworld. Or maybe, just maybe, there actually is another, more mystical country—whether lost or forgotten—somewhere out there across the lakes.

Wyoming

The Treasure of a Forgotten Land

Dreams often play a significant role in folklore. They sometimes show the future, they warn, they provide information. In many stories and legends, individuals are guided by them towards some course of action or to some place where their destiny awaits. Some may marry as a result of dreams, others may avoid certain tasks, and some may even find financial gain. This last aspect looms particularly large in Irish folklore, in which dreams and visions often show the sites of hidden gold and lost treasure. Stories in this vein are common across Ireland and usually follow a similar pattern: a person dreams of a certain distant location where there is great wealth stored away and he or she journeys there to find that the dream is entirely accurate and a fabulous fortune is waiting for them. In some versions there is a supernatural guardian or the treasure may vanish within a few moments, but the dreamer is usually well warned of this event by the vision. If the treasure is lost, it is probably through negligence or stupidity.

The vast amounts of wealth supposedly hidden away at various times in Ireland's troubled history have probably contributed to the rich corpus of folktales that exists on the subject. Treasures of ancient Celtic kings, Norman loot, Viking plunder, and church rents stored away during the Penal times must all be waiting to be uncovered and it is through the medium of dreams that this discovery takes place. A typical story comes from Armagh where a man in that city dreamt of a vast hoard of treasure hidden in a rath, or earthworks, many miles distant. It was reputedly the treasure of several of the ancient high kings of Ireland and dated back to the time when Armagh had been a royal seat. Normally, he would have dismissed the dream but the times were bad in Ireland and there was little work to be had so any money at all was more than welcome.

He decided to check out the peculiar vision. He told a number of local men about the dream and they all insisted on going with him to see if there was any truth in it. The rath had an extremely sinister reputation and the day was very dark and overcast so there was a good deal of fear amongst the treasure hunters. Nevertheless, they set out with picks and spades to see if they could unearth the gold. After several hours' hard digging, they reached a flagstone set deep in the earth. This was just as the man had seen in his dream and in that dream, when he had lifted it something terrible had happened, but he could not now remember what. Nonetheless, they managed to raise the heavy flag and looked down on several large chests of gold. However, there was something else: around the chests was wrapped a massive serpent. It opened a jeweled eye as the stone was lifted. So anxious was the man to get the gold that he stretched forward into the hole to get a handful of coins. At this, the serpent reared up, showing dripping fangs, and with a single gulp, it swallowed the poor fellow whole. Dropping their picks and shovels, the others ran for their lives. From time to time, it is said in the locality, the screams of the original dreamer can be heard coming from beneath a nearby lake. It seems that he is to be continually eaten by the serpent throughout eternity—a salutary warning to anyone who might follow dreams too closely.

In another story, an Offaly man dreamed of going to Dublin, where he would meet in Sackville (now O'Connell) Street an old friend whom he had not seen for years. This man would hand him a key which would unlock the door to a vast fortune. Shortly after, he did go to Dublin and as he was walking down Sackville Street, he happened to bump into a man whom he had not seen since they had been boys together back in Offaly. They adjourned to the nearest pub and began to reminisce over old times back home. The companion mentioned an old story which they had both heard in their youth concerning a hoard of monkish gold hidden somewhere in the ruins of an old monastery near Roscrea in North Tipperary. He mentioned some clues which he had heard in an old tale but added that they were just idle superstition. His companion, however, was not so sure.

He returned home and procured some digging implements. Then he set out for North Tipperary on what might well have been a fool's errand. The area around Roscrea used to be littered with monasteries and there are many stories in various localities concerning hidden treasure dating back to monastic times. However, back in Offaly, he had dreamed the dream again and this time he used the key to open a great door behind which lay heaps of gold and valuable religious artifacts. Although the door was locked, it was also fastened with a great seal on which were a number of words in Latin. The key seemed to break all locks, giving the dreamer access to the treasure beyond the door. He was now more convinced than ever that the vision was trying to tell him something. He went to the place that the old legends had spoken of—a remote, windy cemetery— and, following the clues that his friend had given him, began to dig amongst the roots of a great oak tree on the very edge of the graveyard. He had not dug down all that far when his spade struck the edge of a large box, which he dragged to the surface. It appeared to be fastened with a seal that bore some sort of Latin inscription he could not read. He was able to break this seal and throwing open the chest, found that it did indeed contain gold and religious valuables which made him a wealthy man for the rest of his days. The dream was metaphorical: the "key" given to him by his friend was the set of clues which arose from their discussion, while the seal appears both on the door and on the unearthed chest. As such, the dream was accurate in every respect. In some versions of the tale, the treasure is cursed (as it was taken from a religious institution) and brings the dreamer nothing but ill luck, but in the main, the tale is used to demonstrate the veracity of dreams.

Dreams must have also been important to the Irish immigrants arriving in the New World. To them, the land to which they arrived was unknown and likely held many mysteries and surprises. Immigrants may well have dreamed about sites they had never seen before but upon which they would eventually settle; there are various family tales about them doing so. But the notion of dreams as an indicator of hidden wealth sometimes became fused with a much older quest for treasure in the Americas, a quest which involved lost Indian kingdoms.

Since the first Europeans arrived in America there have been tales of fabulous and extremely wealthy realms lying far away in the unexplored wilds. Such legends came to a head in the mid- to late sixteenth century as Spanish conquistadors began to probe the continent. Spanish leaders took such tales very seriously and mounted expeditions to determine the location of these kingdoms and deprive them of their wealth by colonizing them in the name of Spain. One such leader was Francisco Vasquez de Coronado, governor of New Galicia (contemporary Sinaloa and Nayarit in Mexico). Coronado had sent the priest Marcos de Niza on a voyage to the north, into what is today effectively New Mexico. The priest returned with tales of a wealthy Indian city called Cibola, which was made out of gold. Coronado's interest was raised and in 1540, he mounted a large force of 340 Spaniards, 300 Indians, and 1,000 slaves and fighting men (both native and African) to locate and conquer it. Following the coast of the Gulf of California he reached the Sonora River where he traveled upstream, crossing the Gila to Cibola. Here, he was met with disappointment for the fabulous city turned out to be nothing like de Niza had described it. Rather than a city made of pure gold, it was nothing more than a simple pueblo of the Zuni Indians. Marcos de Niza was sent back to Mexico in disgrace. Coronado, however, stayed on and explored further. He visited several other Zuni pueblos but found nothing of interest. Undeterred he sent out several expeditions, the leaders of which became explorers in their own right. Their brief was to follow up stories concerning fantastic cities and kingdoms which were said to lie in the hinterland.

Melchior Diaz investigated the lands around the mouth of the Colorado River, while Pedro de Tovar was sent northwest where he rendezvoused with Hernando de Alarcon who was heading due north. He heard of a great river far to the west where there were fantastic gold mines and where the Indians were extraordinarily wealthy. Garcia Lopez de Cardenas was sent out to find this river and the mines, and while he failed in this, he did become the first European ever to see the magnificent Grand Canyon. Coronado's captain of artillery, Hernando de Alvarado, was sent east and at Pecos pueblo his force encountered an Indian whom Coronado would later name "El Turco" (the Turk). El Turco told tales of golden cities far to the east and, following some of these tales, de Alvarado and his men became the first known foreigners to partially cross the High Plains. Giving up in this quest, de Alvarado took El Turco back with him to Coronado's winter quarters at Tiguex (present-day Bernalillo, near Albuquerque). The wily Indian regaled the "great general" with even more fantastic tales, including one concerning

Quivira, a rich country in the northwest where there were many gold mines. Coronado himself led the expedition to find it, using El Turco as his guide. He forced a march across the Texas panhandle but seemed no closer to finding Quivira; he now suspected that the Turk was leading him astray. He had the Indian executed. Other guides led him to the area of present-day Lindsborg, Kansas, where he found nothing. Battling savage Indians and disease, Coronado explored further, and crossing a fast-flowing river (now known as the Wichita), he finally found Quivira. The disappointment of Cibola was repeated. Along the banks of the river were nothing but grass-covered mud huts, and the Quivira Indians (later the Wichitas) were extremely poor. They did not own even the smallest amount of gold. In disgust and frustration, Coronado turned back. He wintered again at Tiguex before returning to Mexico in 1542. Only one hundred of his men came back with him. His expedition had been a complete and utter failure, but even so, Coronado remained as governor of New Galicia until 1544 when he retired to Mexico City where he died in 1554.

Coronado was the most famous of all the Spanish treasure seekers but he was not the only one. Many lesser-known conquistadors crossed and recrossed the American continent lured on by stories of marvelous Indian cities and wealthy gold mines in the mountains. Although none of these were ever found, the legends persisted and fused with the myths of the incoming settlers to form a new strand of American folklore. Various gold rushes in several parts of the continent only led credence to these legends of lost Indian mines, and the belief in wealthy lodes soon became staple fare in the developing West.

The most famous of all these treasures was the Lost Dutchman Mine in the Superstition Mountains of Arizona. Legend says that this mine has not been worked since the 1880s when Jacob Waltz, a German immigrant, also known as the "Dutchman," mined it. However, prior to that it was said to be an old Indian mine, part of a forgotten Spanish-Indian empire. Alternately, it had been mined by Mexicans and the occasional prospector before becoming lost to the world. Waltz is supposed to have rediscovered the mine—one of the richest in Arizona—deep in the rugged mountains to the east of Apache Junction. He then made periodic trips into the Superstitions (also known as Hell's Backyard), returning to Phoenix with small quantities of pure gold ore. Waltz is said to have died in Phoenix in 1891 without ever revealing the source of his bonanza gold, thus sparking one of the most enduring legends in the mountains (and, arguably, in the whole of America) concerning lost and forgotten mines.

But did Jacob Waltz exist and if so what had he found? There certainly seems enough evidence to suggest that he did exist and that he was both a prospector and a miner. Researchers have unearthed a Jacob Waltz, born near Oberschwandorf, Wurttemburg, Germany, around 1810 (no baptismal records have been discovered but his age on German census records seems to suggest this date), who immigrated to America in 1845. He arrived in New York City before traveling to North Carolina to pan for gold both there and in Georgia. By the time he arrived at Meadow Creek, North Carolina, the diggings there had been well established and there was little to be had so he moved on to Georgia but found equally little success there. He next appears in Natchez, Mississippi, where he filed a letter of intent to become a citizen of the United States at the Adams County Courthouse on November 12, 1848. It was a shrewd move. In many of the goldfields it was much easier to stake a claim as an American citizen than it was as a foreigner, and as a naturalized American, Waltz could personally register any fortune he found. He planned to move on to California.

Together with another prospector, Ruben Blakney, Waltz worked on the San Gabriel River in California's "motherlode territory" for eleven years. It was on July 19, 1861, that he finally became a naturalized citizen of the United States at the Los Angeles County Courthouse. It was while working on the San Gabriel that he met another prospector, Elisha Marcus Reavis (who would later become known as the "hermit of Superstition Mountain"), who may have told him a legend of a mysterious Spanish-Indian kingdom in the Southwest.

Although Waltz and "Old Rube" Blakney made some money on the San Gabriel, they never struck the longed-for lode. By now the Californian goldfields were beginning to peter out and many prospectors were heading southwest in search of new lodes. Waltz is thought to have joined a group of them (similar, perhaps, to the Peeples-Weaver expedition) around 1863 and headed into the Bradshaw Mountain region of Arizona Territory. This was one of the first prospector bands to enter the area, which was controlled by the Apaches, and as one of the earliest settlers, Waltz appears to have been very active in the region. His name appears on a minor claim filed at Prescott, Arizona, in 1863. His name also appears on a territorial census taken in 1864 where he is listed as a miner, aged fifty-four years and a native of Germany. Further, his name appears on a petition to the territorial governor, John N. Goodwin, demanding a militia to control Apache raids on miner camps in the Bradshaw Mountains. The name of Jacob Waltz also appears on registration documents for the Big Rebel and General Grant claims in the Bradshaw region. He seems to have worked the area right up until 1867.

Following a lack of success in the Bradshaw Mountains, Waltz moved on to the Salt River Valley in 1868 and filed a homestead of 160 acres there. He began making periodic trips into the mountains surrounding the Salt River, presumably to prospect for more gold, and it was said that he was following the old legends of which Elisha M. Reavie had told him. It is thought that he uncovered an already-worked mine from which he was able to draw his bonanza gold between 1868 and 1886. During this time and prior to 1886, he must have braved the dangers of marauding Apaches, who were particularly restive up until the surrender of their great leader Geronimo at Skeleton Canyon.

Jacob Waltz died in Phoenix on October 25, 1891, in the home of a Julia Thomas without disclosing the source of his gold. It is also said that when he died, several large lumps of gold ore were actually found beneath his bed. Julia Thomas was convinced that his mine lay deep in the Superstition Mountains and traveled there with two brothers—Rhinehart and Hermann Petrasch—to look for it. After several weeks lost in rugged and inhospitable country, they returned to Phoenix empty handed. As they were now broke, Thomas produced several fake maps which purported to show the location of a rich gold mine and which she sold to several would-be prospectors. All hunts for the place came to nothing.

But what had Waltz found? The story that he had heard from Reavis may have concerned a legendary and extremely wealthy Spanish-Indian kingdom in the Southwest. This had been based upon the remnants of a far older kingdom of the forebears of the Tanoan Indians and was reputedly founded by Juan de Onate, a conquistador-explorer around 1598. Like Coronado, he had marched north from Mexico and had waged war against the Pueblos, capturing Caypa, on the confluence of the Rio Grande and Rio Chama Rivers. He is also credited with founding San Gabriel del Yunque, the first capital of Spanish New Mexico. Hearing of fabulous gold mines which had serviced a kingdom in present-day Arizona, he had marched on but failed to find them. It was his successor, New Mexico's third governor, Don Pedro de Peralta, the founder of Santa Fe in 1610, who discovered and developed these ancient mines. He did so by forming an alliance with local Indians and together they began to excavate the area, uncovering rich lodes of almost pure gold, just as the forerunners of the Tanoan Indians had done many centuries before. However, they enslaved other local Indian tribes based in many of the pueblos scattered throughout the area, and in 1680, some of these villages revolted, killing many Spanish settlers strung out between Socorro and Santa Cruz de la Canada (near Espanola). They drove the Spaniards south into what is now Texas, to El Paso del Norte (El Paso), and claimed the land for themselves. The conquistadors would not return until 1692, under Don Diego de Vargas, and then only in limited numbers. With the Spanish gone, the Ute, Navajo, and Apache claimed control of the area, harassing the Pueblos. The Apaches, especially, had been driven south by the Comanches and were particularly ferocious throughout the region. Whatever remnants of the former kingdom remained—including the mines—they destroyed, killing settlers and wiping out all traces of civilized occupation. The mines that had reputedly supplied this kingdom with gold (gold trains were supposed to have traveled to Taos and San Gabriel del Yunque) were now more or less lost, existing only in legend and story. It was these legendary mines that Jacob Waltz is said to have discovered. The fact that Waltz never revealed the exact location of the mines only adds to the legend, giving it a greater force and mystery.

Well-developed legends like these—many concerning lost treasures and vanished mines which were sometimes connected to ancient kingdoms—merged with the Celtic notions of dreams and visions as conveyors of information to create a new strand of American folklore. One of the most celebrated, the story of the Lost Cabin Mine, comes from Wyoming and serves to illustrate the fusion of the two ideas.

As the California goldfields began to peter out, a number of prospectors began to look elsewhere for rich veins. One of these was Allen Hulbert, a miner who had been working for three or four years in California with little to show for it. He teamed up with two other prospectors, Cox and Jones, and between them, around 1863, they set out for the Rocky Mountains to try their luck. On his way, Hulbert had an odd dream. In it he saw a small cabin at the confluence of two creeks with gold set outside its door in large bags. In the background was a large, leafless tree which looked as though it might be dying. Investigating further, he found that the sacks were crammed with so much gold that they were spilling out onto the ground and although smoke was coming from the cabin's chimney, nobody answered when Hulbert called. He tried the door but found it locked and, as he turned to help himself to some of the gold, he woke up. The dream had been extremely vivid and seemed very odd but he paid it no heed.

Following the Yellowstone River, the prospectors pressed onwards to the mouth of the Big Horn River and then turned southeast into the Big Horn Mountains to look for gold. They had little success. Then Hulbert dreamed again. Once more he saw the little cabin with the smoke billowing up from its chimney and on the front porch, the oldest man he had ever seen was sitting, drawing on a pipe. Hulbert greeted him and the old-timer told him that he stood on a rich vein of gold which had once served a powerful Indian kingdom stretching right across the Big Horn Mountains. He had built his cabin on what remained of the largest Indian pueblo but the ground was sacred and the cabin passed between one world and the other and could only be found with the aid of dreams. Hulbert had a feeling that the other might have told him more had he not woken up. He told his partners about the vision but they simply laughed and dismissed it. Nevertheless, under Hulbert's urging, they moved farther southeast.

On a river fork, possibly on the north fork of Crazy Woman Creek or on Rock Creek, something strange awaited Allen Hulbert. Where a small stream entered the river stood a small cabin in the shadow of a huge and leafless tree which looked as though it might be dying. It seemed like the place he had seen in the dream although there were significant differences. No smoke issued from the chimney and the cabin was falling in upon itself and looked as though it had been long abandoned. Nevertheless, Hulbert believed that some unknown power had guided them to this region and began to dig close by. He and his companions dug down about seven feet, creating a steep shaft, when they hit a seam of incredibly rich pay dirt. Using sluice boxes and a small dam across the creek, they recovered a bushel of gold nuggets. And each night, Allen Hulbert had the same dream in which the old man came out of the cabin and told him that this was the treasure of a long-vanished kingdom but that he was welcome to it, provided he used it only for good. The prospectors agreed to spend winter at the site and began to excavate a wider area. In the course of this, they unearthed what looked like a man's skeleton, partly clad in buckskin. Allen Hulbert wondered if it was the old man whom he had seen in his dreams and whether it was this man who had raised the cabin in the wilderness. The winter months passed slowly in the mountains.

With the spring, Hulbert set out for civilization in order to register the claim. He met a party of settlers heading into Wyoming and tagged along with them. During his time with the party, he engaged in several games of cards and using his new-found wealth, managed to cheat some of the settlers out of their hard-earned money. That night, in Hulbert's dream, the old man came out of the cabin in an extremely angry mood. Hulbert had betrayed him and for that he would never enjoy the treasure of the lost cabin. As he shook his fist, Hulbert awoke with a feeling of dread. Alarmed by the dream, he started back for the creek. Horror awaited him. In his absence, Indians (probably Arapahos) had attacked the camp and Cox and Jones had been killed. More importantly, the cabin seemed to have completely vanished; not a trace of it remained, although it might have been pulled down by the raiders. The dead tree was also gone. The Indians had not withdrawn all that far and the surrounding woods were full of them. Hulbert had to get out of the area and so, loading up what golden nuggets he could, he headed south, keeping well away from the main trails in case he met a war band. Eighteen days later, he overtook a wagon train headed towards the North Platte River country and joined them on a journey to the Montana goldfields

He appears to have had little success in Montana because in 1864, Hulbert was in Virginia City trying to drum up interest for an expedition back to Crazy Woman Creek. He led a party back into the mountains to look for the mine but they could not find it. Facing repeated Indian attacks, they returned to Virginia City empty handed. In 1866, Allen Hulbert discovered another reasonably rich mine on the Big Prickly Pear Creek which set him up for the rest of his days. He never lost the dream, however, of finding the strange mine beside the ruined cabin. It remained as elusive as ever. Perhaps it did not really exist in this world but in some strange and mysterious realm akin to the Celtic otherworld.

That is one version of the story. There are, of course, several others. In one variant, a group of seven or eight Swedes set out to look for gold in the Big Horn Mountain region during the spring of 1865. They were continually attacked by Indians, who wiped out the majority of the party. Two of them reached Fort Connor/Fort Reno a few miles below Sussex, Wyoming (Fort Fetterman), in October 1865 with seven thousand dollars in gold nuggets. They then made their way to Fort Laramie and then back east to return with ten others. The entire party headed back into the Big Horn Mountain area through Johnston County, where it was said the Swedes had discovered the Lost Cabin Mine that Allen Hulbert had originally located. They were never heard of again and it was assumed that the entire party of twelve had been wiped out by Indians. Before they left Fort Laramie one of the Swedes had a dream in which he saw the small cabin with the old man sitting on the front porch beside sacks of gold. It was this dream which inspired them to go into the Big Horn and probably brought about their deaths.

Many groups have searched for the lost mine but none have found it. The most famous of these prospectors was Thomas Paige Comstock, who gave his name to the Comstock Mine. However, another famous frontiersman who claimed to have dreamed about the lost cabin (and to have found its gold) was the mountain man Jim Bridger. Still another explorer in the area was the Jesuit missionary Fr. Jean Pierre de Smet, who made donations of pure gold taken from some unknown source to various Catholic churches in Arizona.

In some versions of the tale, the cabin is said to lie in the middle fork of Rock Creek but it can only be seen at certain times of the year. At all other times, it is believed to melt away into a kind of otherworld, similar to that mystical realm in which the Celts believed. It is also said that a local rancher, Bill Bryant, found a bottle down at the middle fork that contained a letter from one of the Swedes who had disappeared. What was in this letter is unknown but it was thought to have stated that at least some of the Swedish group were still alive in some place beyond human vision. Of course this might only be pure legend as neither the bottle nor the letter was ever recorded as being seen. There was even once said to be a half-ruined cabin on the middle fork which a rancher named George Yarwood tore down in order to try to find the Swedes' gold but he found nothing. Yarwood is then said to have built a cabin of his own in an attempt to locate the Lost Cabin Mine, but if he did, no trace of it exists today and there is no account as to whether or not he was successful.

Between 1898 and the early 1900s, August Hettinger met up with a man called Morgareidge (it is unclear if this was his real name) who had been hunting and prospecting in the Big Horn Mountains. Morgareidge said he had found a campsite close to a ruined cabin which stood under a large tree. There had been rusted cooking implements, old canvas, rope, and hollowed logs which had been used to make rudimentary sluice boxes. The hunter also showed Hettinger some gold nuggets and told him that along with these had been the skeleton of what appeared to be a very old man. At the time, Morgareidge appears to have been in very poor health and less than a month after his meeting with Hettinger, he died without revealing the exact location of the campsite (and associated diggings) that he had come across. All that Hettinger knew was that it was near a ruined cabin somewhere near the middle fork but he thought that the old hunter had hinted at enough to lead him in its general direction. Doubtless, he would eventually find it. He got several backers together and mounted an expedition into the mountains. Although Hettinger had a general idea where the site was, he could not find it. It is said that he dreamed of the cabin beneath the spreading tree from which an old man came out and chased him away. Apparently he was not welcome in the area and the hidden treasure was not for him. He wandered around for several days, finding nothing, before returning home. Morgareidge's treasure remained as elusive as ever. From time to time, other travelers in the region claim to have come across rotted corpses and the remnants of decaying sluice boxes which shortly disappeared. The last such "discovery" was in the 1920s.

So what is the Lost Cabin Mine? More importantly, who is the ancient occupant who lives there but only appears in dreams? Is he some sort of hermit, like Elisha Reavis in the Superstitions? Or is he a spirit from the otherworld guarding an ancient treasure of a long-forgotten kingdom? Is he merely the ghost of some long-dead prospector, protecting his claim from unwelcome visitors? Did the pure gold, which Allen Hulbert uncovered once, finance a vanished civilization in the region, perhaps remembered only in legend or folktale? Finally, does the cabin itself sometimes slip out of one world and into another? The answers may very well lie lost forever in the vast mountain wilderness of the Big Horn.

Part 2
Mysterious and Sacred Places

Connecticut

The Place of Noises

The peoples of the Celtic world not only experienced visions of the fabled otherworld, they sometimes heard it as well. In many ways, this was far more terrifying. Instead of seeing strange shapes in clouds, water, or in the air, individuals were assailed by sounds and voices from these sources. In Celtic society, such noises were believed to be the sounds of spirits communicating with the mortal world to instruct, warn, admonish, or prophesy. Great attention was paid to them although many of the sounds that were heard were unintelligible and had to be interpreted by the Druids, the Celtic priests of the early period. Sounds might emerge from deep wells, from trees, from rocks, or simply from out of the natural landscape—any place where spirits were believed to dwell. Later, Christian tradition sometimes took the view that these were the sounds of angels speaking from holy wells or sacred shrines to convey God's will to his people. More often, however, it declared that the noises were in fact made by demons trying to tempt the faithful or lure them from the Christian path. Such beings, to emphasize their point, often accompanied their noises with physical manifestations in the landscape such as a trembling of the ground, storms, lightning, and other natural phenomena. These voices, as described by those who heard them, were certainly suggestive of demons. They were mostly low, gruff, almost mechanical in their tone although sometimes they could be high-pitched and shrill. These latter sounds were attributed to the fairy kind: dark and evil sprites who were concerned with doing mortals great harm. This notion was strengthened by the fact that the noises were usually heard at specific locations, places that were sometimes associated with the fairy kind.

As the belief in the otherworld began to develop in the Celtic mind and some sort of definition was placed on the realm (although it has never really been properly defined), other notions began to creep in. These sounds were not only the noises of fairies and sprites, they were the voices of the dead coming from the afterlife, calling out to the living, probably in torment. Just as it was unwise to listen to the blandishments of demons and fairies, so it was not good to pay close attention to the cries of the dead that rang across the landscape from a world unseen. Many of these voices and cries were heard at night when darkness pervaded and they were strongly associated with ghosts and unquiet souls. Once again, they were placed at specific locations—trees, rivers, etc.—possibly where some act had been committed or that had some association with the departed—old graveyards or burying grounds.

For example, at a stone cairn near the village of Dungiven, County Derry, in the North of Ireland, a voice was heard to call out at certain times of the year, usually around Halloween or May Eve, the name of the next to die in the community. The cairn, an overgrown heap of stones, was situated in a small stand of trees that was supposedly badly "fairy haunted," providing a link between the modern day and the pagan fairy beliefs of the past. Few people would venture near the cairn after dark when the spirit that dwelt there was supposed to speak. Similarly, a standing stone in County Cavan (Irish Republic) was said to cry with a human voice when someone in the surrounding countryside was to die. Various locations are given for this site, but many of them seem to be located around Blacklion, near the border between the Irish Republic and the North of Ireland. It was an evil thing to hear this sound and in some variants of the tale, the hearer listens to his or her own name being called—a signal of approaching death. These variations often relate the cry to that of the banshee, a warning, supernatural creature of Irish fairy folklore. Not far away, Lough Naman Finn on the side of Belmore Mountain in Fermanagh, was said to scream with a human voice when mist gathered on its surface, particularly early in the morning or at twilight. To hear the scream meant illness or death. It is generally said that three nuns were killed there by a local bailiff named Hassard during the nineteenth century and this is the cause of the lake's screams, but no one is truly sure. There seems to have been a tradition of strange noises there for much longer and it is to be noted that no fish can live in the water of the lake.

Scotland, too, has its strange and supernatural sounds. For example, on an island in the middle of Loch an Eilean near Aviemore in Speyside a spirit has been said to wail on certain nights. It was thought that this was a demon commanded by the dreadful Wolf of Badenoch (one of the sons of Robert II of Scotland) who had constructed a castle there and was known to deal with witches and warlocks in the Highlands. Although no real explanation was ever given for these noises— they were deemed to be incredibly mysterious—it was widely believed that they had their source in the otherworld.

With immigration to America, many of these old beliefs and legends made the transition across the Atlantic. The American landscape was just as wild and rugged as any in Scotland or Ireland and was just as suggestive of spirits dwelling in caves, rivers, and deep forests as the land which the settlers had left. Moreover, many of the Indians who lived in the wilds had their own stories of strange noises and mysterious voices, and these blended well with the tales of the otherworld and the creatures there who sometimes called to mankind. Strange and brooding geographical features, deep forests, caves, and chasms all across the country were imbued with some sort of malign intelligence which sometimes manifested itself in sounds or voices. Settlers told of eerie voices that spoke in sinister tones deep in the woodlands, thus developing a corpus of mythology concerning communications (whether understood or not) from another, supernatural world. The demons and ghosts which had beset them in both Ireland and Scotland were just as potent in America, if not more so. Now they combined with Indian myths to create terrifying mythologies which smacked, amongst the early settlers at least, of the work of the Devil in this new and mysterious land. The founding settlers considered these to be the pagan spirits of an earlier time which refused to relinquish their hold on the land they had formerly inhabited.

As settlement of the American continent continued, other considerations came into play. The country experienced two serious conflicts: the American Revolution in the eighteenth century and the Civil War in the nineteenth. The numbers of dead in both these wars reached horrific totals and added to a developing tradition of ghost lore which was beginning to establish itself in the nightmares of the American people. Memories of the awful slaughter etched themselves into the consciousness of the growing communities and soon the noises and sounds heard in the remote hollows and woods were connected in the popular mind with the dead and usually with some terrible or tragic event which had occurred in the vicinity. Accidents and murders were also added to the emerging folklore, and as the echoes of the Civil War died away, they were replaced by tales of bloody battles against the Indians, all of which created ghosts and phantom noises in specific localities. This was just as it had been in the Celtic west from which many of the settlers had come.

At the upper end of Indian Creek, Unicoi County, Tennessee, for example, the family of William Lewis was attacked by marauding Indians during the fall of 1780. A harsh winter the previous year, coupled with unseasonable weather in spring, had depleted the Indians' crops and the recent French and Indian War had made them edgy. The first frost of 1780 had now passed, to be followed by a period of warm weather known as Indian summer, a time when the tribes were often at their most restive. Nevertheless, William Lewis and his eldest son went fishing one bright afternoon. As they returned to their cabin hidden in the forest, they heard the war whoop of an Indian band and realized the worst. The cabin was in flames, Lewis's six-year-old son had been beaten until his face was no longer recognizable, his wife had been brutally murdered, and his daughter had been carried off. The barbarism of the attack shocked Lewis beyond words and threatened to drive him to insanity. He was later able to bargain for the return of his daughter and of another son from an Indian hunting party by bartering a rifle and a powder horn which he had about him. The original perpetrators of the terrible and barbaric act were never brought to justice.

The brutality of the incident left its mark on the lands surrounding the upper part of Indian Creek. From time to time, persons in the area have heard the sound of crackling flames, an echo of the cabin burned more than two hundred years ago, and the anguished screams of a woman or a small child as they are butchered by Indian raiders. The sounds are said to be repeated over and over again and then they fall silent for long periods, sometimes as long as several years. These sounds are still considered an evil thing to hear by the communities round about.

Not far away in East Tennessee, at a place known as Piney Flats (midway between Johnston City and Bristol), the ghost of a Union soldier continually cries for help. During an exchange there in 1863, during the Civil War, Confederate sharpshooters (so the legend goes) used a small copse of trees near the main trail as a location to pick off Union patrols as they rode through the area following a bloody battle at Jonesborough, the county seat of Washington County. A small group comprising three Union soldiers came up the trail past the copse, pursuing stragglers from the Confederate forces that had retreated behind the Greene County line. As they rode past, several snipers hidden in the brush opened up, killing two of them outright and injuring the third in the leg. The bullet clipped an artery and the man fell to the ground, bleeding profusely as the snipers fled. Tearing his shirt, he made a makeshift tourniquet and called for help. None came and although he called and called, he was answered only by silence. By morning he was dead. Several days later, the three bodies were discovered by neighborhood boys who brought their parents to inspect the awful find. By now crows, buzzards, and wild creatures had attacked the bodies, leaving them virtually unrecognizable. As no one knew their identities, the three men were given a Christian burial in the local cemetery and this part of the war was soon forgotten. Or so it seemed.

Many years after, following the end of the war, a traveler was passing the copse when he heard somebody calling for help. He knew nothing of an ambush in the locality or of a dying soldier and went over to the trees to see who was calling. There was nobody there although the traveler could still hear the voice, now crying with an added urgency. When asked who was shouting, the voice suddenly fell silent and was replaced by the sound of the wind in the branches overhead. Convinced that he had been hearing things, the traveler told his queer story in a hostelry in Piney Flats itself. Soon people began to make the connection with the ambush and with the three Union soldiers who had died, one of whom had quite clearly bled to death. The voice which spoke from the trees was that of the latter. Once one person had heard it, many others in the locality did likewise and the story, together with the sounds themselves, passed into rural folklore.

The copse is today part of a private farm and "No Trespassing" signs have been put up all around it. Even so, it is said to remain haunted by odd noises, particularly one which sounds like a human voice calling for help. It is a test of bravery amongst the local youth to spend the night in the "hainted copse" for a dare. Some of them even say that they have seen the spirit of the dying Union soldier glowing amongst the dark trees although there are those who say that the voice has an even older, more pagan origin than the Civil War.

Legends of voices and sounds from comparatively recent and also extremely ancient times can be found not only in northeast Tennessee, but also all across America, many tied to specific local sites. In northwest North Carolina, a ghostly choir is frequently heard in the air around Roan Mountain. Old-timers say that the sounds are a choir of angels practicing for Judgement Day but the noises are clearly pre-Christian as they appear in the legends of the Catawba Indians who once inhabited the Pisgah Forest and laid claim to the surrounding region. A reference to the singing was also made by John Strother, who surveyed the area in 1799 to mark out the Carolina/Tennessee border. The most chilling account, however, is given by another surveyor named Libourel who went through the Roan in 1873. Speaking many years later, he claimed to have entered a cave somewhere near the summit of the mountain and found the source of the music. Those who sang, said Libourel, were not angels; they were the skeletal dead. The beautiful music which haunted the top of Roan Mountain came from the crumbling skulls of long-dead corpses—some Indian, some European. All exhibited deep gashes in whatever flesh still clung to their bones. Libourel was convinced that he was listening to the Choir of the Damned and fled the site. He never returned, but the story that he told lingers as a connection between the sounds of another world and the dead.

Arguably one of the most famous of these "sound sites" is to be found in rural Connecticut, near what was originally the location of the village of East Haddam. The site at which these noises are heard dates back to the Indians, but there is little doubt that these old legends have been mixed with Celtic beliefs to form a basis for local folklore. The old Indian name for the area, according to the New England historian Samuel Drake, is Machemoodus, which means "the place of noises," and it is well named. Since records have been kept, queer sounds have been heard there by a great many people, some of whom have recorded their experiences. The area was, according to many of these accounts, greatly disturbed by strange roaring sounds accompanied by frightful quakings and tremors of the land all around, causing great alarm to the people who lived there.

One of the earliest recounts of the eerie occurrences is given in a letter from the Reverend Mr. Hosmer, a local minister, to a Mr. Prince of Boston, Massachusetts, in August 1729. He states that the area is a very old one and was at one time used for Indian powwows, being a site where the Indians communed with their spirits and where their gods spoke to them to direct them and give advice. With the words of the gods came a trembling and shaking of the ground and this continued together with peculiar noises long after the Indians had departed from the region. The explanation that was usually given was that the Indians' gods were angry because the settlers' god had now come to the region and they were making their displeasure known in a tangible form. The Reverend Hosmer himself claimed to have heard nine or ten such sounds—thundering roars, screams, and fearful if distant shouting—together with the shaking of the earth within the space of five minutes on one occasion. These sounds, he went on, had occurred in his parish at regular intervals for about twenty or thirty years and if anything, they were getting more terrifying.

The sounds would begin, the Reverend Hosmer reported, "like a slow thunder, coming down from the North." They would then take on a noise like cannon shot or musket fire which would seem to pass right under the settlement and beneath the very feet of those who lived there. Houses would shake and crockery would fall over and break. But all was not yet finished for the sounds would then turn into screams, voices talking, or shouting a long way off and unseen explosions which reverberated around the whole community of Haddam. He went on to state the danger of the "shaking ground" but added that recently (around 1729) the noises had become fewer in number and that their effect—the trembling and shaking of the earth—had become less violent. Indeed, he went on, there had only been two such occurrences within the past year (1728-29).

Some scientific figures in the community had stated that the sounds and vibrations were due to the movement of air in subterranean caverns far below the surface of the earth. The noises were not voices at all but were made by wind trapped in underground tunnels. Hosmer was not so sure. He dubbed the sounds "Moodus noises" and hinted that they might, in fact, be of supernatural origin. Indians, he pointed out, tended to shun the region because they feared the wrath of their own gods. An old Indian who lived in the area had averred that his gods would take revenge on anyone who settled in the place because it was a sacred site, and the good reverend thought there might be something in this. The site was the abode of pagan, pre-Christian powers who must be treated as demons and expelled by the power of prayer and of praise to the Lord.

Whether or not the noises had a scientific basis, it was never fully investigated. Hosmer's rather romanticized religious viewpoint seems to have won the day as far as the settlers of East Haddam were concerned. Many of the locals took to wearing amulets and talismans to protect themselves from whatever evils the noises brought with them. There seems to have been a particular belief that outbreaks of disease and minor epidemics occurred around the same time the noises were heard and that the two were somehow related. Strange lights were also seen flickering around the area and along various rivers, further adding to the terror many people felt. This, of course, gave further credence to the notions of demons and evil spirits in which the New Englanders seem to have passionately believed. Prayer and praise, however, seemed rather ineffective against the worst of the sounds and so local people resorted to other means to banish the noises.

Around 1731, a certain traveler passed through East Haddam. Several accounts mention him but our main record comes once again from the Reverend Hosmer, who gave a brief description of his activities. The traveler was one Dr. Steele, an "educated and book-learned man" who came apparently from England. He was intrigued by the Moodus noises and made several enquiries about them. The inhabitants of the settlement related the old Indian legends to him and this seems to have piqued the doctor's curiosity even more. He took up residency in East Haddam and is said to have opened a blacksmith's shop there. He worked in his forge only at night and it was believed that he was, in fact, engaged in some form of occult sciences within the confines of the place. At the same time, the noises around the area seemed to grow in intensity and the quakes appeared to become even more ferocious. The people, now utterly terrified, approached the doctor and asked him what he was doing. The magician replied that he was engaged upon a great supernatural experiment in which he was attempting to grow by occult means a great carbuncle far below the surface of the world which would rob the arcane forces making the noises of their powers. The carbuncle would absorb these forces and when they were magically removed "from the bowels of the rocks," the area would be at peace. Not only this, but Dr. Steele also made replicas of the carbuncle he was creating, which he sold to the people of the community as a form of protection during the quakes and tremors. He seems to have had a ready market throughout the locality. Skeptics might be tempted to say that he had created the market himself out of the gullibility and superstitions of his clients. Steele further declared that the "Place of Noises" was actually the site where a very powerful wizard (whether Indian or other, he did not specify) had been buried and the sounds were caused by the groanings and turnings of the magician's evil soul. The spirit had drawn other evil forces to itself and it was these which were tormenting the good people of East Haddam. They could only be exorcised by the creation of the underground carbuncle, which nobody ever saw. Yet, Dr. Steele rapidly gained wide acceptance of his beliefs and gradually acquired a large following amongst the people of the district.

Several months after the doctor's arrival, the noises (which now seemed to have reached something of an intensity) began to subside and gradually die away altogether. It seemed that Dr. Steele's "occult experiment" was bearing fruit. No sooner had the sounds started to diminish than the doctor himself suddenly packed up and stole away from East Haddam overnight. Nobody saw him go, but in the morning, his forge was deserted. He was never again seen or heard from and for a time, some people wondered if there actually ever had been a Dr. Steele. No one knew where he had come from or where he had gone. It was even suggested that he was an angel sent by God to do battle with the evil spirits that were creating the eerie sounds. He is said, nevertheless, to have left behind him several magic books—supposedly written in ancient Hebrew or in some other archaic tongue—which could be used to "re-energize" the underground carbuncle lest the noises return, which, eventually, they did.

By the 1830s, vague tremors and faint but uncanny sounds were once again experienced in the East Haddam area. The Moodus noises had returned, albeit in a much more moderate form than previously. At first, they were little more than the suggestion of far-away thunder accompanied by a faint vibration under the ground, but as time went on, they seemed to increase in frequency and scale so that by the early 1840s they were almost as severe as they had been in the late 1700s. Many people in the East Haddam community remembered Dr. Steele and his occult experiment to create the underground carbuncle. It seemed that the unseen artifact had now worn away and the dark Indian spirits had returned. Many people claimed to have heard the strange noises—which now sometimes resembled voices crying and men shouting—and even more were terrified by the strange shaking of the ground which was now so ferocious in places that it resembled an earthquake. Local ministers claimed that the disturbances were caused by the ghosts of long-dead Indians holding an eternal powwow at the Place of Noises.

Once again, a mysterious figure showed up to deal with the eerie phenomena—this time in the form of a traveling preacher, Robert Edge. Edge is an enigma who appears in the folklore of several New England communities and seems to be something of a cross between a man of God and a shaman. As with Dr. Steele, no one knew very much about him and virtually nothing about him has passed into history, but he was certainly credited with occult powers, including the abilities to heal and to curse. He was also widely regarded as something of an exorcist. For a little while he lived with a local family during which time he conducted a number of tent missions in the district, preaching terrible "fire and brimstone" sermons graphically concerned with the Day of Judgement and the end of all things, many of which are said to have terrified his listeners even more than did the frightful sounds. During his stay in East Haddam, he is also alleged to have discovered the mysterious books left behind by Dr. Steele. Where these had been located is unknown, but Robert Edge seemed to have very little difficulty in tracking them down. Taking these books with him, he is said to have gone to a hill just as the sounds began again and read out words and phrases in an unintelligible language. These were read in an imperious and authoritative tone. Surprisingly, the noises seemed to respond to his commands and while they did not disappear altogether, they seemed to decrease in both frequency and volume.

Shortly after his visit to the hill, Robert Edge disappeared—to where, no one knew—just like Dr. Steele before him. For a while after his disappearance the noises continued, but they were steadily growing more and more infrequent and had less of an impact on the area. Gradually, they became so infrequent that they passed into rural folklore and were little more than a local memory in the communal mind.

There is one last twist to the story, however. As the War Between the States moved towards its bloody climax around 1864, the noises and the odd vibrations returned. Once again, they were not as loud or as strong as they had been, but they were certainly disruptive enough to be noticed. And, as before, some of them resembled distant thunder, voices screaming, or a number of men chanting and, as before, many locals associated them with the old Indian powwows and the calling of spirits which had once taken place around East Haddam. Some people, however, stated that the sounds might have a different source: they were the voices of spirits which might have come with the settlers from the Celtic lands across the sea and they had taken possession of the area. This idea was more or less a fusion of settler and Indian beliefs. Still others supposed that the awful bloodshed which characterized the Civil War (even though rural Connecticut was relatively free of it) had somehow activated the spirits once more. The wanton spilling of blood all across the American continent had re-energized the appetites of the ancient forces and they were making their presence known in East Haddam again. There seemed to be something in this thesis for almost as soon as the war ended, the sounds and tremors began to diminish once again and a relative peace returned to the area.

Since then, there has been little to report. On occasion, certain individuals in the area which was formerly East Haddam claim to have heard peculiar noises or eerie voices calling to them or to have experienced slight tremors in the ground, but there has been nothing like the frightful tumults and quakings which characterized the region during the late eighteenth and early nineteenth centuries. Many of these reports are simply dismissed and even the name Place of Noises has been all but forgotten, even in the locality. The spirits seem to have been stilled at last.

Although the East Haddam experience has been all but forgotten, some fragments concerning it do survive. One such fragment is to be found in the shape of a long poem by John Brainard, which was later turned into a local ballad. A little East Haddam girl sang the poem in its entirety for Samuel Drake when he visited the region around 1883. While the poem itself is too long to recount in full, the last verse states:

The carbuncle lies in the deep, deep sea,
Beneath the mighty wave,
But the light shines upward so gloriously,
That the sailor looks pale, forgets his glee,
When he crosses the wizard's grave.

Kansas

The Gateway to Hell

One of the most fundamental beliefs in the patchwork panoply which characterized Celtic "religion" was that of the otherworld. The concept has never been properly defined and was probably as mysterious to the ancients Celts as it is to modern interpreters. Briefly and simplistically stated, it is that beyond normal vision and experience lay a realm which was unseen but just as real as the everyday world. This domain was the abode of fairies, spirits, ghosts, and other uncanny creatures which were anything but mortal. It was a land of enchantment and magic, but also of great danger. Time passed very differently there—a few minutes in the otherworld might well be several years in the mortal sphere—and those who accidentally found their way into this land might find, upon their return, that time had literally passed them by.

At certain times of the year, the barriers between this mortal world and the otherworld were exceptionally weak, and it was then that creatures from that other realm could pass over into our own or when unwitting mortals could, by accident, cross into the other sphere. These times were on dates such as Halloween or on May Eve. Most of those who did cross into the otherworld never returned and those who did were changed utterly. They were often more dreamy and less interested in the affairs of the everyday world; some might even show symptoms that would be classed today as bordering on mental illness. This condition was supposed to have been brought about by their glimpses of the otherworld.

Descriptions of this realm, taken from those who visited it, varied greatly. Some visitors described it as a beautiful, happy place populated by fairies and friendly spirits; others who returned said that it was a bleak, dismal landscape in which the dead and other *sheehoguey* (unnatural) things dwelt. For the earliest Celts, it was a place to which their heroes went upon death and was a domain of endless battle, hunting, and feasting, probably akin to the Viking Valhalla. Gradually, however, it became a general dwelling place of the dead and came to be considered an eerie and disturbing kingdom. From this world, the dead watched the living, and demons and malign forces prowled its borders ready to entice or snatch away mortals as the fancy took them. The otherworld gradually became a place to be feared.

In ancient Celtic mythology, too, there were disturbing elements concerning this hidden realm. Oisin, the fabled poet and son of the Irish hero Fion MacCumhail (Finn McCool) was lured away into a wonderful land by a fairy queen who had fallen in love with him. Under her spell, Oisin lived in the otherworld for a number of months, being feted by the queen and composing music and poems in her honor. However, he soon became homesick and asked to return for just one day to the land of his birth. This request the queen granted on the condition that he visit the mortal world on horseback and that he never once dismount or set foot on mortal earth. However, when he did return to the mortal realm, Oisin found that it had utterly changed. Although he had been no more than several months in the otherworld, over two hundred years had passed in his own country and the days of gods and heroes were gone forever. On his way to his old homestead, he came upon several men trying to move a large rock by the side of the road and he was surprised by how small and puny they were. In a proud show of strength, Oisin offered to aid them and leant down from his horse to move the boulder with one hand. As he did so, his saddle slipped and he fell to the ground. As soon as he touched mortal earth, the weight of years was upon him. He became an old, old man and eventually crumbled away to a fine dust which blew away in the wind.

Even though this tale comes from Ireland and is part of the great Fenian Cycle (named after the Knights of the Fienia), similar stories can be found all over Scotland, England, and Wales. In Scotland, for instance, musicians of particular talent were carried off into the otherworld where they performed for the fairies. Even as late as medieval/early modern times, we can find legends of fiddlers being carried away into fairy mounds and hills, which were widely regarded as entrances to the supernatural realm. The two most famous fiddlers who did actually vanish and whose whereabouts were never discovered were Thomas Cumming (Tam-an-Tournan) and Farquar Grant (Farquar o' Fashie), who were believed to have been carried off into an underground fairy hall inside Tomnahurich Hill near Inverness and who are still believed to be playing for the fairy folk there.

It was widely suggested that, even aside from times when the veil between worlds was thin, there were places in the countryside where the otherworld touched our own, mortal sphere. These were also spots where foolish or incautious people could cross over from one world into the other and were to be steadfastly avoided. Such places comprised physical, geographical features such as ancient hills, standing stones, fairy forts and rings, and lone trees which were alleged to be gateposts to the fairy world or to the otherworld of the dead or the damned.

As Christianity spread, the notion of the otherworld took on a more chilling and sinister significance. The church sometimes taught that this realm was akin to hell itself and that only the souls of those who had not died in Christ were taken there for torment. This perception also found its way into rural folklore and turned the otherworld into a terrible place where evil spirits and fairies dwelt who were continually seeking to draw human souls into their own dreary kingdom. The otherworld was now established in the social and religious consciousness as a terrible place indeed. And, of course, the old gateways to this domain remained. These were usually spots associated with former pagan worship and indeed many of them seemed relatively sinister. These sites were usually located in dark and gloomy glens or in the ancient earthworks of former aboriginal inhabitants—the raths, forts, hills, and mounds of Celtic antiquity. The church equated these places with entrances to hell, that domain in which evil dwelt and which decent Christians should avoid. Gradually, tales grew up around these places which made them seem even more daunting and mysterious.

Because Celtic culture and tradition was primarily orally based, the Celts were great storytellers. They wrote nothing down and so history and tradition were handed down by word of mouth from one generation to the next. This means they had to have extremely good memories, and historians such as Peter Berresford Ellis have argued that there were certain classes of Druids (or holy men) amongst them who acted as "rememberers" and who were regarded as custodians of the local tradition. There may well be something in this argument as in many rural areas in Ireland, Scotland, and indeed in some parts of Wales, there are venerable men who act in the role of a *seanachie* (man of lore) and who remember genealogies and old stories regarding a particular location. In order that dates, stories, and histories were easily remembered, they may have been embellished in order to aid recollection. Bits and pieces of other stories may have been attributed to them or certain points in them may have been exaggerated. This was part of the storyteller's art. As regards some of the locations in the countryside which were deemed to be part of the otherworld, it may be that some additions to the tales about them were made. Places which actually looked sinister or which had a mysterious air about them could be regarded as being part of the evil realm which coexisted alongside our own and tales may have been composed in order to enforce or exaggerate that perspective. Thus, eerie tales frequently grew up in the Celtic mind around sites which were not really deserving of them. And there were many such sites all across the Celtic world.

One of these lies in the North of Ireland, in County Antrim, at a place known as Dundermot. This mound is actually no more than the site of an old Norman fortification, possibly dating back to the twelfth or thirteenth century. It was, according to tradition, built on the site of an extremely ancient Celtic rath and this is consistent with the way in which the early Normans used the landscape, turning and modifying already defensive sites to their own advantage and purpose. Today, it is little more than a large hillock overgrown with a few dark trees, standing in the middle of a tilled field near a modern main roadway. During Norman times, it would probably have been topped with a small defensive fort and later it would have stood close to a main coaching road that connected Dublin with Derry City. Over the years, queer legends grew up around the place. Lights were reputedly seen amongst the trees on the top of the mound and it was soon decided that this was a gateway to the fairy kingdom or, worse, to hell itself. It was said (although there is no real evidence for this) that the enclosure upon which the fortification had been built had been used for ritual, perhaps even sacrificial, purposes and that terrible deities had been summoned there. These had lingered on long after the

Normans came. It was even said that on certain nights of the year (May Eve and Halloween), a door opened in the side of the mound and fairies or the spirits of the dead trooped out to wander about the countryside. They had the power to carry off individuals from the surrounding countryside back into the otherworld with them.

These old tales were given a fresh impetus when, around 1797-98, a coach was said to have vanished somewhere in the vicinity of Dundermot. It was, allegedly, a coach from Dublin traveling through Belfast to Derry and was driven by a Limerick man, Thomas McHarg. In Belfast, which at the time was a hotbed of political intrigue prior to the 1798 Rising of the United Irishmen, McHarg was supposed to have been handed a package which he was to deliver to the army barracks in Derry within two days. If he did so, he would receive a substantial bonus. Taking his young daughter with him on the driver's box and with a seventeen-year-old boy, James Orr, armed with a pistol, riding the postilion to guard against robbers on the road, McHarg set out for Derry. As he did so, a fearsome rainstorm broke over the east Antrim hills. Stopping at a change house in Antrim Town, McHarg noticed that the rain was growing worse and showed no sign of abating. The woman of the house urged him to stay for the sake of the little girl but the driver was adamant. "Neither God nor the Devil himself can keep me from getting to Derry," he famously announced as he hitched a team of fresh horses. Then he set off into the storm.

He passed through several small villages and at each one, he asked the same question: "Is the bridge at Glarryford still up?" Beyond the village of Cullybackey, the coaching road crossed the Garry Bog and the Clough River and there were two main crossings for coachmen and their teams, one at the hamlet of Glarryford and the other at Dundermot. Although Glarryford was considered the best for coaches—there was a small inn there—the bridge there was uncertain and was liable to be damaged during heavy rain by the swift-flowing Clough River. Coachmen tried, as far as possible, to avoid Dundermot because the bridge there was narrower and because of its sinister reputation. No one was able to tell McHarg if the bridge at Glarryford was still standing. The coachman whipped his horses to an even greater frenzy, trying to beat the storm, and thundered off in the direction of the hamlet. However, it appears that the Glarryford bridge had indeed been swept away and it is thought that McHarg detoured to cross at Dundermot. His coach was never seen again.

It was probably attacked and destroyed by highwaymen or by the bands of localized militia which rode back and forth across the area at the time. Yet, at certain times of the year, Dundermot mound is said to open and what is known locally as "Black Tom's coach" rattles out into the wider world. If a traveler meets it upon the road, the coachman perched on the driving box with a little girl beside him will always ask the same question: "Is the bridge at Glarryford still up?" To give a reply or to speak to him at all is to invite death within the year, and local people will tell you of those who have met a grisly fate in this way or who have avoided destruction by keeping silent.

Whether or not Thomas McHarg actually existed is unknown and there are no records of him outside the legend. Nevertheless, the tale is a persistent one in the area. Curiously, it parallels another well-known story from New England concerning a certain Peter Rugg who traveled between Concord and Boston (again with his daughter) during the early nineteenth century. According to the tale, Rugg made the same challenge to God and/or the Devil and is condemned to wander the road until the Day of Judgement. Many people claim to have seen him, just as many others claim to have seen Black Tom's coach. As in the Celtic version, the appearance of Peter Rugg is always said to presage death for the viewer.

If Dundermot is the "gateway to hell" then there are a number of other such infernal portals scattered around the world. It is said that there are quite possibly seven such gates. There is at least one other alleged entrance in Ireland, a small island near St. Patrick's Purgatory in Lough Derg. In the United States, there is rumored to be one somewhere near New York, perhaps a reflection of the Celtic storytellers' art blossoming in America. If the Celtic world was filled with dark and gloomy places, then America was even more so. And, given the religious perspective of the colonists, it was also logical to think that these places were, perhaps, the outer reaches of hell. This was consistent with Puritan teaching which stated that the gates of hell were closer than anyone imagined. If Dundermot was an entrance to the demonic realm then there were bound to be others within the developing United States.

A particularly infamous one lies in the American heartland. Between the Kansas towns of Lawrence and Topeka lies the tiny hamlet of Stull. As settlements go, it is not a particularly impressive place—little more than a few houses, a store, and a couple of churches—and yet Stull has achieved something of a reputation for itself and continues to draw what the locals describe as "unwelcome visitors" throughout the year. The reason is the graveyard, which is considered by many to be one of the major gateways to hell. In fact, so notorious has the hamlet become that in 1992, the rock band Urge Overkill released a compact disc entitled *Stull* that bore the picture of the cemetery, together with its ruined and falling church, on its cover. Each year around Halloween droves of sightseers descend on the place, much to the irritation and even anger of the locals, who claim that such visitors only serve to desecrate the graves of their families. There have also been rumors of witchcraft and black magic ceremonies being carried on by "outsiders" within the cemetery. Indeed the situation has now gotten so bad that the Douglas County Sheriff's Office patrols the immediate area and its officers have the power to issue $100 fines for trespassing to those interlopers they find inside the cemetery boundaries. They also have the power to escort these people out of the hamlet. Despite these measures, interest in Stull remains extremely high and there are at least half a dozen Web sites on the Internet devoted to the discussion about the site.

Although stories concerning Stull are legion—many involving diabolical revels and appearances by Satan himself—there is no real history to them for the notion of it as hell's gateway is surprisingly modern. The hamlet started out as the tiny settlement of Deer Creek in the mid-1800s. It was comprised, as far as can be gathered, by solid, hard-working farming people who were deeply religious and circumspect in their ways. Although small, Deer Creek community was large enough to have its own post office since it lay on a postal route to Topeka. The postmaster there was Silvester Stull, whose nationality varies between German and Polish and whose date of birth is given as March 19, 1862. He was the son of one of the community's original inhabitants, Isaac Stull, who was allegedly regarded as something of a village patriarch. Given such a worthy local background, it was only natural that Silvester Stull should take over the position of postmaster on the relatively prestigious Topeka route. He married in Deer Creek a lady named Bertha Koehler, who appears to have been German. She bore him eleven children, all of whom survived and were reared near the site of the ruined church in the hamlet. At that time it was still a thriving place of worship and it is possible that all Silvester's eleven children were baptized there. When he retired, however, Silvester Stull moved to Orange County in California, where he died on July 4, 1931. He is reputedly buried in Orange County's Fairhaven Memorial Park. However, the tiny community he left behind had changed the name of their settlement in 1899 to reflect his contribution as postmaster there. The post office in Stull was closed in 1903. The name "Stull" is therefore not, as many have claimed, derived from the word "skull," which associates it with evil rites and witchcraft.

Stull did, however, have a number of factors which would later lead to its rather sinister reputation. In the 1970s, it had a gloomily picturesque ruined church sited on a rise above the hamlet; it did share the same zip code as nearby Topeka—666, the number of the Devil; and, as early as 1905, records show that the principal route past the hamlet was known as Devil's Lane. It was also near another sinister Kansas landmark known locally as the Devil House. Located at the junction of 93rd Street and Paulen Road, south of Topeka, the house was a two-story stone farmhouse which had long been left abandoned. There were rumors that the place was badly haunted and that its almost inaccessible and boarded upper story was frequently visited by demons. One investigator claimed that the downstairs of the place was used for black magic ceremonies and that he personally had seen burnt candles, animal carcasses, and inverted crucifixes there—symbols of local coven activity. The reputation of the Devil House may well have impacted the legends about Stull.

Nearby Lawrence, of course, also has a bloody history. In the early years of the Civil War, the town was used as a base by pro-Union guerrilla forces such as the Kansas Red Legs and the Jayhawkers under the command of James Lane, who raided deep into Missouri. At five o'clock on the morning of August 21, 1863, a group of Confederate partisan raiders led by William Clarke Quantrill entered the town to take reprisal for an alleged Union attack on Osceola, Missouri. It was Quantrill's declared intention to burn the town to the ground and "take Jim Lane's heart back to Missouri" (Lane had to escape by running through cornfields in his nightshirt). Quantrill's orders were to "kill every man and burn every house." While his troops were doing this, the Confederate officer enjoyed breakfast. The slaughter was horrific and over 120 houses were burned; some were found with charred bodies inside. The legacy of this awful killing undoubtedly left a blight on the surrounding countryside.

Old tales of bloody terror may also have influenced the development of strange stories around Stull, even though it did not feature in the massacre. It is difficult to say how the hamlet's eerie reputation was acquired, but it is worth studying as it demonstrates how the early Celts may have developed and embellished stories about allegedly sinister places.

The stories seem to have begun in the early 1970s, a time when America was gripped by what might be described as "Devil fever." In 1971, William Peter Blatty released his now-famous novel of demonic possession, *The Exorcist,* and in 1973 came the blockbuster screen adaptation which shocked the country and spawned a thousand imitations. Films such as *The Omen* and Michael Winner's *The Sentinel,* which centered around a gateway to hell in the middle of a busy city, were a significant part of U.S. cultural fare at the time. As in medieval days, people were obsessed with the idea of demons lurking everywhere and of the imminence of the Devil.

All this "demonism" had more or less passed Stull by. There were some old ghost and witch stories about the place but no more than in any other small community. One of these, dating apparently from the mid- to late 1960s, concerned a large tree which grew in the cemetery of the old Emmanuel Hill church. The church itself was a ruin, having been abandoned in 1922 when its congregation outgrew its confines and moved to a more modern place of worship. The tree—a massive spreading pine—had somehow managed to encompass one of the nearby tombstones in the churchyard so that the funeral marker appeared to have become part of the growth itself. The stone marked the final resting place of Bettie and Frankie Thomas, both of whom had died in 1879. Somehow an unfounded story began to circulate that these two were witches and had been involved in diabolic rites in Stull churchyard. As late as 1969, stories were spreading amongst the teenagers of Topeka that the Emmanuel Hill church had been burned down by Satanists and that black masses had been conducted in its grounds. Nothing could have been further from the truth, but this story was to have implications a little later.

In 1974, an article appeared in the University of Kansas student newspaper, *The University Daily Kansan,* concerning Stull and headed "Legend of Devil Haunts Tiny Town." It was in keeping with the Devil-obsessed mood of the times which had been created by *The Exorcist* and claimed to have been based on widely accepted local mythology. It went so far as to detail the alleged supernatural experiences of persons who had visited Stull churchyard as well as a "widespread" belief that the hamlet was one of only two places on Earth where the Devil appeared in his full and terrifying majestic form. The article went on to assert that this legend had been "told and re-told" in the locality "although it has probably never been recorded" and that "some people say they heard it from grandparents and great-grandparents."

The story, of course, owed more to the imagination of the writer than to any rural folklore; however, a freshman from Bonner Springs did say that her grandmother had told her that the Devil made an appearance in Stull each year around Halloween and had actually driven her past the old church when she was about ten or eleven in order to see it. The young woman told the paper that the experience of viewing the site had stayed with her for years afterwards. Several other freshmen claimed to have heard that an early mayor of Stull had done a deal with the Devil, allowing him to appear within the limits of the settlement in return for diabolic favors. Another variant of the story concerns the murder of the mayor by a stablehand in the early 1850s. The site of the terrible deed was an old barn which was later converted into Emmanuel Hill church, which was in turn gutted by fire. Although a fine and terrifying tale, this could certainly not have happened as the original settlement of Deer Creek—which consisted of only six families in 1857—was unincorporated and too small to warrant a mayor. In fact the hamlet has never had a mayor. There was also a tale that a witch buried within the precincts of the Emmanuel Hill church had borne a child to the Infernal One and that this child still lived around Stull as a werewolf, manifesting itself on certain nights of the year.

These supposed folk legends were no more than a rehashing of horror paperback books and monster movies and had no basis whatsoever in local tradition. Nevertheless, they continued to flourish and grow almost as urban myths until they were more or less accepted as fact. And there were additions to basic tales. Some people spoke of three- to four-hour memory lapses when visiting Stull cemetery; others spoke about being gripped by invisible cold hands as they approached the old church; others speculated as to whether or not the tales owed their existence to extraterrestrial involvement and there were hints at alien abductions from the region. Everyone, it seemed, had either a story or a theory regarding Stull.

Even denials by the pastor of the Stull church and by Robert Smith, then associate professor of anthropology at the University of Kansas, who openly stated that the stories were a creation of university students and not actual folklore, did little to stem the flood of tales. On March 20, 1978, a crowd of almost 150 people (mainly University of Kansas students) gathered in Stull cemetery to await the Devil's appearance. It was also said that those buried there who had died violent deaths or had practiced Devil worship would rise at the hour of midnight to dance with Satan. However, as was waggishly pointed out, the only spirits which appeared in Stull that night came out of a bottle. Nevertheless, the stories continued unabated and grew more and more fanciful with each telling.

One man stated that a sinister wind had sprung up as he visited the old church late at night and had blown out a candle that he was holding and left him unable to move. Numerous individuals claimed that the Devil had been appearing in the cemetery from as early as 1850, ignoring the fact that the church was not built until 1867 and the burying ground itself was not laid out until 1869. By 1980, the legends regarding the tumbleweed community had become so widespread that they were starting to appear in the national press. The *Kansas City Times* outlined the story, stating that the hamlet shared the dubious pleasure of the Devil's visits with a remote plain in India and that, at these locations, he gathered together all those who had met with violent deaths around the world. Other papers took up the story and added fresh details. The Devil, it was claimed, returned to Stull on the first night of spring in order to visit the grave of a sorceress who had been buried there following a protracted witch trial in Kansas. (The fact that one of the headstones in Emanuel Hill cemetery bore the name Wittch only added to the legend.) Stull, claimed another article, shared its name with a town in England where witch persecutions were carried out, and there, too, the Devil appeared in awful majesty. Photographs also appeared, allegedly taken in Stull cemetery, which showed a werewolf-like figure crouching, ready to spring. This was supposedly the werewolf son of the witch and the Devil, though it bore a closer resemblance to an actor in a rubber mask. Yet another newspaper added to the myth by stating that Stull was, in fact, one of the "seven gateways to Hell which are scattered across the world."

It is this which is the most persistent myth about Stull and which draws more curiosity seekers than any other. Somewhere in the vicinity of the fallen church, runs the legend, there is an opening in the ground with a flight of worn steps which leads down into darkness. This is the entrance to hell and the steps end at the very gates of the domain of the damned. Of course, there are many differing accounts as to where these steps are actually located: some say they lie to the right of the ruined building; some say they are to be found behind it; others still say that they lie within the retaining walls of one of the family plots. This plot is reputed to be that of Geneva Stull (a descendant of Silvester?), who died in 1920. It is said that if anyone descends these steps—even part of the way—time will pass at a different rate (recalling some of the stories of the passage of time in the Celtic otherworld) and though the individual assumes that only a few moments have passed, weeks and even years will have gone by in the mortal world. There is no evidence that such steps even exist but this has not prevented throngs of thrill seekers from arriving in the hamlet to look for them. Nor has it stopped numbers of "experts" from logging onto the Internet, claiming to know where the staircase to hell is and giving vague directions to them. In language reminiscent of the Winner film *The Sentinel,* many warn of dire consequences for those who investigate—a sure invitation for them to do so.

By 1989, the crowds at the Stull cemetery on Halloween night hoping to see the Devil emerge from hell had grown so large that the Douglas County Sheriff's Office had to station special deputies around the site to discourage ghost-busting teams and to charge those who were caught in the graveyard with criminal trespass. Nonetheless, estimates of between five and six hundred arrests were made and vandalism at the site was rapidly becoming a major concern. At other times, it was thought, those involved in witchcraft and the occult were traveling to Stull to carry out ritualistic practices in the old church. The walls of the place were becoming daubed with slogans and graffiti, and beer cans and fast-food containers were starting to litter the cemetery—what in fact should be a place of rest. The mood of the locals began to change from one of bemused bewilderment to outright anger as they saw the graves of their loved ones desecrated in such a fashion. Most of them claimed never to have heard anything about the ghostly and devilish legends and that they were certainly not part of the folklore of the area.

This did not stop the newspapers from printing even more lurid and colorful stories. The *Kansas City Times,* for instance, continued to recount tales alleging that, according to local legend, the original settlers in Stull had all practised witchcraft and some were descended from those who had fled from Salem, Massachusetts, because of the witch trials there in 1692. It was further alleged that a witch had been hanged from the great pine tree in the cemetery and that in penance for their occult ways the inhabitants of Stull had built the church at Emmanuel Hill, which had later been destroyed by fire. It went on to say that the ruin was reputedly possessed by evil spirits and that the date above the doorway had been mysteriously removed. None of these allegations had any basis whatsoever in local folklore and were hotly denied by the residents of the hamlet. Not that this made any difference for university students from places like Lawrence, Tecumseh, Lecompton, and Topeka; all declared that they had heard stories about Stull at their grandparents' knees. Every story seemed to have a fresh variation which somehow appealed to the popular press and caught the collective imagination. Items on Stull began to appear in *Ghost Trackers' Newsletter* and in such publications as *Haunted Places: The National Directory,* all of which added to its notoriety. Of course, the picture of the ruined church and the title track on the Urge Overkill *Stull* CD circulated the hamlet's name amongst a much younger Gothic audience.

The inhabitants of Stull refused to tear down the old church. Many have relatives buried within the ancient cemetery and are sentimentally attached to the ruin on Emmanuel Hill. There has also been a fear that if they did so, such an action might only lend a greater credence to the legends. But each year, as the church fell further and further into rot, the numbers of beer cans, cigarette butts, and shards of glass seemed to grow within its crumbling walls despite the nightly patrols. (It is believed that no bottle marked with the sign of the inverted cross will shatter within the precincts of Emmanuel Hill and many visitors have tested this superstition.) For a while, there was some talk of trying to restore the ancient building, but there were few funds and the action got no further than just talk. Recently, things have changed in Stull. Even as this chapter was being written, the old church on Emmanuel Hill mysteriously collapsed and is now no more than a pile of rubble. It seems to have been torn down but nobody can say for sure who undertook the demolition and it is said that the land's owner gave no permission for it. There is now nothing there but a pile of rubble, another mystery to add to the growing legend surrounding the hamlet. One thing all locals agree upon is that there are no steps leading down to hell anywhere in the Stull cemetery.

Yet, such matters will not always rest. In 1993, as part of an American visit, when Pope John Paul II flew to Colorado in order to conduct a mass there, it is reported (in no less than *Time* magazine) that the pontiff requested that his plane take a route around Kansas and into Nebraska and then down to Colorado, thus avoiding eastern Kansas, where Stull is located. It was rumored that the Holy Father did not wish to fly over the unholy opening to the infernal regions. Of course, this may be just rumor, but perhaps the pope might have known something that the rest of us do not.

So, is Stull really one of the seven gateways to Hell? Probably not; and perhaps the brooding bulk of Dundermot mound in the North of Ireland is a much better bet.

New Hampshire

The Willey House

For the territorial Celts, demarcations, particularly with regard to land, were extremely important. These might be in the form of boundaries or borders and signaled a passage from one area or sphere of influence into another. In a political sense, they sectioned off one Celtic kingdom from another, and some of the early kingdoms were exceptionally small, maybe no more than forty or fifty miles across. The borders between them, therefore, became very important. They were the extent of one ruler's (or warlord's) territory and the beginning of another's domain. Natural boundaries such as forests, fast-flowing rivers, or mountain ranges often marked the distinction between the settled, known land and wild, unexplored areas. Such regions were usually considered the abodes of monsters, witches, and other eerie creatures.

But the boundaries had a religious and supernatural significance as well. Just as borders demarcated the lands of mortal, terrestrial rulers, so they denoted where the mortal world ended and the realm of the gods or mystical beings began. For the Celts, the gods and supernatural forces did not live in some remote place—beyond the clouds or on some distant mountaintop—they were all around, and so were their spheres of influence. Areas around rocks, standing stones, and trees were under the rule of such beings and often lay outside the mortal domain. The passerby, therefore, needed to know where the boundaries were as to stray into the spirit areas could prove hazardous or even dangerous. Religious or sacred enclosures were well cordoned off and no one would enter them except possibly priests or Druids themselves.

The Celts also believed that beyond the perception of ordinary mortals lay the otherworld. Within this sphere of existence lived the dead, fairies, gods, and all sorts of unworldly beings, many of which were hostile to mortals. A veil separated this world from our own mortal world and kept it from human sight. Sometimes and at certain times of the year, however, that veil was thin and creatures from the otherworld might cross into our own. Alternately, some mortals might (usually accidentally) cross into the otherworld.

Crossings and passages across boundaries and borders, then, began to acquire a special significance since they provided a way from one realm—or sphere of existence—to another. Even physical crossings such as bridges and ravines, gullies, and passes began to attain an almost supernatural significance. Physical gateways, too, held a similar symbolism since they also led from one place to another—perhaps even into another world. For example, the celebrated green children who turned up at the village of St. Mary's-by-the-Wolfpits in Suffolk during the mid-twelfth century claimed to have come from an underground kingdom known as St. Martin's Land through a system of tunnels and caverns, guided by the sound of a Christian bell. Made when a great tree had been uprooted, the hole in the earth through which they entered our world was said to have been sealed by a Norman knight, Sir Richard de Colne, for fear that others from their world would invade our own. Certain trees in both Cornwall and Brittany were avoided by locals as they were considered to be gateways into a world of ghosts and spirits and to venture too close to them was to be sucked into this other place. The trees were believed to be gateposts or boundary markers between the two worlds, as were large stones, rivers, and other natural parts of the landscape.

Perhaps no geographical feature was so rich in such symbolism as the mountain pass. Mountains provided a formidable and often impenetrable barrier between one part of the world and another—between one realm and another—and in some cases, represented the end of known experience. A pass that led through a mountain range, therefore, connected differing regions and kingdoms and may even have had a supernatural element to it. It was, in both mythology and reality, a way into another world—a world which was relatively unknown and beyond experience. It was also a way for invasion, either by an actual army or by unknown and possibly supernatural beings. In later Celtic times, mountain passes became of paramount strategic importance and had to be defended. Fortresses and castles were built there for the purpose of defence, but the supernatural element still lingered. It was around such passes that mysterious entities loitered, perhaps threatening the raised fortifications more than any invading military force. And, as mountain passes became integral parts of greater travel, stories of ghosts and demons terrified those who journeyed there. Vampires, fairies, and trolls waited in some gloomy ravine to destroy and devour passing travelers as soon as the sun went down. The roots of such a belief lay in Celtic lore.

With the coming of the Christian faith, these beliefs were slightly adapted. Gateways, for instance, were considered to be especially eerie (particularly gateways set in the enclosing wall of a church). It was here that the ghosts of the dead lingered, perhaps unable to enter sacred ground. Thus litch (or lych) gates, where the coffins of the dead were rested before proceeding to the funeral service, were places of some supernatural danger. The notion of passage from one place to another was becoming firmly set, even in the Christian mind.

America, as the first colonists were to find, was a land of forest and mountain. If there was to be any communication between the settlers then roads had to be constructed and many of these ran through heavily treed and mountainous frontiers. The notions that dark and gloomy passages were filled with supernatural danger loomed large in the Western mind. These ways were truly roads into the unknown and dangers such as rockslides, highwaymen, or Indian attack frequently took on added and mysterious dimensions. And, of course, to actually live near one of these places was to invite supernatural menace and disaster.

In mid- to late 1832, a group of riders rested their tired horses on a high bluff near Crawford Notch in New Hampshire's White Mountains. Around them, sheer mountain walls rose towards the clouds and in front of them was the Notch, a narrow pass through the cliffs down which a chilling wind blew. Against its blast, the horsemen drew their coats more tightly around them. One of them, a young man from Salem, Massachusetts, named Nathaniel Hawthorne, would later become one of New England's most celebrated writers and would record that experience, which had remained with him:

> It was the middle of September. We had come since sunrise from Bartlett, passing up through the valley of the Saco, which extends

between those mountainous walls, sometimes with a steep ascent, but often as level as a church aisle. . . . We had the mountains behind us and mountains on each side, and a group of mightier ones ahead. . . . It is, indeed, a wondrous path. . . . This is the Notch of the White Hills. We had now reached a narrow passage, which showed the appearance of having been cut by human strength and artifice in the solid rock. There was a wall of granite on each side, high and precipitous, especially on our right and so smooth that a few evergreens could hardly find foothold to grow there. This is the entrance to the romantic defile of the Notch . . . passing through a deep pine forest, which for some miles allowed us to see nothing but its own dismal shade. . . .

Writing many years later in his *Sketches from Memory,* Hawthorne evokes skilfully the awe, majesty, and mystery of the gloomy pass through the White Mountains. The air which came from this dark passage, he states, was "now sharp and cold" and he was struck by a kind of "unpleasantness" which hung about the Notch like a dank shroud. The sensation would never leave him and he would return to Crawford Notch a number of times after, when he wanted to write some of his stranger tales. He would also meet with the owner of an inn located near the entrance to the place—Ethan Allen Crawford. Crawford was a mountain man in the strictest sense of the word—huge, brawny, and bear-like—and it was his father who had founded the inn at the Notch and who had given the pass its name. However, the Crawfords had not been the ones who had discovered it.

Crawford Notch was first fully explored by white settlers around 1771. Most of the earliest pioneers had kept close to the coast, where they could be serviced and supplied by shipping, with very few venturing into the interior forests and mountains. A hunter named Timothy Nash, out on a foraging expedition, climbed a tree at Cherry Mountain in order to get his bearings and noticed a deep, shady valley cut into the mountain wall. Assuming that it had been cut by the Saco River, he made his way up there and explored it, reporting his find to Gov. John Wentworth back in Plymouth. It subsequently emerged that this pass and the trail which meandered through it had been known by local Indians for at least one hundred years but that they had kept it secret from the incoming white men. Canadian Indians used the route as a surprise trail on raids against their neighbors or to free captives which had been taken by the settlers on the coast, but the place had an eerie and supernatural reputation even amongst these warriors. The ghosts of the dead were supposed to linger in the shadows along the edges of the valley and might attack travelers as they passed along it. These, however, were only Indian tales, but the Notch had already attracted other more terrible and bloody stories amongst the settlers themselves.

The trail had been known to the local military as early as the late 1750s but for security reasons that knowledge was kept from other settlers. In 1759, the noted Indian fighter Maj. Robert Rogers was sent to Canada together with two hundred of his Rangers to attack the Indian village of St. Francis de Sales, just southwest of Quebec, and to rescue many white New England captives there. The expedition had political implications as well. The Indians were supported by the French and it was widely rumored that French guerrilla bands were using the village as a base for raids into New England. Rogers carried orders to destroy the village and to put it beyond any French use. A strict Protestant, he carried out these orders with relish, not only attacking the village and butchering hundreds of Indians, but also sacking and looting the Catholic chapel of St. Frances, burning it to the ground. From the chapel they carried off much silver plate, golden candlesticks, and a ten-pound statue of the Virgin Mary, made completely out of silver. The carnage done, the Rangers headed for home. They were pursued for twenty days by angry Indians and had to fight their way back to what is now the American border. Rogers decided that it would be better if his force were to split up into a number of groups, each of which would make its own way across the White Mountains as best it could. Ragged and weary, the major and several of his men eventually made the British fort at Charlestown, New Hampshire, many days later. The majority of his forces, however, were hunted down, massacred, and scalped by the outraged Indians. Some died from sickness and starvation in the mountains. A group of nine survivors carrying some of the looted treasure, including the statue of the Virgin, met up with a group of supposedly friendly Indians who offered to take them across the mountains by a series of secret trails. One of the scouts led them into the dark and gloomy mountain pass which is known today as Crawford Notch. After poisoning one of them with a snake's fang, the guides left them lost and wandering amongst a crooked maze of mountain trails and gullies. Only one Ranger made it back to civilization. He was wild and mad, ragged and dirty. In his bloody knapsack, he carried six knives and a large piece of human flesh on which he had apparently feasted for the last eight days. Although he had survived, he had only done so by eating his comrades and the horror of his actions had unhinged his mind. He was so crazed that in the end he had to be shot like a mad dog. As for the plundered holy treasures that these men were carrying, the golden candlesticks were found on the banks of Lake Memphremagog in 1816 but most of the plate and the ten-pound silver image of the Virgin has never been recovered. The legend of lost treasure coupled with treachery and cannibalism only added to the mystery and romance of the Notch.

However, when Timothy Nash reported in Portsmouth that he had explored the valley in mid-1771, the merchants of the port were especially pleased. Now the settlements of the north could be linked with the developing colonies of the west, and a road could be established from Portsmouth to the uplands of what the Indians called "Cooes Country" along the Connecticut River. Nash and his fellow explorer, Ben Sawyer, were granted land in and around the Notch; their brief would be to develop it so that it was passable for packhorses. Soon Nash and Sawyer were able to transport a barrel of tobacco from Lancaster to the sea and then a barrel of whiskey from Portsmouth to Lancaster. However, both Nash and his partner were overly fond of the products they transported and began to drink all the whiskey before it reached Lancaster. It was due to their persistent drinking and unreliability that Nash and Sawyer eventually lost their claim to the lands around the Notch, but the trade route had now been opened. Pack trains of goods wound their way up from the coast while others made their way down to the sea. Some disappeared, like that led by Enoch Fennel, a seasoned scout who set out for Lancaster and simply vanished somewhere near the Notch. Probably some of them were beset by Indians, others by highway robbers after the goods they carried, others still may have simply gotten lost, but these disappearances were enough to start up the old rumors concerning the pass once again. Old Indian legends regarding spirits which dwelt amid the Notch's gloom were revived and tales concerning the cannibalistic ghosts of Major Rogers' lost men were told. The mystery around the pass deepened with each telling. There were increased Indian attacks in that area too. Ethan Crawford was later to call the Indians of the region "great drunks" who carried their *uncuppy* whiskey with them at all times in moose bladders attached to their waist belts. In their drunken state, they frequently attacked settlers near the Notch and some trade trains wending their way along the main trail.

Nevertheless, the pass still drew rugged characters who were determined to carve out a living for themselves in that wild country. One of these was Ethan Crawford's grandfather. His grandmother, too, seems to have been an individual of some spirit. Her name was Hannah Rosebrook and she came from Vermont. Once, when attacked near her home by a drunken Indian wielding a hatchet, she is said to have given him the "evil eye," making him retreat in fear. She is presumed to have married Ethan's father, Abel Crawford, contrary to her own father's wishes, and in order to escape his anger Abel and Hannah traveled some thirteen miles through the pass to build their own house on the other side of the mountains from Mr. Rosebrook. This would become known as the Crawford House.

The first house up on the Notch was built in 1793 by Nat Davis, Abel Crawford's son-in-law. Nat had hoped to remain there for some time but he found the pass too gloomy and the stories surrounding the place far too frightening to stay. Shortly after building the home, he abandoned it. The next house was built by innkeeper Henry Hill. By now there was an established road through the White Mountains and Henry thought that he would cash in on merchants using the pass. Later, he also tried to make a living from those who were traveling between the Crawford and Rosebrook houses. Henry had few guests in the summer and none at all in the winter. Eventually, he too abandoned the gloomy place and returned to Plymouth. In 1824, Ethan Crawford took over the property and planned to open it as the Notch House, a hostelry of quality and distinction. However, the legends persisted. Eerie voices like the souls of the dead screaming in torment or the sounds of soldiers being butchered were heard echoing along the mountain's corridor. At least that was what the old folks said—more probably it was nothing but the wind in the pass. Ethan brought down hay for the winter to the Notch barn and prepared to welcome his first guests. However, the pass was blocked with snow in drifts deeper than even Ethan had ever known and the winter seemed so cold and so long that he was reluctantly forced to abandon the idea of his grand hostelry.

In the autumn of 1825, Samuel Willey, Jr., and his wife, Polly Lovejoy, moved into the old house up at the Notch. Sam Willey was an optimistic (perhaps too optimistic) businessman and was determined to make the guesthouse idea a success. He set to work with a will, repairing and refurbishing the house, which had been allowed to deteriorate over successive winters. Building on Ethan Crawford's idea, Sam planned to turn it into the best stopover for people traveling through the Notch. He hired two live-in farmhands, Dave Nickerson and Dave Allen, both from North Conway, to help him build up the property. The two men came during the early summer to work in what was then an idyllic location, but gradually the beauty of the place wore off. Evening appeared to fall very early and without warning in the pass and the surrounding mountains made the place seem unnaturally dark in the late afternoon. As night approached, the Notch was eerily silent. Not even a bird sang and the only sound to be heard was the distant rush of the Saco River as it poured through a deep gully beyond the pass and twenty feet beyond the house and barn. As winter set in, snow and ice began to form, the latter hanging in dagger-like points from the edges of the towering cliffs that rose for two thousand feet behind the buildings. Storms closed off the Notch with drifts of deep, deep snow during that first brutal winter.

Spring came again and the Willey House, as it was now known, opened for business. His first guests were few and far between and were mainly businessmen traveling through the Notch to spring markets. However, as the year rolled on, the number of guests increased slightly and Sam Willey predicted that the scheme would soon become financially viable. His wife, however, was less certain for the gloomy pass was starting to frighten her. From time to time, she thought she saw shapes amid the darkness of the towering cliffs and she sometimes imagined she heard voices calling to her from away up in the Notch. Her children, too, were unsettled by the mysterious place and claimed that they heard evil-sounding laughter, crying, and screams from the mountains round about. As spring arrived, the ice sheets on the upper slopes began to melt with a sinister crackling sound and on occasion, large boulders would fall and drop into the pass, some of them bouncing and shattering in the backyard.

The spring passed in a brief blur and winter seemed to melt into summer. The great walls of the Notch held the growing heat, making it sultry and almost unbearable. As summer progressed, the weather became even more oppressive. Men working on building a road through the Notch were forced to seek shade—sometimes in the Willey House. And, of course, there was the rain. When it did rain, it fell in torrents, pouring down from the upper mountains and loosening the rock and dirt up there. Ethan Crawford recounted an incident which occurred in June 1826 when he and several others were working on a road crew digging ditches through the Notch. As they were working, an especially heavy thunderstorm broke and they were forced to flee down the Notch and take shelter in the Willey House. Sam and Polly welcomed them and even made them some food, which the men gratefully accepted. As they were eating, there was a roar from somewhere outside and, crossing to the window, one of the men saw a movement on the slopes to the west side of the house. Rock and gravel tumbled down, taking all in front of it, even young trees. It moved with an agonizing slowness, drawing closer and closer to the building, but when it reached a level part of the land just above the building, it stopped. The Willeys had seen their first landslide.

Although they had been spared, Polly Willey was determined to leave the house for the safety of her children. Sam pleaded with her to stay and he eventually persuaded her by promising to have a horse and buggy ready at all times for an immediate escape. He also had a stout shelter built near the Saco River in case the family should have to vacate the house because of avalanche. Reluctantly Polly agreed but both she and the children were very unsettled. The young ones cried continually or called out in terror every time a queer noise (and there were plenty) drifted down the Notch. Polly herself was tormented by terrible dreams of dead soldiers and rocks which swept away both her home and her children into the Saco River. And occasionally loose stones would bounce off the roof, frightening everyone. The two serving men even threatened to return to Conway, and Sam was obliged to raise their wages to encourage them to stay. His dream of a thriving business up in the Notch was steadily going sour.

Polly's dreams grew worse. In one nightmare, she saw her home and her children being carried away by an avalanche while she stood powerless and the whole Notch rang with the sound of demonic laughter issuing from an unknown source. Once again, she spoke of going back down the mountain to live in Plymouth and once again Sam talked her out of it. Business was not good. Few riders now stopped at the Willey House and the pack teams which went past were running to tight timetables and had no time to rest. He needed them all to pull together if they were to make a success of the place. He had sunk good money into the venture and he did not want to lose it.

The morning of Monday, August 28, dawned hot and dry like many others. Behind her house, Polly noticed that an ominous mist covered a number of the mountain peaks and that the mysterious sounds in the Notch had increased. She heard noises that sounded like people talking farther along the pass although she knew full well there was nobody there. By noon, the day had started to darken and black clouds began to roll in from the west, promising a storm. It was not long in coming. By early afternoon, sheet lightning was flickering across the sky overhead and torrents of rain were falling on the mountain slopes. The two Daves had to bring in the animals and take shelter in the barn to escape its severity. Water began to pour into the Notch, coming down from the uplands above, as the two workmen made their way up to the Willey House to sit out the storm with the family there. It was the worst tempest they had experienced, and it continued for the rest of the day and well into the night. Rocks began to tumble own the slopes and bounce from the roof of the building, making all those inside jump in terror. Everyone gathered their chairs round the fire—there was no sleep that night—and prayed that the violent weather would end. Over one thousand feet above their heads, they heard more rumblings and larger and larger stones hit the roof of the Willey House. Across the road, the river rose and broke its banks, threatening to flood the building and barns. The children screamed while Polly wept and the farmhands prayed and trembled. Almost in desperation, Sam Willey read from his Bible the Eighteenth Psalm: "The Lord also thundered in the heavens. . . . Hailstones and coals of fire, He sent from above . . . He took me . . . He drew me out of many waters. . . ." As he read aloud, the entire mountain chain seemed to rumble in response.

Six miles away, twenty-four of Ethan Crawford's sheep drowned as the rising Saco River flooded the other end of the pass. The waters also swept away Ethan's sawmill, and as one of the Crawford farmhands looked out he shouted, "The earth is now all covered with water—it's like the Flood—an' even the hogs is swimmin' for their lives!" All Ethan Crawford's crops were destroyed by the rising floods and a couple of his outbuildings were carried away.

As the storm passed on down the Notch with clearer weather coming in behind, the Crawfords began to sort out the mess that was now their farm. They had no time to worry about their neighbors on the other side of the pass. Crawford, however, had a guest staying with him, a John Barker, and it was he who set out into the Notch, hoping to make his way through the rubble and destruction which littered the place and spend the next night at the Willey House. It was a foolhardy journey but somehow Barker made it, tired and exhausted after traveling only six miles over boulders and fallen trees. He arrived at the Willey place just as darkness was setting in. He paused, waiting for a call from the house, but none came. Smoke was curling from the chimney and the house gave the appearance of a normal home. But everything was still and silent and when Barker reached the door, there was nobody there to greet him. He went in. The remnants of a fire smouldered in the hearth, around which a circle of empty chairs had been placed. Looking around, Barker saw that money and papers had been spread out on the bar and that a Bible lay on the floor, open at the Eighteenth Psalm. But nothing moved, not even the Willeys' dog—which Barker knew.

He concluded that the Willeys were probably farther up in the Notch inspecting storm damage or else they and their farmhands had fled to safety in the nearest town, Bartlett, where Sam Willey's father lived. Deciding to wait until they returned, John Barker made himself a meal and stretched out on the couch and, exhausted by his journey, fell into a deep, sound slumber. He was wakened sometime during the night by a deep, loud moan which seemed to come from just outside the house. It was not a human voice which called him but a low, guttural roar which persisted into the night. Barker remembered the old supernatural tales concerning the Notch and at first refused to investigate, terrified of what he might see. As dawn was breaking, he eventually ventured out. A barn had collapsed during the storm and an old plow ox had been trapped by a fallen beam and been hurt. Barker managed to free the wounded animal and then began to search further, trying to discover what had happened to the Willeys. He noticed great piles of mud, stone, and gravel which seemed to have come down from the upper slopes of the Notch and which had crushed a number of the outbuildings and brought trees crashing down onto the floor of the pass. There had been, he concluded, a devastating landslide which had come down the mountain behind the house. The avalanche had somehow split into two, separated by a large overhang of a boulder which rose directly behind the building, and in doing so had missed the Willey House completely.

Puzzling over the mystery of the abandoned house but still convinced that the Willeys were somewhere else in the locality, Barker made his way down to Bartlett, observing as he traveled down the Notch that the Saco River had risen almost twenty feet at certain points. In Bartlett, he found no trace of the family, although Mrs. Lovejoy, Polly's mother, reported that the Willeys' dog had arrived at her front door the day after the storm howling and whining. When anyone approached it, it would cower and howl mournfully and it was later seen running backwards and forwards up and down the road towards the Notch, whimpering as it went. It later disappeared and was never seen again.

Following Barker's report, Sam's brother, Ben Willey, organized a search party to go up to the Notch and find out what had happened. On the way there, they met the Crawfords coming down, and together both teams went up to the Willey House and started clearing up the debris around it. This was on Wednesday, two days after the storm. It did not take them long to find the mangled body of Polly Willey under a boulder that was so heavy it took seven men to shift it. She had been trapped close to the front door, still clutching her badly crushed youngest child. Later that same day, the searchers found Dave Allen's body, also under a large boulder which had slid over one thousand feet down the mountainside. Sam Willey's body was found in the Saco River two days later, having been washed farther down the Notch. Sally Willey, the youngest of the girls, was fished out of the Saco River near Bartlett almost a week later, while Dave Nickerson's remains were found under a twenty-foot pile of rubble soon after. Three other Willey children— two boys and another girl—were never found. Had they too been crushed by the avalanche or did they escape and like the dog were so traumatized by the shock that they wandered off into the maze of gullies and canyons surrounding the Notch?

It was ironic to note that had everyone stayed in the house, they would have emerged from the experience relatively unscathed. Although there was evidence of some flooding on the first floor of the Willey House, the landslide had utterly missed the building. However, something seemed to have lured all nine occupants out to meet the tons of earth and rock that came crashing down from the upper slopes. Maybe they had all fled in blind panic. In fact, that was how Nathaniel Hawthorne described it in his *Twice Told Tales*: "they quitted their security and fled right into the pathway of destruction."

The Willey House lay abandoned for eighteen years after the terrible tragedy. And yet, conversely, the Notch became more popular than ever with travelers and sightseers. During the summer months, when the blossoms were out, the pass acquired a beautiful and romantic ambience that was unrivaled anywhere in New Hampshire. And, of course, it was, as Hawthorne put it, "a great artery, through which the lifeblood of international commerce continuously throbbed between Maine on one side and the Green Mountains and the shores of the St. Lawrence on the other."

When passing by the abandoned building, traders would raise their hats and women would bow their heads before a great pile of stone which was said to be the unmarked grave of Polly Willey and two of her children. Sometimes, passersby would also add a rock or small stone to the pile out of respect. Stories of their ghostly cries and of fearful sobbing along the Notch began to be told, and the whole area was treated as a "hainted place" for many years after.

It was not until 1844 that the Willey House was taken over by Ethan Crawford and reopened as a hotel. Nathaniel Hawthorne frequently stayed there and was on his way up into the Notch in May 1864 to spend a night there with his old friend and former president, Franklin Pierce, when at Pemigewasset House in Plymouth he died peacefully in his sleep. In 1898, the old Willey House mysteriously burned to the ground and today not a trace of it remains. The awful tragedy and the eerie reputation of the mountain pass, however, have never been forgotten.

In many ways, Crawford's Notch corresponds with Celtic beliefs regarding passes, tunnels, and crossing points. It led between two different regions (the north and west), essentially what was two different "countries." In accordance with ancient Celtic lore and belief, it began to acquire certain supernatural legends about it: that it was the dwelling place of Indian spirits and that it was haunted by the cannibalistic ghosts of Major Rogers' ill-fated expedition into Canada. It was said by the old people in New Hampshire to be pure foolishness to build a house in the Notch, no good could come of it. And of course, tragedy bore that warning out and, in a sense, reinforced it. So great a grip did this story have on the New England mind that ghostly tales regarding the Notch and the old Willey House are still being told in rural New Hampshire. And who is to say that there is not, perhaps, more than a grain of truth in them?

North Carolina

The Devil's Tramping Ground

For the early Celts, the landscape around them was a terrible place abounding in unseen deities, spirits, and demons. Wells, rocks, rivers, and hills attracted forces that were capricious in nature and could just as easily be dark and malignant as friendly and welcoming. There were, too, the problems of the defensive earthworks left by former peoples—raths and ringforts—which dotted the landscape. Such sites were frequently regarded as places of mystery where supernatural forces gathered and kept a sullen eye upon the affairs of puny mortals. These forces waited within such places to trap the unwary and excise awful penalties for those who entered them in an irreverent manner or without the deity's express permission. These places either became areas to be avoided or sites of ritual worship.

Groves of trees also became a focus for worship, particularly groves of oak trees, which have been popularly associated with the Druids (Celtic pagan holy men). It was even thought at one time that the word "Druid" had its origins in the ancient Greek *drus,* meaning "oak," thus making the Druids "men of the oak tree." The Classical writers Pliny the Elder and Strabo make this connection. Recently, however, this has been called into question by such Irish scholars as Dr. Daithi O hOgain, who points out in his *Myth, Legend, and Romance: Encyclopaedia of the Irish Folk Tradition* that the favorite tree of the Druids was clearly the rowan and that hazel trees were also important. Whichever tree was sacred or magical, groves of them were clearly central to early Celtic worship. Within the confines of the grove, the god lived and had to be worshipped. The Roman historian Lucan (39-65 A.D.) wrote about such places in part III of *Pharsalia* ("Civil War") as follows: "Nobody dared enter this grove except the priest: and even he kept out at midday between dusk and dawn—for fear that the gods might be abroad at such hours."

The Gaulish (Celtic French) name for a grove was *nemeton*—*nemed* in Irish—and this has been incorporated into the names of relevant deities such as Nemetona and Armetia, showing how important worship in groves may have been.

Hills and high places, too, were home to powerful supernatural beings. Because they were so close to the skies, where, increasingly, deities were believed to live, their summits often became sites of veneration. Here the god could descend from the clouds and hold court amongst his or her worshippers. Consequently, many gatherings in Ireland and Scotland were held on the summits of hills or on exceptionally high places. Festivals such as Blackberry Sunday (at the end of July) or May Eve (April 30) obviously had their origins in the worship of the Celtic world.

As the Celtic lands gradually became Christianized, the common perception of these sacred pagan places changed. Rather than being the abode of gods and spirits, which were worshipped, they became the haunts of demons and fairies, which were to be abhorred and avoided. Those who still visited them were engaged in black magic for these were now sites where the Devil himself or his demonic agents held court. Forts and hills became places of even greater fear and began to have a significant impact upon local folklore in many regions. Groves and mountaintops now became places of mystery and evil, particularly if they had some strange or unnatural feature about them—for instance if no grass grew there or they were especially bleak or isolated.

One such place is Bredon Hill in the English West Country. It may have been a place for ancient and mystical rites, but during the mid-twentieth century, it acquired a particularly sinister reputation. In May 1939, a man named Harry Dean met a peculiar death there, an incident which has remained shrouded in mystery ever since. His body was found in a deserted quarry on the hill and he had apparently been strangled. However, his body had been laid out in accordance with some ritual: a large boulder had been placed at each of the four cardinal compass points and Harry's body was found beside the southernmost one. A coroner's court was hastily convened and despite the overwhelming evidence of strangulation, a seemingly inexplicable and highly questionable verdict of accidental death was returned. Obviously, some fear of the place is still rife in the area, even in legal circles.

Not far away stands Meon Hill, a noted Warwickshire landmark. It is said that this hill was created by the Devil, who expressed his displeasure at the building of the nearby abbey at Evesham by picking up a clod of dirt and hurling it across country at the sacred place. Thanks to the prayers of St. Egwin, the holy abbot who founded Evesham in the year 717 and was watching over the building, the missile fell short and became Meon Hill. Local legend suggests that the summit of the hill was used for witchcraft rituals in the distant past and on February 16, 1945, a report in the *Stratford-upon-Avon Herald and South Warwickshire Advertiser* stated the following:

OLD MAN'S TERRIBLE INJURIES
Inflicted with Billhook and Pitchfork
TRAGIC DISCOVERY AT QUINTON

Warwickshire police are investigating what may prove to be a murder of a particularly brutal character. On Wednesday night, following a search, the body of a 74 year-old farm laborer, Mr. Charles Walton of Lower Quinton, was found with terrible injuries at Meon Hill where he had been engaged in hedge-laying. A trouncing hook and two-tined pitchfork are said to have been embedded in his body. Mr. Walton, who lived with his niece, was a frail old man. He suffered considerably with rheumatism and walked with the aid of two sticks.

The billhook and pitchfork had been used ferociously, and the body of the old man was badly mutilated. In fact, the fork had been driven right through his neck, pinning his body to the ground. His throat had been cut and his chest had been slashed with a crude sign of the cross. Horrified by the murder, the local constabulary called in Chief Inspector Robert Fabian of Scotland Yard to investigate. Fabian had an almost 100 percent record at solving murders but this was one which eluded even the great detective. However, the case interested a certain academic, Dr. Margaret Murray, an eighty-five-year-old Egyptologist at London University and author of such books as *The Witch-Cult in Western Europe* and *The God of the Witches*. Five years after Charles Walton's death, Dr. Murray published some of her considerations regarding the murder, stating that more sinister and occult motives should be investigated. It was, she was sure, connected with witchcraft and the hill itself. Charles Walton had long been considered something of a wizard in the locality and perhaps the murder had to do with his alleged uncanny powers. There was also the proximity of Bredon Hill to be considered. After all, another peculiar murder had been committed there. Both murders remain unsolved but even today, few local people will talk about either of them.

The notion of the occult significance of hills and groves has transferred itself to the New World and similar examples to those quoted above are to be found in various American states. One such state is North Carolina, where many Celtic Scots-Irish settled in the nineteenth century. Here, many of the famous "balds" of the northwestern region form part of the Appalachian chain. These are mountains which, although heavily timbered on the lower slopes, refuse to support any such growth (or which support only minimal growth) on or near their summits. Their names reflect a long and complicated history—Rumbling Bald, Standing Indian, Parson's Bald, Clingman's Dome, etc.—and some of them are also known by the epithet of "woolly heads" because of the light gorse which grows on their tops. Some have a rather dark tale connected to them. For example, Grier's Bald reflects the story of one David Grier, a strange, mad hermit who lived there and shut himself off from the world following the rejection of his proposal of marriage by the daughter of local military man Col. David Vance. There were rumors that Grier trafficked with dark spirits up on the balds and that he used dark magic in order to make the girl fall for him. In the end, he became involved in disputes with neighbors and killed one of them in a fight. Although acquitted on the grounds of insanity, he was later killed by one of the dead man's friends. His unquiet spirit is said to haunt the mountaintop as a penance for dealing in dark matters. Of course, there are Indian legends too. Local Cherokees said that the spirits came to the bald mountains to consider the affairs of men, and they were places where men might vanish. There might be something in this, for much of North Carolina has heard the story of the Reverend W.T. Hawkins, the so-called shepherd of the hills, who mysteriously vanished near Timber Ridge in the beautiful sapphire country in the northwest of the Tar Heel State in the early days of the twentieth century. No trace of the seventy-three-year-old Methodist minister, much famed for his kindliness, has ever been found.

Many other mysterious regions and geological features across

North Carolina have, over the years, become associated with the occult and the Devil in the same way that the groves and hilltops of the Celtic world gradually assumed a diabolic aspect. Many local names bear testimony to the Enemy of All Mankind—Devil's Glen, Devil's Seat, and Devil's Courthouse (near where the Reverend Hawkins is said to have disappeared)—however, few have a more sinister reputation than an area of Chatham County known as the Devil's Tramping Ground.

Chatham is a historic county with a tradition that stretches back to the Revolutionary War. It was settled around 1771 by settlers who moved north from the Cape Fear region, and the county was named after the British earl of Chatham, William Pitt, who also gave his name to the county seat at Pittsboro. The original village of Pittsboro was known simply as Chatham County Court House and the British general Lord Cornwallis is said to have spent a night there during his march to Wilmington, after the Battle of Guildford Court House. Around the same period, the English sympathizer Col. David Fanning and his band of Tories attacked the village while a court-martial was in progress and captured forty-four persons as part of a localized campaign of terror. This gives the county a turbulent past stretching back over two centuries and one which lends itself to supernatural occurrences—especially those connected with the Prince of Darkness. It is in the West of Chatham, about ten miles from Siler City, that the Devil's Tramping Ground lies.

The Tramping Ground is a circular area of land completely devoid of any form of vegetation. It lies in the midst of a grove of trees on the edge of some private property. Roughly forty feet in diameter, it is surrounded by pines and scrub oaks which cast strange shadows around its edges. Nothing will grow there except a kind of wiregrass sprouting on its outer periphery. It has always been as it is today—bare and grassless and utterly sinister. Today, a rural highway runs near it and a solitary sign at the community of Harpers Crossroads points curiosity seekers in its direction.

As far back as anyone can remember, legend has designated this area as the spot where the Devil was to be found, walking backwards and forwards in a circular motion, thinking, scheming, and plotting all the evils that he would unleash on the unsuspecting world. It is said that he comes there late at night and departs before it is light. No one has ever seen him—no one has ever dared go there as soon as darkness has fallen—but the spot and story are well known all through the county. Some people have left objects in the area to see if they are disturbed the following day; such objects invariably and inexplicably disappear.

The oldest of all the legends refers to the Indians who inhabited the region when it was known as the Great Flats. It is said that local tribes periodically met either at or close to the spot for religious celebrations and festivals, feasting, and counseling. It was reputedly a place where the spirits gathered and the braves called on them to give success in hunting and warfare. Some have argued that the ground was originally worn down by the constant tramp of moccasined feet moving in endless war dances there.

A second Indian tale links the Tramping Ground to yet another North Carolina legend—that of the lost Roanoke Colony. Years before white settlers came to the region, a confederation of Indian tribes met in pitched battle at the scene of the Devil's Tramping Ground. Soon the ground had soaked up the blood of their dead, dying, and wounded. The leader of one of the factions was Chief Croatan, who was killed in the conflict. The remainder of his tribe buried his body with due ceremony and ritual at what is now the very center of the bare spot. They named the area Croatan in honor of their fallen chieftain before fleeing north to avoid further casualties. The Great Spirit was said to reside there, watching over the fallen chief's grave and keeping the area completely bare. It was to this particular spot which the members of Sir Walter Raleigh's Roanoke Colony were heading when they abandoned their coastal settlement. They left behind the word "Croatan" on a tree to inform others of where they had gone. When they reached the Tramping Ground, they were swallowed up into some magical otherworld, leaving no trace behind. Legend further states that no birds will perch or build in the trees around this accursed spot, perhaps because of Chief Croatan's ghost, which is said to haunt the site. It is said that no dog will cross that bare ground but will turn tail and flee.

There are two scars in the earth, both on the edge of the Tramping Ground, and there are two small holes in the very center of the phenomenon. These were allegedly made by treasure hunters and suggest another legend, one of fabulous hidden wealth. It is said that during the Civil War, a group of Confederate guerrillas made away with a Union army payroll but bluecoat soldiers followed close behind. As the Northerners drew ever closer, the Confederates reached the Devil's Tramping Ground. Here they paused to bury a gold-laden pay-chest, digging deep into the strange, sour soil. While they were so engaged a Union patrol came on them and called on them to surrender. In reply, the Confederates opened fire and in the exchange all of the guerrillas were killed, their lifeblood seeping into the bare and hungry earth of the Tramping Ground. Cautiously, the Union soldiers made their way to collect the pay-chest that lay in a hole near the very center of the clearing, but as they approached it, it suddenly sank out of sight as though pulled under the earth by an unseen hand. The soldiers ran from the site in terror.

Several years later, a couple of treasure hunters, hearing of the lost pay-chest and assuming that it held a fabulous cache, came to the Tramping Ground to look for it. With spades and shovels, they crossed to the center of the bare spot and began to dig. Suddenly, the ground in front of them opened and out of a deep, dark hole rose a massive gray-scaled serpent with red and shining eyes. It bared fanglike teeth and swooped towards the terrified hunters who, like the terrified Union soldiers before them, fled back into the woods. All that remained were some marks where they had been digging. In other variations of the tale, a terrible black hag rises up and threatens the hunters, who run for their lives.

The tale of the serpent is interesting. Serpents have traditionally been connected with the Devil and the story suggests that the infernal master is somehow guarding the stolen Confederate treasure. Strangely, a similar story comes from County Roscommon in Ireland where, on the death of the tyrannical landlord and priest-hunter Robert Ormsby, a terrible gray worm or serpent rose up out of the open grave and swallowed the coffin—thus the Devil claimed back his own. Could the story from Ireland have been translated to this remote area of North Carolina?

The Reverend Edgar Teague, a retired minister living a short way down the road from this terrible place, tells a story of some men who were willing to challenge the curse of the Devil's Tramping Ground. These were a group of young men from Bennett who dared one of their number to spend a night within the confines of the bare circle itself. He accepted the dare and took a sleeping bag and some blankets to the woods with him. The Reverend Teague goes on to say that he himself was driving home on that same night when he passed a blanketed figure in the car headlights running for his life. It was the young man who had accepted the dare. When the blanket was removed, the youngster screamed in total and utter fear. He was not physically harmed and seemed sound in limb, but he could not remember what had happened to him in the confines of the circle or what had terrified him so much. Ever after, goes on the reverend, the boy was regarded as strange by the local community—dreamy and withdrawn and seemingly wrapped up in a world which nobody else was aware of. His personality had completely changed. This incident only added to the sinister reputation the spot enjoyed.

Various attempts have been made to explain the phenomenon. Perhaps the most convincing has been offered by officers of the North Carolina State Museum. While conducting soil tests in the area, museum curator Henry Davis, together with state geologist J.L. Stukey, ran some experiments around the Devil's Tramping Ground to measure levels of sodium chloride—common salt—content. While in the vicinity they encountered a number of salt licks, which had probably been caused by long-vanished buffalo and deer. There were also, they noted, instances of wiry vegetation which thrived on brackish water such as that found in coastal regions and which carries a high saline content. There was also evidence of heavy salt deposits in the immediate area of the Tramping Ground. Davis then put forward the theory that the Devil's Tramping Ground was little more than an area so loaded with salt that no significant vegetation would or could grow there. Further tests were carried out in the area and while these appeared to at least partially back the curator's theory, they did not completely solve the mystery.

The Soil Testing Section of the North Carolina Department of Agriculture ran a series of field tests on the Tramping Ground itself, using soil samples which were taken from the very center of the circle. The results were checked by two chemists—Dr. I.E. Miles at division headquarters and W.A. Bridges at Wilson—who came up with some strange results. The soil taken from the center of the circle was utterly and completely sterile. Moreover, it was highly acidic. While a heavy concentration of salt might produce a partial sterility, it could not wholly account for the complete lifelessness of the sample that was taken. Mr. Bridges noted, "Although there may be other factors of a physical nature that would make this a sterile soil, our findings show that plant life will not be supported on a soil that is so acid and so low in the necessary soil nutriments." It was almost, remarked one observer, as if the soil had come from somewhere else and was not of Earth at all. Maybe it came from that strange and alien otherworld in which the ancient Celts believed. No one could explain why, if the soil was so poor, the immediately surrounding area was fertile enough to support grasses, flowers, and trees. Even history shows that the spot has been infertile for as far back as memory will allow. Indian legends always speak of the place as being barren. The only answer, said the locals, was that this was a place reserved for dark spirits and was where the Devil himself was abroad.

There is another mystery too, one not fully explained away by scientific, soil-testing means. Why will no animal go near the spot? One story, told by a Mr. Dixon, a lawyer from Siler City, recounts a hunting expedition through the woodlands around the Tramping Ground. He had with him, he states, two exceptionally fierce dogs— good possum hunters—that were "afraid of nothing." They broke through the undergrowth and came out on the very edge of the Devil's Tramping Ground. Suddenly, both hounds simultaneously emitted mournful howls and fled back into the brush. No amount of coaxing would make them approach that spot again. Another hunter in the area recounted a similar experience with his dogs and stated that whenever he bent down to touch the bare earth of the circle, he found it curiously warm against his skin. It was, he said, as if a fire had been lit there in some very recent time and the heat was still somehow retained in the ground. Other hunters have noted that sometimes birds in flight have appeared to wheel and dart away rather than fly over the area and that the tiny animals which live in the undergrowth all around tend to shy away from the place. Certainly none of them will try to cross it. What is it they fear about the area?

A number of locals have claimed to have seen strange shapes flickering near the center of the Tramping Ground, although whether they are human or animal is not specified. There are suggestions of cloven hooves, but this may be simply additions brought about by the association with the Devil. There are some stories, however, of great spiders—far bigger than any ordinary spider—that sometimes scuttle about the area. Many people tend to give these creatures a wide berth.

A local doctor from Graham recalls how as a much younger man he was near the Tramping Ground when suddenly some sheep which must have accidentally wandered onto it came pouring out through the woods in great distress—one animal after the other in a straight line. It was, he says, a most peculiar sight. If the place had been simply a salt lick, the animals might have stayed there. Could it be that the absence of bird or animal life on the Tramping Ground is indicative of the presence of the infernal master? And might the heat in the ground, experienced by several hunters, come directly from hell itself? Or might the circle be the gateway to some arid and sterile other realm which lies just beyond our vision? Could there simply be some straightforward scientific explanation which has not been discovered yet?

Certainly the Devil's Tramping Ground would appear to be an eerie place, surrounded as it is by myth and legend. While there may be some perfectly rational explanation for this barren area, it, like the balds, has sparked echoes of the ancient Celtic belief which the colonist brought with them to the New World—that there were groves and shrines which were the sole domain of the gods and that no mortal should ever venture into them. The connections with the Devil are perhaps of more recent, Christian origin. Nevertheless, it may be that the Father of Lies does indeed visit Chatham County in order to meditate and scheme. Furthermore, it could be that all the woes of the world are plotted in a remote corner of North Carolina. Who can say?

Part 3

Witches, Wizards, and Uncanny People

Maryland

The Evil of Patty Cannon

Within Celtic society, witches were not initially viewed in the conventional sense—that is, as evil midnight hags ready to bring harm and misfortune upon their neighbors. This stereotype is a much later one, arising in the Christian West during the late medieval/ early modern period. The Celtic witch was an integral part of the community in which he or she lived. Such witches followed from the shamanistic/Druidic tradition which had been central to the early Celtic religious perspective. They acted as healers, foretellers of the future, and preservers of local lore. They had a knowledge of illnesses and of the herbs which remedied them as well as how to avert misfortune and disaster. They might, for example, be able to control the weather or ensure that the corn grew or that game was plenty. Moreover, they were at one with nature and could often advise on natural things. Their power was often considered as absolute but always beneficial.

Nevertheless, such people had their darker side as well. While others healed and cured, they would curse and bring misfortune upon those around them; while others brought good weather and aided in the ripening of the harvest, they called down storms and blights upon the grain; while others prepared love potions, they created poisons and disease in the community. They fought with their neighbors and blighted the lives of those around them. And it was out of this side—the darker side of the power—that the first stirrings of the now-familiar Christian stereotype grew. The church, of course, took a dim view of the alleged powers of such people. Where did they obtain those powers? it asked. Not from an ancient Celtic tradition which linked the practitioner with the natural world, but from the Devil, the master of evil. Consequently, to deal with such "wise people" was to invite damnation of one's immortal soul.

Even with the disapproval of the church, in many Celtic lands—Ireland, Scotland, Cornwall, etc.—these "wise folk" continued to exercise great influence within their own localities. The Cornish wise woman Tamsin Blight (or Blee) and her rather dubious husband acted as "pellars" (repellers of illnesses, which were believed to be caused either by witchcraft or demons) all over Cornwall throughout the early nineteenth century. They were even consulted by people from as far away as Wales. Similarly, Irish people traveled great distances to consult with Biddy Early in County Clare and Moll Anthony at the Red Hills in County Kildare during the same period. Other people, too, ventured down to County Kerry to see the famous "fairy doctor" Maurice Griffin. Such people were considered beneficent and were deemed to be working (no matter what the clergy said) for the good of the community. There were others, however, who claimed similar powers and who were prepared to use the awe and mystery in which they were held against their neighbors. Such witches were counted (and rightly so) as agents of the dark powers and of the Devil himself.

One of these dark people was the Cornish witch Madgy (or Madge) Figgy, the witch of St. Levan, near Land's End. This fearful harridan was both despised and feared within the villages around the southern part of Cornwall and is reputed to have leveled terrible curses upon all those who crossed her—curses which often came to fruition. Madgy was predominantly a "weather witch," a sorceress who could create storms and bring down hail and rain upon the fishing communities which dotted the coast, making it almost impossible for any boat to leave harbor in order to ply their trade. She lived in a tumbledown cottage not far from the village of Raftra and local people avoided the place like poison. And with good reason for it was well known that Madgy Figgy was not only a witch, she was a criminal. Together with a gang of hardened men, she lured ships which passed along the coast onto rocks near Perloe Cove or summoned up storms which would drive them into the reefs near Tol-Pedden-Penwith, a sheer cliff face rising straight out of the sea. Indeed, on the western part of the promontory itself rose a series of cubical masses of granite known as "the Chair Ladder" or sometimes as "Madgy Figgy's Chair" as it was here that the old crone was said to sit to call down her storms upon unsuspecting vessels.

On one occasion, according to legend, Madgy lured a Portuguese Indiaman, a ship operating for one of the East India companies, into Perloe Cove by occult means. There the ship was dashed to pieces by a terrible tide, drowning everyone on board. As the bodies washed ashore, Madgy and her gang emerged from the landward rocks and proceeded to strip anything valuable from them without compunction. The ruffians then buried the corpses in a narrow green glen nearby, marking each grave with a stone placed at the head of the corpse. The haul from the wreck must have been a good one for many of the women round about—the wives and sweethearts of the wreckers in Figgy's gang—were kept supplied with fine dresses and small pieces of jewelery for many months afterwards. Even girls working in the fields were often bedecked with the finest brocades and wore gold ornaments on their arms. For a long time afterwards, gold and gems continued to wash up on the sands around Perloe.

But there were other stories about Madgy Figgy too. These were about how she flew through the air like some great bird, mounted only on a piece of ragwort, casting spells which brought bad luck on all the houses over which she passed. She was also said to raise the dead from the graveyards across which she flew and to steal things from rich men's dwellings, which she often entered invisibly. There was no end to her magical powers or her wickedness.

Once she wrecked a French vessel passing along the Cornish coast, dashing it on the reefs around Land's End. Amongst the dead who were washed ashore was the body of a rich foreign lady very grandly dressed and with jeweled rings on her fingers and gold chains about her neck. This body, like all others, was stripped almost immediately, and on the back of the corpse, Madgy and her cohorts found a mark which was said to bode evil for them all. Many of the gang simply wanted to leave the gold and jewelery which had been taken but the dreadful old Figgy (she was quite well advanced in years at this time) drew a knife and threatened them all. She was more than a match even for the most hardened members of her gang, and they all secretly feared her alleged dark powers. She said that the strange woman's wealth held no terrors for her and that she would take it all herself. There were none who disagreed with her. All the valuables which had been taken from the body were carried to Madgy's hut where they were placed in a great old chest which was kept in a dark corner under some sacking. The foreign woman was buried nearby with no gravestone to mark her resting place. That night, however, and on succeeding nights, a strange, bluish light drifted ashore, just where the wreck had been, and went up to Tol-Pedden, where it seemed to seat itself in Madge's Chair for a while. Then it made its way to Figgy's cottage and, drifting into the ramshackle building, settled itself on the chest in the corner and disappeared. This happened on several nights and was witnessed by a number of people. Everyone was terrified, believing it to be a ghost, except for Madgy Figgy herself, who said that she knew all about it.

One evening a strangely dressed, very dark-skinned foreign man arrived at Figgy's door when Madgy was not there. Figgy's husband, however, was at home and the stranger indicated by signs (for he could not speak English) that he wanted to see some graves. He did not, he motioned, require a guide. Nevertheless, Figgy's husband went with him and together they climbed up to the grave where the foreign woman had unceremoniously been laid to rest. There, he gave full vent to his grief. He then sent Madgy Figgy's man away and waited there until dusk fell and the strange light appeared. As usual, it made its way down to Madgy Figgy's cottage and, going inside, settled on the old chest, now covered up with sails and other fisherman's lumber. The stranger swept these things aside and, opening up the chest, took out certain artifacts which he placed in a canvas bag he carried. He did not, however, take any of the valuables. He rewarded the wreckers with costly gifts and left them; nobody knew where he went or even where he came from. Now Madgy Figgy was truly triumphant. "One witch knows another, living or dead," she declared, "and yon African [for such she supposed him to be] would have been the death of us if we hadn't kept the treasure and if it hadn't been for my own powers of which he was greatly afraid. Now we have good gifts and no gainsaying 'em!" The incident added greatly to Madgy's reputation in the locality, and she and her gang continued with their wrecking and plundering almost without interruption.

Madgy made the most of her increased notoriety, cursing her neighbors whenever they refused to sell her a pig so that the animal died shortly after. And she was not the only such sorceress. Another Cornish witch known only as "Old Joan," who lived at Alsia Mill, cursed the hogs of her neighbor Madam Noy, who was regarded as something of a harridan and perhaps as a sorceress herself, so that they took the "swine fever" and died. It is thought that Old Joan, like Madgy Figgy, was also involved with the wrecking gangs which frequented the Cornish coastline.

In some cases, criminal activity and alleged witchcraft were intertwined. In the Christian mind, the antisocial behavior of the criminal was strongly connected to the diabolical powers of the witch and over the years, the two became inseparable within some localities. This perspective was carried to the United States, where it took root in parts of New England. In a land were the law assumed control only slowly, criminals often flourished and some of them relied upon the reputation of supernatural powers to protect them from the forces of justice. One such person was Patty Cannon.

Along Route 392, heading towards the Delaware border and just inside the Maryland state line, stands a sign that reads, "Patty Cannon's house at Johnson's Cross Roads where the noted kidnapping group had headquarters as described in George Alfred Townsend's novel *The Entailed Hat.* The house borders on Caroline and Dorchester Counties and the state of Delaware." The area, now known as Reliance, Maryland, was once the haunt of one of the most notorious characters in the development of early America, and it is said that her ghost sometimes returns to waylay travelers and create mayhem in the countryside. Patty Cannon was a murderess, kidnapper, and black marketeer and headed a ruthless gang which caused unrest throughout the region (and even further afield) for many years. Even today, her deeds are remembered around Reliance and have been documented in George Alfred Townsend's book *The Entailed Hat.* She is remembered as a woman of great physical strength and a grim, personal determination.

Little is known about Patty's origins, but she is described as "gypsyish" and incredibly swarthy. It is not known if Cannon was her true surname or one which she adopted to disguise both herself and where she had come from. Some said that she might have come from Canada; others say from Eastern Europe. It might have been that she was wanted elsewhere under another name and that she fled to Maryland to avoid capture, changing her identity in the process. She lived in the late 1700s and early 1800s, a time when the United States was settling down after the Revolutionary

War and trying to establish some sort of cohesion after a turbulent period. New states were being formed and the absence of a unified political system coupled with the primitive law enforcement of the time served to aid Patty in her nefarious activities.

It is known that Patty had at least one daughter, either legitimate or illegitimate. This girl, whose name is not known for certain, married one Joe Johnson, who owned a tavern at a crossroads near the Maryland/Delaware border. Although Johnson was something of a rogue himself, he was in nowhere near the same league as his new mother-in-law and was respectable enough to give his name to the area in which he lived, Johnson's Crossroads, which would later become part of the town of Reliance. At the time, however, it was an isolated and relatively lawless place and was said to have already been frequented by robbers and highwaymen who dealt with Johnson himself, who established close relationships with many of them. Now his mother-in-law, having moved into the Johnson tavern and using it as a headquarters for her illegal activities, took over those relationships and began to recruit a number of these footpads into her own gang. Around her, she assembled equally ruthless cutthroats who followed her every command. Their main source of income was the capture of free blacks whom they sold as slaves although they carried out highway robbery and kidnapping as well. In the early 1800s there were a number of landholders in the Maryland/Delaware area who were quite willing to buy slaves without question on the black market and this fact was continually exploited by Patty and her gang. Indeed, Patty Cannon was one of the prime movers in the Maryland illegal slave market.

The outlaw band were responsible for many disappearances throughout the state and the law seemed powerless to do anything about it. Suspicion had long fallen on Patty Cannon and her son-in-law but no one could prove anything. Law enforcement operated in a haphazard fashion in many states and there was a general lack of concern amongst whites regarding the fate of the free blacks and erstwhile slaves who disappeared. Besides, with a fluctuating state line, there were legal difficulties in obtaining a prosecution. The problematic definition of the Maryland/Delaware border made the coherent enforcement of law almost impossible in the area, and when officers from Maryland showed up to question Patty she refused to answer on the grounds that she considered the tavern to be in Delaware—something which the authorities had to check out, thus allowing Patty and her gang to slip away. Other times, they simply crossed the border and so eluded capture.

Patty's reputation was steadily growing throughout the region. Her continual ability to avoid arrest was drawing comment and suspicion from every quarter. There were suggestions that Patty herself was a "conjure woman" who had outwitted the law through magical means. Stories spread that she and her gang came and went about their criminal activities invisibly—sometimes under the very eyes of the law officers, who apparently saw nothing at all. It all added to the legends concerning her.

Between Maryland and Delaware lay an almost undetectable network of dark and meandering trails which cut through overgrown bottomlands and across overgrown ridges. These had been infrequently used in the days of the Indians but few of them had even known the foot of man. Patty, of course, knew every one of them and used them to move her victims from place to place without detection. Here, too, were hidden hollows and valleys where the gang could rest unseen and well away from the forces of the law. It was the capacity to move about and hide which earned Patty Cannon her "supernatural" reputation, a dubious accolade which the woman herself encouraged.

Foul mouthed and argumentative, she frequently fell out with the people around Johnson's Crossroads, cursing them and threatening to hex them if they crossed her. Sometimes things happened to those with whom she argued. Whether these were caused by Patty and her gang themselves or whether such "accidents" were no more than coincidence is open to question; nevertheless, many people of the region attributed them to Patty's witchcraft. It was said, for example, that on certain moonlit nights the Devil, riding on a black horse with red fiery eyes, visited Joe Johnson's tavern to converse with the awful harridan and to plot mischief against God's people in Maryland. Joe Johnson, probably acting on his mother-in-law's instructions, never denied such rumors. If anything, he encouraged them. Even when the expanding and developing settlement changed its name from Johnson's Crossroads to Reliance, stories of the nightly visitations continued amongst the populace. It was said, too, that Patty traveled the area in the guise of a crow, spying at people's windows in order to ferret out their best-kept secrets. And, in the tradition of Celtic witches, it was even said that somewhere in the tavern, she kept a magic mirror in which she could see what was happening in houses throughout the area and as far away as Delaware. She was a known blackmailer and it was widely reported that she obtained her information through occult means. These were simply tales but they were encouraged by Patty and by other members of her gang to ward off the curious and those who would seek to inform on her. The authorities, therefore, found it almost impossible to obtain evidence against her.

Many people knew that Johnson's tavern was the headquarters and a kind of way station which the Cannon gang used in the transportation of slaves. Their victims were allegedly kept chained in a series of attic rooms until they could be moved along the dark trails to somewhere else. Patty herself was said to have overseen their confinement and there were rumors of tortures and beatings within the place. The tavern was relatively isolated but even so cries and screams could often be heard in its vicinity at late hours of the evening. At the back of the inn lay a series of unmarked graves where the bodies of those with whom she had been overly zealous were buried. Many suspected what was going on, but nobody dared to speak of it, much less take any action. The police had no evidence with which to charge Patty. All that was to change by the late 1820s.

In the spring of 1828 or 1829, a farmer plowing a cornfield near the tavern made a grisly discovery. His plow struck something half-buried in the earth and, thinking it to be a large stone, he bent down to pull it out. The "stone" turned out to be a human skull and as the horrified farmer dug further, he unearthed more and more human bones, some which carried iron shackles. These were the remains of the slaves whom Patty and her gang had tortured and murdered. One of those skeletons, it was whispered, was Patty's own husband (even though it is unclear whether she ever had a husband). The authorities now had their evidence. Patty's terrible career came to an abrupt end in 1829 when law enforcement officers swooped upon Johnson's tavern and arrested her. She was taken to Georgetown, Delaware, where she was placed in custody. She was charged with murder and awaited trial. Many people thought Patty Cannon would finally be punished but many others expected her to avoid the hangman's noose. The latter were right for she never even made the trial. While in prison, Patty committed suicide by taking some poison which she had reputedly secreted in the hem of her voluminous black skirt. The nature of the poison is unknown but certainly she was skilled with poisons and was able to dissolve a small portion of the mysterious substance in some drinking water before gulping it down. For her, death was almost instantaneous. The number of people who died at her hands will never be known, but it is estimated to have been well over a hundred. Some people claimed that justice had been done and by her own hand.

Years went by and even though Patty Cannon was dead, her name lingered on in the streets of Reliance, the town formerly known as Johnson's Crossroads. The tavern which Joe Johnson, now himself dead, had once owned still stood, as did the house where Patty had lived (some two hundred yards from the tavern itself), strong reminders of the evil which Patty and her followers had released within that small community. Of course, there were those who refused to believe that she had died in the Georgetown jail at all. It was claimed to have been one of her last, great supernatural tricks. Somehow, she had escaped from the jail and had left a "stock"—a lifeless magical representation of herself—in her place, making everybody believe that she was dead. Patty was living somewhere in another part of the country, said some commentators, still carrying out her evil. It was a tale widely believed across Maryland and Delaware.

Johnson's tavern changed hands several times, not remaining long in the possession of any one owner. Many of its owners felt distinctly uneasy about the place and there were rumors that somehow Patty was still around it. There were secret rooms, ran the stories, which had never been discovered and where the rotting skeletons of former victims still lay. After her magical escape from Georgetown, the witch had taken up residence in one of these and, with her mind now crazed with the horror of her past actions, only came out at night to wander about the building. At least, this was the basis of the tale. Other stories said that her ghost haunted the building, bound by divine will to the scene of her most heinous crimes. This was no insubstantial phantom but a tangible, murderous specter which rattled doors and windows and threatened those who slept in the old tavern. Yet further tales told that it was not Patty herself but the ancient powers she had drawn to the place which remained there or it was the troubled ghosts of those whom she had slain.

In January 1982, the tavern was bought by a retired Marine Corps colonel, Mr. Jack Messick, who taught at the nearby elementary school. Together with his wife, Rose, and their four sons, they moved into the old building. Just before they did so, however, strange stories concerning Patty Cannon and her gang began to resurface in the area. Her ghost had been seen wandering on lonely back roads, sometimes alone, sometimes leading a line of chained, wailing victims towards the state line. There were also tales of a treasure, part of Patty's ill-gotten gains, which were supposed to be buried in the same field where the bones had been discovered. There were other stories that part of the gang's loot had been hidden somewhere in the tavern itself. If it existed, the Messicks never found it.

There were also stories concerning the previous owner of the tavern, who had been convinced that he was not alone in the old place. There were strange noises, strange whispers, sounds like furtive footfalls, and he came to the belief that Patty Cannon herself was sharing the house with him. At that time, the tavern was also used as a museum with tourists and visitors being led through the old place for the price of a small admission to inspect the "dungeon" where Patty had "entertained" her unwilling guests and had perpetrated the majority of her most horrid crimes. Late at night, however, there were sounds like strangled cries coming from deep in the tavern and these unnerved the owner so much that he had sold up, claiming the place was too badly haunted for him to continue to live there. The vengeful spirit of Patty Cannon, he claimed, prowled its corridors as soon as the sun began to go down. With his departure, the ghostly goings on seem to have ceased.

In all the time he and his family have lived there, Jack Messick has never experienced anything of a supernatural nature. In the master bedroom, there is a trapdoor to an attic where presumably the wretched slaves were kept and, according to the previous owner, this would open from time to time of its own accord. On one occasion, he claimed to have seen a tormented black face staring down at him. Since the Messicks have come to live there, the trapdoor has remained firmly closed. The family do not use it, nor do they seem especially troubled by the old house's turbulent history. The only disturbance they seem to have is from ghost hunters and treasure seekers who turn up at their door at unsociable hours.

Maybe Patty Cannon has returned to the scene of her former crimes. Perhaps her unquiet ghost cannot rest because of the weight of her sins. Maybe it is some vestige of the power which she once wielded which abides in the very stonework of the old building. Who knows? Patty certainly did conform to the ideal of the Celtic witch in later times—that woman who was outside the parameters of decent society and outside her own community. She was a criminal and, quite possibly, a murderess. Thus, in ancient Celtic belief, the evil which she unleashed through her terrible actions might linger on, even though she herself is long dead. Such dark forces could often act independently of their originator and manifest in various forms—sounds, smells, odd glimpses. Perhaps the tales of ghostly activity can be contributed to nothing more than the frolicsome activities of local youths who, building on the sinister reputation of Patty Cannon, have played tricks on the local populace. This is the explanation currently given by many people around the area. But can anyone actually be sure? One thing is certain: the dark shadow of Patty Cannon undoubtedly reaches across the years, touching the hearts and minds of the people around Reliance even today.

Massachusetts

The Quaker Seeress

For the Celts, as for many other peoples of the ancient world, a knowledge of the future was essential. It was, for example, extremely useful for local rulers or warlords to know the outcomes of their actions before a proposed battle or for a farmer to know whether the harvest would be good or bad in a given year. In the Celtic world, the task of prognostication fell to the Druids—pagan holy men and women—who advised their masters and mistresses, the kings and queens of the Celtic world, through the interpretation of signs and signals through which the spirits who governed mortal lives foretold the future. It is interesting to note that this prognostication was usually by interpretative means rather than, say, by full spirit possession, as was common in some other cultures. The Druids possessed abilities denied to others which enabled them to determine the will of the gods and relay it to the rulers and people. Amongst the signs they interpreted were the movement of birds, the formation of clouds, or the swirls of water in a river, all of which were indicative as to what the spirits or gods were thinking.

"The Druids," Greek philosopher and historian Dio Chrysostom stated, were "well versed in the art of seers and prophets." Irish and Scottish Druids in particular seemed to enjoy something of a reputation for augury, and second sight (the "seeing" of future events) was prevalent in the Highlands and Western Isles of Scotland as late as the twentieth century, according to author and folklorist Lewis Spence. Certain rituals known as *tagharim*—an ancient word originally meaning "echo" but which had come to mean divination by occult means—were being carried out by "specialists" in some of the more remote areas of the Highlands and islands. This involved the practitioner wrapping him- or herself in the skin of a newly slain bull and withdrawing to the vicinity of a waterfall to meditate or sleep (*dercad*). This practice induced what might be described as an altered state through which the spirits made their presence known. Not only would the seer reveal glimpses of the future, but they would also answer any questions which might be asked, with the sleeper acting as a kind of medium or interpreter.

The Irish *Tairbhfheis,* or bull sleep, employed a much more formal, ritualized ceremony and was only used on great occasions and for much more specific purposes than community divination. Because of their great strength, bulls held a special place in the beliefs and mythologies of many ancient peoples, in particular the Celts. A bull was sacrificed and its bloody carcass was made into a foaming broth. A warrior well respected in the community was chosen to eat the bull flesh and drink the broth and, after consuming as much as possible, was permitted to lie down to sleep while the Druid chanted around him, calling on the spirits to make their will known through him. While he slept, dreams would come to him which would, hopefully, reveal the name of the next rightful high king of Tara.

The bull sleep was considered to be an infallible method of determining the will of the spirits and of discerning future events, but there were also others. The best-known method of augury in the Celtic world involved the entrails of chickens or other fowl. The writer Diodorus Siculus notes that in all Celtic countries birds were extensively used in prognostication by the Druids. This method was so successful, apparently, that chickens were adopted by certain Roman legions in order to determine military strategies. Yet another form of Druidic divination was through the *coelbreni,* or omen sticks. Here, the druids took hazel wands, each inscribed with a few words of the sacred language, *ogham* (a system of lines and intersections carved on either stone or tree bark), which they cast upon the ground. Meaning (and the will of the spirits) was interpreted from the lie of their fall.

Prognostication, therefore, played an important role in ancient Celtic life, not only for the leaders, kings, and chieftains but for the common people as well. The Celtic world, some historians have argued, appears to have been obsessed by augury, and much of the early Celtic social mind was centered on ways of disclosing the future. This did not change much with the coming of Christianity. Celtic Christianity (as opposed to the Roman model) placed great emphasis upon the foretelling of future events. However, rather than surrounding it with ritual or associating it with the summoning of spirits, the Celtic church believed such foretelling was a direct gift from God and that those who professed it were in some way extremely holy. Indeed, the foretelling of future events was the sure mark of an early saint. This was no more than a fusion of both pagan and Christian beliefs, but it was an extremely important one. Just as it had in the pagan world, prophecy became an important facet of the Christian one and, throughout Celtic countries, was probably used to demonstrate God's power and to draw new converts into the faith.

Even following the perceived amalgamation of both the Roman and Celtic churches following the historically and ecclesiastically famous Synod of Whitby in the year 664, much of old Celtic belief permeated the new church (which was essentially Roman in tone, concentrating on teaching and dogma instead of the mysticism which had characterized the Celtic model). This would continue into medieval times with monkish oracles and wandering holy men who predicted events in individual lives. Once again, the source of these abilities was given as the result of a holy life or as direct communication with God, who revealed such things to the chosen.

Nor did the interest in future events end with the arrival of Protestantism. Indeed, in some ways, the new dogma intensified it. Central to the philosophies of some of the stricter Protestant sects was the notion of predestination. Because God is omnipotent and omniscient, ran the argument, he knows the entire history of creation from its foundation to its end. Through this, he also knows the future. He knows, for example, who will be worthy enough to be with him in paradise from the moment of their birth and what will happen to them during the course of their lives. And he can reveal portions of such knowledge to those whom he considers holy enough to receive it. These were the elect, usually the foremost members of the religious Protestant sects and men and women of supposedly unblemished character. As in the ancient pagan world, the lives of these people revolved around signs and portents through which God made his will manifest. Just as the ancient Druids had done before them, these worthies interpreted the world around them and relayed their deliberations to their various congregations. Usually God made his directions (and the course of future events) known at times of great stress and difficulty for his people. Thus, in periods of pestilence, warfare, plague, and natural disasters, religious leaders, both Catholic and Protestant, proclaimed supernatural knowledge of forthcoming events which came directly from God himself in order to either reassure or to warn his followers.

The notion of foretelling the future as a gift, whether from God or from some other source, continued across the centuries in the Western Isles and Highlands of Scotland. This was an ability with which many seers were born (although some certainly acquired it in later life)—to glimpse the future, to foretell births, and more importantly to presage deaths. In some cases, it was a gift which the recipients did not want and was considered to be more of an affliction than anything else. The gift was known as the *Taibh-searachd*, *taibhs*, or simply *taish*, more commonly known as the "second sight," and much of this prophesy centered around local issues. Although these were the humdrum predictions concerning everyday life, this ordinariness did not to take away from the supernatural nature of the act itself and those who had the gift were often regarded with awe and respect within their communities. A description of one of these seers experiencing the *taish* on the island of Skye in the Hebrides is given by Martin Martin in his invaluable *A Description of the Western Isles of Scotland Circa 1695* in which he says that the eyelids of the person were erect and the eyes continued staring until the object (viewed only by the seer) vanished. He goes on to state that one of the Skye seers had eyelids which turned so far inwards that he had to draw them down with his fingers.

The most famous of all seers in the Highlands was undoubtedly Coinneach Odhar Fiosaiche—Sombre (or Dun-Colored) Kenneth of the Prophesies—a name given to Kenneth MacKenzie, the prophet of Seaforth in Ross-shire, also known as the Brahan Seer. He is a rather shadowy figure and it is possible that there may have been more than one person using that name at various times. According to Alexander MacKenzie, who collected the prophesies of the Brahan Seer in 1877, he was born on MacKenzie land at Baile-na-Cille on the island of Lewis in the seventeenth century. Somewhere between 1660 and 1675, he came to live near Loch Ussie in Ross-shire and worked on the Brahan estate of the Seaforth

MacKenzies, who were his distant kinsmen. It was here that he began to utter prophecies concerning not only local events but also the fates of certain Highland clans themselves. It is thought that the seer was blind in one eye and that he had a small blue, hollowed stone which he raised to the sightless pupil and through which he could see future events by using what he called "the cam [blind] eye of prophesy." Throughout his life, he was gloomy and sarcastic and came to his end when he insulted the parentage of some of his employers, was indicted for witchcraft, and burned, seated on a tar barrel at Chanonry Point at Loch Ussie. His blue stone was hurled into the waters of the loch and has not been found.

Yet, the Brahan Seer was only one of the prognosticators of the relatively modern Celtic world. Throughout the Highlands and islands of Scotland, seers such as Christian MacCaskill, Lachlann MacCullough, Donald MacKinnon, and even the famous Petty Seer (Rev. John Morrison, minister of Petty near Inverness) flourished in local communities. In Ireland, too, such "wise women" as Biddy Early of Clare and Moll Anthony of Kildare, together with "fairy doctors" such as Maurice Griffin of Kerry, were regularly consulted in order to ascertain the future. Biddy Early, perhaps the most famous of them all, was supposed—like the Brahan Seer—to possess a blue bottle in which she could behold future events and relay them to her astonished clients. This was thrown by a priest into the waters of Kilbarron Lake in County Clare and remains lost. In County Limerick, an evil sixteenth-century abbess at Shanagolden Nunnery—"a woman of the Fitzgeralds," the local aristocracy— acted as a "cup tosser," using tea leaves in order to interpret the future. It is said that no local noble would make war on another without consulting her first—harkening to ancient Celtic days. Such people were denounced as witches and wizards by the regular clergy mainly because of their individual and often irreligious stance. The practice of fortune telling, then, had a long and deeply rooted tradition within the Celtic world, even in relatively modern times. In some parts, too, it had also an anti-clerical slant to it that made established orthodoxies extremely wary of it.

When the first Puritan Protestant settlers arrived in America, they brought many of the beliefs of predestination and precognition with them. Early wars against the native Indians, diseases, and disasters placed the first colonies under pressure and called for greater knowledge of the future. From time to time, local prophets (usually claiming God's authority) appeared amongst the New England settlements warning of approaching doom or terrible catastrophes—many of which did not actually occur. Simon (or Samuel) Winthrop, for example, turned up in the general vicinity of Boston in Massachusetts around the late 1650s claiming visions of colonists being massacred by Indians, great storms, and earthquakes, which generally terrified the largely mercantile populace of the town. Winthrop appears to have been something of an eccentric character, almost a hermit, who lived in the woods, but he cited that God had chosen him specially to deliver these prognostications. The fact that he was considered to be "simple" and was also something of a drunk did not diminish the authority of his message or the terror which his alleged visions engendered. In the end, none of his dire warnings came to pass.

Of course, in a colonial America whose social parameters were governed by religious orthodoxy, questions could be raised as to whether these visions of the future came directly from God or whether they came from some other source. This was of particular importance if that which was prophesied failed to come true. A kind of rule of thumb relating to visions gradually emerged: those which were proclaimed by God's elect (i.e. the Puritan divines) were considered to be true and have divine authority while all others were considered to come from the Devil and were issued simply to mislead God's people. The Enemy of Mankind, it was thought, was continually seeking ways to undermine blessed authority in this new land and would use all of his wiles to do so. Winthrop, for example, might well have been a Catholic or an Anglican (Episcopalian) and so his word was not to be trusted. He was threatened with a charge of witchcraft and of trying to subvert divine rule and was driven out of Boston. Those who received their powers from the Evil One—in other words, their messages contradicted the religious orthodoxy— were counted as witches and were often accused of practising dark magic.

In the highly charged religious atmosphere of Puritan New England, witchcraft was thought to be everywhere. It lurked amongst the "heathen" savages who dwelt in the deep forests and swamps that surrounded the settlements, and the Devil, always very close to the isolated communities, continually sought to lead God's saints astray in this new and savage country. In such a credulous age, dark powers thrived all across the colonies. Winthrop, for instance, was sometimes linked with the notorious Mrs. Ann Hibbens, who was executed in Boston as a witch in the early pre-Salem witch hysteria of 1656. In actual fact, Mrs. Hibbens, the wife of a leading Boston merchant, may have been no more than a sharp-tongued virago and was probably a little too full of her own importance, but any attempt to divert from the communal orthodoxy was treated as the work of the Devil. Evil and individualized behavior or ideologies were therefore sometimes treated as witchcraft. This would certainly have included attempts at prognostication by various "wise" women and men.

Books concerning the topic of witchcraft flourished. Most notable was Cotton Mather's *On Witchcraft* and *Wonders of the Invisible World*, unfettered accounts of the workings of the Devil in New England; they were countered by the Baptist Robert Calef's scathing *More Wonders of the Invisible World*. Calef took a more pragmatic approach but so deeply was the notion of witchcraft entrenched within the New England mind that when he came to publish *More Wonders of the Invisible World*, a closely argued attack on Mather around 1700, no printer could be found anywhere in Boston willing to accept it. Calef's work was publicly burned in the yard of Harvard College on the orders of the new college president, Increase Mather, the father of Cotton Mather and the author of such works as *Cases of Conscience Concerning Evil Spirits*. A great crowd turned up to cheer as the denunciation of witchcraft was consigned to the flames. Such was the hold of Puritanism and the witchcraft ideal upon the minds of many New Englanders.

Arguably, few other religious groupings were abhorred and persecuted so much by the Puritan fathers of New England than the Quakers. Their absence of regular clergy and their interest in a liberal social justice made them anathema to the formal and rigid Puritan authority that governed the colonies. Nor were they afraid to speak out against measures adopted by the Puritan elders which they considered to be hypocritical or prejudicial to the communal well-being. The Quaker Deborah Wilson walked naked through the streets of Salem, Massachusetts, in the 1660s "as a sign of the spiritual nakedness of town and country" and for this was uncharitably whipped with thirty stripes. Following in her footsteps, another Quaker, Lydia Wardwell, alarmed the congregation of a Puritan meeting house at Newbury, Massachusetts, by appearing naked at their door on the Sabbath morn, at a time of public worship, and berating the preacher inside. For this, Wardwell—"a young, chaste girl of tender years"—was tied to a post outside the local tavern in Ipswich, where the court sat, to undergo a similar whipping. The famous Quaker Mary Dyer, originally from Boston but living for a greater part of her life in Rhode Island, publicly denounced the elders of Boston in the town square in 1659 and was arrested. Driven out of the town, she returned again and again with the same message, prophesying that the colony would suffer wrack and ruin if it did not turn from the unlawful (before God and man) edicts of its elders. In the end she was arrested in May 1660 and was publicly hanged as a warning to all Quakers who would prophesy against the ruling Puritan orthodoxy.

Yet, no prophet fits in with the old Celtic ideal of a seer so well as the Quaker Margaret Brewster. However, we have to be extremely careful as any account we have was written after her death and by Puritans who were not sympathetic to Margaret or to her faith. In the accounts, she is frequently denounced as a witch although there is little proof that she practised, either intentionally or unintentionally, any form of black art. Such literature is in all probability no more than Puritan propaganda directed against the Quakers generally.

Little is known of Margaret Brewster's life prior to 1677 although it is possible that she lived in the Boston, Massachusetts, area. It is also quite probable that she came from a relatively wealthy family background and may have been originally a Puritan herself. A number of Puritans for various reasons (usually because they disagreed with the rigid orthodoxy of the Puritan church) converted to the Quaker faith and this gave further concern to the Puritan elders of Massachusetts. Whatever her origins, Margaret Brewster was widely regarded as having a gift through which she could determine future events. This ability, she said, was a present from God himself and gave her a special authority in early Massachusetts. She was said to have been visited by a number of local people from the Boston area who came to consult her on personal matters and to find lost property. This Margaret did with some flair. No accounts are given as to how she accomplished this, but her visions were certainly counted as dramatic and struck awe into the hearts of her clientele. It was said that she could talk directly with God. Most of her prophesies seem to have concerned themselves with purely local issues, but she is also credited with forecasting the American Revolution and the War of 1812. The Puritans tolerated her remarkable gifts without much comment (maybe they were afraid that she *could* speak directly to God!) but that was soon to change.

On a quiet Sabbath morning in July 1677, accompanied by a number of the foremost members of her faith in the area, Margaret Brewster presented herself at the door of the Old South Meeting House in Boston. A sermon was in progress but she appeared to pay scant heed to that. Throwing wide the door, she walked slowly up the aisle accompanied by two followers. She was barefoot—having taken off her boots, stockings, and riding habit in the doorway—and, according to some accounts, carried a great staff in her hand like some Old Testament prophet. She was also bareheaded (a mark of great sacrilege in a Puritan church) and her loose hair hung about her shoulders. Her face was smeared with soot while her head seemed to be sprinkled with ashes. Many people knew who she was and were rather afraid of her, so many drew back as she passed. Ignoring the old minister, she made her way to the pulpit and, climbing into it, proceeded to address the congregation. A general account of what she said is given by Judge Sewall, a member of the congregation who kept a diary concerning life in early Massachusetts. The appearance of the "prophetess Margaret Brewster," says the diarist, "occasioned the greatest and most amazing uproar that I ever saw."

The lady Quaker threw her head back and appeared to go into some sort of trance with her eyes rolling backwards in her head—in the fashion described by Martin Martin regarding the seers of the Scottish Western Isles—before delivering her stark prognostication. Great doom would fall upon the colony, she prophesied, and it would come very swiftly. It was the judgement of God and would show his great displeasure with the sin, which was rampant there. She rattled her staff and struck it against the side of the pulpit and, says Sewell, "caused much terror and alarm." There was a general chattering of men while the women either screamed or dropped in a dead faint with the entire congregation surging to and fro, occasioning the greatest disturbance that was ever heard inside those sacred walls. Louder and louder, she prophesied doom and famine, plagues and pestilence. At last, constables had to be brought in to take her and her companions away to the local prison, where they were incarcerated.

Margaret Brewster was arraigned before the Boston court on several charges, including those of blasphemy and defamation (she had apparently named a prominent Puritan elder, accusing him of the most heinous perversities). The constable who had arrested her was brought forward but, to the utter amazement of the court, said that he was unable to identify the woman in the dock. Several other witnesses professed their own minds to be similarly clouded. One old woman exclaimed that the defendant appeared before her "in the shape of the Devil," much to the alarm of everyone present. A murmur went around the court suggesting witchcraft and this was enough to secure a conviction against the seeress. She was sentenced by the court to be whipped up and down the streets of Boston "at the cart's tail" and to be driven out of the locality. This was carried out within days.

The event brought relations between Quakers and Puritans to a head within Massachusetts. Many Puritans within the Boston area turned against their Quaker neighbors, attacking them and destroying their property. The Quakers responded in kind and for several months there was confrontation between the two churches. However, the fury soon spent itself and the Quakers returned to their places of worship, according to Samuel Drake, "in such formidable numbers that the multitude of offenders became their safeguard."

Little is known of Margaret Brewster after her public chastisement but it is thought that she remained somewhere in or near the Boston area practicing as a kind of prophetess and wise woman. It is thought that she was consulted by many of the local people anxious to know what the future held, including several prominent Boston merchants who wished to ascertain the success of ventures upon which they were embarking.

The tradition of foretelling the future did not end with the punishment of the Quaker seeress. Edward "John" Dimond, the celebrated "Magician of Marblehead," was widely known and widely respected throughout Massachusetts during the early days of the eighteenth century. Dimond was a tall, moody man who lived in a large colonial home at Little Harbor, Marblehead, then a relatively prosperous fishing town. The date of his birth is something of a mystery although it is thought to have been around the time of the Salem witch trials of 1692. From his early life, however, he is known to have suffered from visions and trances, some of which would last for days and were certainly in the style of the old Celtic seers. His eyes would roll back in his head, and he would neither speak nor eat but would emerge from the episode fully refreshed and with a curious knowledge of future events and of occurrences well beyond his own community.

With some money, which he had inherited from his father, John purchased the town's Old Burying Hill, although why he should have wished to acquire this particular location is not clear. Much of the place was overgrown and it was surrounded by dense woodland and trackless foliage. John chose to spend much of his time up on the hill and it was here that he experienced many of his visions. It was also whispered amongst the town's churchmen that he was practising black magic in the thicket there. It was even suggested that he was digging up bodies for the purposes of necromancy. Certain people even claimed to have heard him speaking directly to the Devil amongst the leafy tracks which ran down from the Burying Hill and into the woods.

A generation earlier, John Dimond would almost certainly have been burned as a sorcerer, but the horrors of the witch craze which had gripped Massachusetts in the late seventeenth century had made New Englanders a great deal more cautious and circumspect. So the Marblehead magician and his eccentric ways were tolerated in the fishing community. Besides, the magician's alleged supernatural powers were becoming indispensable within the Marblehead area. Local residents, including local law officers from the townships round about, consulted him regarding the retrieval of lost or stolen possessions or to find the perpetrators of petty crimes. While he did not have a 100 percent success rate, Dimond's abilities of recovery were extremely impressive. Some of these "powers," however, may have been little more than elementary deduction in the style of Sherlock Holmes or through paying close attention to rumor and gossip.

Nevertheless, that was not the extent of his abilities. For instance, he appeared to be able to predict the uncertain weather around Marblehead with uncanny accuracy. Before a storm hit the New England coast, John Dimond would climb to the summit of the Old Burying Hill where his presence would alert the locals to the approaching inclement weather. It was also said that he conversed with the dead as they lay below their tombstones. He must have seemed like some graveyard specter himself, talking and sometimes shouting to the heavens above. It was said that from this lofty place, he could talk to the masters of fishing vessels on the ocean. In the midst of the storm, he could give them directions and warnings, telling them to steer clear of rocks or to avoid shoals and sandbars.

If Dimond took a disliking to anyone, he could place a curse upon them so that their boat would never reach port again. His celebrated disagreement with Capt. Micah Taylor of the *Kestrel* was clear proof of that. Taylor openly ridiculed Dimond and called on him "to do his worst, for he had no fear of him." The *Kestrel* sailed out of Marblehead harbor on a clear, calm morning with no hint of ill weather. At the same time, John Dimond climbed to the summit of the Old Burying Hill and began a weird chant. Almost immediately, the skies began to darken and a strong wind blew in from the west. A gale tore in from nowhere and lashed the New England coast with a terrible ferocity. The *Kestrel* never returned to Marblehead harbor. Every fishing boat which John Dimond cursed was either lost at sea or suffered some handicap which prevented it from returning safely with a catch.

John Dimond also appeared to have a preternatural knowledge of things taking place in other settlements. This was an era when men did not travel very far and although the townships were relatively close to each other, there was only a sporadic interaction between them. While in his trances, John Dimond was said to travel well beyond Marblehead to places like Concord, where he was said to have witnessed a house fire and was able to name those who stood about it, and Boston, where he witnessed a serious accident and was again able to mention names. When the news of these events reached Marblehead, the people already knew about them through the offices of John Dimond. Whether or not he had occult powers is uncertain, but he certainly enjoyed a great and widespread reputation because of them.

John Dimond's granddaughter Molly was born at 42 Orne Street,

Marblehead, in 1738. The house in which she was born—an old colonial frame house—stood directly opposite the old, nearly overgrown path which her grandfather had frequently taken to ascend the Old Burying Hill. Shortly after her birth, it became clear to those who knew her that she had inherited some of her grandfather's abilities. She had a phenomenal memory, and upon her return home from school she could repeat word for word conversations which she had had or which she had overheard in class during the course of the day. In addition, when friends came to call she would accurately reveal, for the benefit of all present, some of the thoughts they were harboring—much to their embarrassment. She also dabbled in predictions in the front room of her Marblehead house. As a very young girl, she is credited with predicting the Revolutionary War, the defeat of John Burgoyne's British troops at Saratoga Springs, and the final victory of the American forces at Yorktown. By doing so, she earned the enmity of many influential Marblehead traders and merchants, many of whom were pro-British Tories.

By all accounts Molly was a remarkably plain girl with a long, sad face, slightly hooked nose, and extremely thin lips, together with a large head, which seemed out of proportion to the rest of her body. She may also have had a slightly "wry," or crooked, neck, which gave her head a lopsided appearance. She must have presented a strange and unsettling figure and consequently, few young men came forward as suitors. Doubtless many were also put off by her rather queer reputation throughout the community. Nevertheless, at the age of twenty-two, some time around 1769, Molly married Robert Pitcher of Marblehead and, soon after the marriage, the couple moved to nearby Lynn.

Throughout the early 1770s, Molly Pitcher's fame as a clairvoyant and seer spread throughout Massachusetts and beyond, and many made their way to the Pitcher house, some traveling great distances. The house in which Robert and Molly lived nestled at the foot of Lynn's famous "high rock," which gave it an almost mystical and supernatural aspect in its own right. Robert acted as agent for his wife and frequently boasted to friends of the uncanny accuracy of her prophesies—perhaps in an attempt to drum up business. Probably, Molly Pitcher's prophecies were no more accurate than many of the other mystics and prophets of the day. However, the setting of the consultation and Molly's rather strange physical appearance may have added some awe and eeriness to the occasion. She also seems to have been an extremely serious woman who had a gift for plain speaking, a trait much valued amongst the stolid New England families. If, for instance, a seaman consulted her as to whether or not he would return from a voyage, Molly Pitcher would tell him without any frills, qualifications, or apologies. It was also said that she did not suffer fools gladly and those who went to her for entertainment were frequently told some unpleasant but accurate truths about themselves so that they went away severely chastened. Most of Molly's clientele, however, were merchants from around the Marblehead and Lynn areas who came to visit her concerning trading ventures in which they were engaged. In the days when severe storms often swept the New England coast and pirates lurked amongst the offshore shoals and islands ready to pounce on trading ships, a knowledge of events was vital to the success of any enterprise.

Like her grandfather, Molly acquired a reputation for casting curses—especially against sea captains and the crewmembers of the various boats that sailed from Marblehead harbor—many of which were particularly virulent. It was said that she could call down deadly fogs in which ships would be lost for long periods (a warning) or wrecked and their crews drowned (the final curse).

By 1813, the year of her death at the age of seventy-five, Molly's reputation as a clairvoyant and wise woman (in the strict Celtic sense—although one might be tempted to say "witch") was renowned all over the East Coast of America. Her name even prompted the poet John Greenleaf Whittier to write a long poem in her honor dedicated to her amazing powers of prediction. This was published in 1832 but by the end of the nineteenth century, her name was all but forgotten, just as her grandfather's had been before her.

The power of prophecy as manifested by Margaret Brewster, John Dimond, and Molly Pitcher held echoes of the ancient Celtic Druidic tradition of prophesy. Their tradition continues to this day for many people around the Marblehead area still claim to have psychic powers. One more unusual seer recently featured in the local press, apparently a dog from Dorchester, near Boston, "saw" that his young master was in the hospital and went to see him there. Maybe the ancient traditions stretch into the animal world as well.

South Carolina

The Amazing Dr. Buzzard

In many tightly knit Celtic communities, wise women and fairy doctors played a crucial societal role. While not formally recognized by their neighbors as witches in the conventional sense, these people took on all the attributes that might be described as witchcraft. Their knowledge of herbs and potions, for example, was usually unequalled by anyone else in the community. They became healers and physicians, their skills meeting the majority of illness that beset their localities. Indeed, in Ireland, some healers were so skilled that their services were sought all over early continental Europe by European rulers. The O'Malleys of County Mayo, widely known as the "Western Owls" because of their great wisdom, were at one time believed to be the greatest doctors in the Western world.

The tradition of the local healer assumed an even greater importance in the eighteenth and nineteenth centuries when medical practitioners were widely scattered (and usually out of reach for those living in rural areas) and their attention was extremely expensive. Into the breach stepped a local healer who often acted as both doctor and midwife to become, understandably, a vital figure in any community. In many instances, such people could treat both humans and animals, adding to their worth in localities that placed economic dependence upon livestock. However, such "wise" or "cunning" people usually had other, perhaps more supernatural attributes as well. As has been noted elsewhere in this book, they frequently also had clairvoyant powers. Through these they could sometimes predict the future or could see what was happening in other parts of the countryside. Using these uncanny skills, such people could often detect those who had stolen property or find lost or mislaid items for which their clients were searching. In this respect, they became detectives and retrieval experts. Many of these "powers" were most probably nothing more than shrewd deduction, guesswork, or a knowledge of local gossip, but they were also in the main accurate and served to establish a reputation surrounded by awe and mystery for the individual concerned.

This mixture of local doctor, detective, and diviner was needed by every small society. However, such individuals were also regarded as remnants of the old, pagan ways of life and as Christianity began to spread across Celtic lands, the new religion regarded them with a mixture of suspicion and hostility. Because of their position within society many of these "wise" people did not conform to the norm that the church expected from its adherents. For instance, many of them were women who often did not behave in what the clergy considered to be a wholly feminine manner. They might drink, swear, and fight, displaying conduct that was more appropriate to men than to their own gender. Others simply ignored the dictates of the clergy; they were above such things, they may have felt. In response, the church denounced them as suspect. They were, after all, representatives of an old way that Christianity sought to replace (but which it frequently did not. These old traditions simply continued beneath a more superficial Christian surface). Not that the "cunning people" took much notice of what the church said anyway.

All over the Celtic world, there are instances of so-called wise people who impacted their local communities and even beyond. Their names appear time and time again in folklore. In Ireland, Biddy Early and Moll Anthony operated in Counties Clare and Kildare, respectively, while the celebrated "fairy doctor" Maurice Griffin carved a reputation for himself in County Kerry. All of them appear to have acquired their powers in supernatural ways. Biddy Early, for example, was supposed to have possessed a blue bottle which she received from the ghost of one of her former husbands, Tom Flannery of Carrowroe, or else she had won it in a game of cards with a fairy man near Kilbarron Lake. Moll Anthony possessed a glass that would allow her to glimpse the future. This had been given to her by the fairies on the Hill of Grange where she lived. Apparently, she was on the friendliest of terms with them. Maurice Griffin, on the other hand, had obtained his powers by drinking milk from a cow that had been touched by a fairy cloud on the hills near Tralee. There were other wise people, of course, up and down the Irish countryside whose names have been lost to history but who were relatively famous in their own time.

In addition to the fame their supernatural abilities brought them, Biddy Early, Moll Anthony, and Maurice Griffin shared the dubious distinction of having being denounced by the church. The nineteenth-century wise woman Biddy Early, in particular, was the subject of a number of sermons from the pulpit in Feakle, County Clare. Most were directed at her behavior, which, the clergy considered, left much to be desired. For instance, she formally married at least four times and, when an extremely old woman, to men much younger than herself. It is a double standard, of course, that in nineteenth-century Ireland it was not considered unusual for an old man to marry a young girl but when an old woman married a young man it was considered to be witchcraft. The clergy believed that she had put "the glamour," the magical art of illusion, on some of her husbands, making them think that she was a young girl in order to get them to marry her. She drank, continually smoked a pipe, and ran a card school in her cottage up at Kilbarron Lake to which many of the young gamblers of the countryside went. This unladylike behavior was scandalous in itself and was almost guaranteed to offend the local clergy. However, Biddy also practiced healing and was said to have made certain potions for her clients, including love potions, which were condemned by the church. Although she died after making her peace with the priest in Feakle (whose name according to tradition was Father Fawley) and after receiving the Last Rites, Biddy's confrontations with the church, particularly with young and zealous curates, were legendary.

Although not as colorful as Biddy Early, Moll Anthony enjoyed a similar reputation and mistrust of the local church. It was said that she could cure animals—and some humans too—simply by touching them. This raised questions amongst the local clergy, who were wary of her anyway, as to the true source of her powers. As she lived in a mud hovel on the slopes of the reputedly fairy-haunted Hill of Grange, it was assumed that she received her skills from these demonic beings. Like Biddy Early, Moll entertained card schools and hurled imprecations at the local priest when he remonstrated her because of her gambling. It is not known whether she became reconciled to the church before her death, but it is quite possible that she was not. In any case, nobody knows the exact date of her death, no more than they do the date of her birth.

Maurice Griffin was widely regarded as a healer and "far-seer" all across Kerry. His home is given as being the hill of Dun Lean in the north of the county, but many other areas farther south claim him as their own. Griffin is famous because as an eloquent man and a "hedge philosopher" he engaged in many debates with local priests on the nature of his own powers. He reminded one priest, for instance, that he "avoided misery by foretelling" and that he "cured many by his own powers which the Church for all its miracles, could not do." Looking directly at the priest Maurice Griffin said, "Some say that you have power, your reverence, but if you have, you are not foretelling or curing. Mine are different powers entirely." By this, he was asserting that his powers were just as beneficial to the community as those offered by the priest. When he was able to tell the holy man some personal details about himself, the clergyman undertook not to "meddle with him" again. It was said that on his deathbed, Maurice Griffin passed his powers on to his wife—such powers could only be passed across the sexes—and that they died with her.

In Cornwall, too, wise people flourished. Many of them were known as "pellars," which was taken to be a shortened form of "repeller" as they drove away disease, misfortune, or curses. The most famous of all Cornish pellars was Tamsin Blight (Tammy Blee), also known as "the Witch of Helston." She was born in Redruth in Cornwall around 1798 into a poor family about whom virtually nothing is known. For the greater part of her life, Tamsin seems to have lived on her own, a single woman plying her trade as a pellar, issuing charms and conjuring and claiming to be of "true pellar blood" stretching back into Celtic antiquity. This was a dangerous thing to do, for local magistrates and the local clergy looked unfavorably upon so-called pellars and conjurers and there may have been some church-inspired hostility towards the trade in rural areas. In 1835, when she was aged thirty-eight, it is known that Tamsin married a widower named James (or Jemmy) Thomas. Like his new bride, he was not a wealthy man and he appears to have been employed at a pumping station at a local Cornish tin mine. Marriage would have given Tamsin stability and relative respectability within the Cornish community, and Jemmy's employment as a boiler man would also have provided them with a regular income. However, Tamsin did not give up her pellar's trade and her reputation actually increased all across Cornwall. So celebrated did she become and so many people came to consult her (some from as far away as Wales) that Jemmy was able to give up his work in the mines and the couple were able to move from Illogan to Helston.

Here Tamsin enjoyed even greater success as a pellar while Jemmy, now acting as a conjurer and claiming occult powers for himself, began to acquire a rather unsavory reputation. He claimed that he possessed a dark magic by which he could contact demons and spirits in the manner of some of the western Renaissance high magicians. It is probable that he had a smattering of "book learning" with which he could impress his clients and it is also possible that he used gibberish sprinkled with Latin words as part of his esoteric formulae. There were also some allegations of homosexuality— then a crime in England—laid against his name. It was said that he slept with several young men as part of a ritual to lift a curse which he assured them they were under. Despite his own relative fame as a conjurer or wise man there is little doubt that Jemmy's activities did much to damage Tammy's reputation. By now it is doubtful they were even living together as man and wife as Jemmy pursued his own career and the seduction of gullible young men. It is also thought that he was involved in petty crime such as burglary and the selling of stolen goods. He charged extortionate fees for elaborate and meaningless rituals and he was frequently drunk. Is it any wonder that Tamsin tried to disassociate herself from him?

By that time she was also linked to another, more authentic Cornish wise man: Matthew Lutey of Curey. The Cornish folklorist William Bottrell informs us that Lutey had captured a mermaid and in return for releasing her into the sea, she rewarded him with the occult powers of a pellar. Just what the relationship was between Lutey and Tamsin Blight is unclear, but it has been suggested that some of Lutey's powers were somehow transferred to the witch of Helston, making her even more famous.

Tamsin died in 1856, still enjoying a widespread, if tarnished (due to Jemmy's continuing activities with which she was linked by association) reputation. Jemmy survived her by almost twenty years. His death is recorded in the newspaper *West Briton* as occurring on February 26, 1874. Ironically, at the time of her death, Tammy's reputation had started to revive somewhat. She had become a seller of charms and talismans which were much sought after from Cornwall to Wales to the Scilly Isles. These charms were designed to lift curses or ward away evil luck and were extremely elaborate. Many of the amulets she dispensed were little more than pieces of paper with supposedly mystical words written on them. Some of these words had been straightforwardly copied from books, maybe purchased in London, relating to magic in the High Middle Ages and were more in keeping with Aleister Crowley, another Cornish wise woman. It is highly doubtful if either Tamsin or Jemmy even knew what they meant. For an extra fee, bizarre designs could be added to increase the potency of the charm. One of these Bottrell describes as "a headless cherub" or "a brooding angel or bird" drawn on one side of the paper. This was probably Tamsin's own design, around which she had placed words written in pencil or cheap crayon which looked mystical but meant very little: nalgah, tetragrammaton, etc. On some others, she wrote quasi-Biblical names—Jehovah, Jah, Elohim, Adonay, Have pity an a poor woman—together with a multicolored hodge-podge of esoteric and indecipherable symbols. She also sold rings and pendants which were supposed to bring luck and fend off evil spirits. Many of these had been bought in the markets of London and were little more than cheap trinkets, but Tamsin made a considerable fortune for herself—most of which she is thought to have drunk away—by selling them. Such was her fame that, even after her death, her name lived on and survives as the premier Cornish witch, wise woman, or pellar.

There were others too—both male and female. Matthew Lutey, Tamsin Blight's contemporary, was considered one of the foremost conjurers in Cornwall during his lifetime. Anne Jeffreys—"the woman who talked with the fairies"—both cured and prophesied around St. Treath, Camelford, and Bodmin during the mid-seventeenth century, while Old Doll Pentreath of Penzance and John Nancarrow of Marazion were both considered to be witches and conjurers in the eighteenth century. Old Doll's claim to fame (and possibly John's also) was that at the time of her death in 1777, she was reckoned to be one of the last native speakers of Cornish in England. Both could curse in this arcane tongue and it was believed they were issuing spells against those who crossed them.

Both were probably quite harmless. The same, however, could not be said of another eighteenth-century Cornish crone Madgy (or Madge) Figgy, the witch of St. Levan, who reputedly could call down fearful storms, raising winds and savage seas to menace passing shipping. In fact, old Madge was the leader of a gang of smugglers and wreckers who operated in the St. Levan area and much of her plunder came from ships which ran aground on the treacherous rocks of the region. Her power over the elements was said to have been granted to her by the Devil and could only be used to create death and disaster, heartbreak and ruin. In addition to this, it was widely believed that Madgy had the power to curse those who crossed her or to lift curses and issue cures—for a fee of course. She was a person who might reasonably fit the stereotype of the "wicked witch." However, most wise people and conjurers were largely benevolent individuals.

The notion of the wise woman followed the early settlers to America. In the new colonies, the settlements were scattered and isolated, very much as they had been in the Celtic west. They were also extremely tightly knit with wise women and conjurers resuming the central role they had occupied in Irish and Scottish communities. In the places where the Scots-Irish settled, such people flourished. In rural areas, medicine was fairly rudimentary and many local doctors would not travel into the remote regions to tend to those who were sick and ailing. Their services also tended to be quite expensive, more than many country people could afford. So they looked to the so-called wise people. In the Appalachians, for example, "granny women" acted as midwives at mountain births and usually, with their knowledge of herbs and unguents, tended to those who were sick. Their services were sought throughout the hill country and beyond. Stolid mountain women had no wish to have men around at the time of birth and if the town doctor happened to be a man, he was largely ignored in favor of the granny. They combined a rudimentary medical knowledge, an almost supernatural understanding of herbs and potions, and superstition in a way the local people knew and trusted. They could cure fevers and chills, banish burnings, and stop blood, often by their very words or by quoting a relevant verse from the Bible. They could also tell if mountain people had been "witched" (bewitched by a neighbor) or not. They became integral and respected members of their communities, just as they had been in Celtic Europe. But there were some differences too.

The Scots and the Irish were not the only immigrants to come to America. Amongst the Germans, Italians, Poles, Swedes, and others who flooded into the developing country were Africans. Some came as slaves, others as itinerant workers and they brought their own belief systems with them. Central to many African communities was the idea of the tribal witch doctor or "juju man," an individual who could communicate with the spirits. While not exactly the same sort of belief as the Celtic wise woman, the two held many characteristics in common and it was only natural that, in some respects at least, the two figures might merge to form a kind of communal wise man/woman that demonstrated elements of both traditions.

One of the more celebrated conjurers was the legendary Dr. Buzzard, who practiced his mystic arts around Beaufort, South Carolina. "Dr. Buzzard" was not, of course, his real name but it is the one which has passed into regional folklore. Like Marie Laveau, the famous voodoo queen of New Orleans, and Darky Kelly in Dublin, it is quite possible, even probable, that there was more than one individual bearing the name (there are thought to have been at least three individuals using the name "Marie Laveau"). They were all probably of African origin, but a few stories vaguely suggest that Dr. Buzzard may have been white (or at least coffee colored). Whatever his ethnicity, and although he is often described as a "juju man" or "conjure man," he neatly fits into the criteria which characterized the Celtic wise people: he cured sickness, he foresaw the future, he lifted curses, and at times, he issued curses of his own—imprecations which always worked. And like Celtic sorcerers of old, he could change shape, usually into a cat, stoat, or owl.

Although many of his clientele certainly included the white Scots-Irish settlers of South Carolina, most of those who came to Dr. Buzzard were local Gullah people. The Gullah had their origins in slavery and were thought to come from Angola to work on the rice plantations that made South Carolina prosperous. They brought with them beliefs such as voodoo, gris-gris, and mojo and their conjure men and "root doctors" proliferated through the Carolina swamplands. On the plantations they worked cheek-by-jowl with Irish immigrants and it is reasonable to suppose that two belief systems—that of the Celtic wise woman/man and that of the African conjure man—merged into some sort of bicultural form, a curious hodge-podge of primitive spiritism and formalized Catholicism which appealed to many of those of a more Celtic origin. Amongst the Gullah, there were a number of "doctors"—Dr. Fly, Dr. Bug, Dr. Crow, Dr. Turtle—all of whom conformed to Celtic ideals and were consulted by the Scots and Irish. The most famous of these root doctors was Dr. Buzzard. His reputation as a wise man survived into the mid-twentieth century.

Possibly the most famous of all those who used the title "Dr. Buzzard" was Stephany Robinson, who died in early 1947. This Dr. Buzzard, who was reputedly the son of *another* Dr. Buzzard, lived at Oaks Plantation on St. Helena Island, just off the South Carolina coast. Writer Samuel Hopkins, who had met Robinson on a Beaufort street in 1943, described him thus: "At first sight, the elderly man might have been mistaken for a bishop in the A.M.E. [African Methodist Episcopal] Church. He was tall, slightly bowed, benign of expression and soberly dressed in quality black." Even in the austere days of World War II, Dr. Buzzard maintained an aura of "quality" about him, from his dress and the fact that he drove a brand-new Lincoln automobile. Like Tamsin Blight, Dr. Buzzard dispensed potions, charms, and talismans—some written in "dog Latin" to impress his Irish (Catholic) clients.

Dr. Buzzard is especially famous throughout the South Carolina Lowcountry for his ongoing feud with the sheriff of the area, J. E. "Ed" McTeer. McTeer was from the oldest Celtic Carolina stock and was a descendant on his mother's side of the Heywoods, who had put their name to the Declaration of Independence. His maternal grandmother had been a seer in the strict Celtic tradition and Ed McTeer himself had reputedly inherited the second sight from her. He became sheriff of the Lowcountry in 1926, taking over from his father and setting up his office in the Beaufort County Courthouse. However, he soon ran into some problems. Formerly healthy people began to take sick and die for no apparent reason, strange individuals showed up in court and fixed prosecution witnesses with a steely and disconcerting stare that caused them to forget crucial testimony, mysterious powders appeared on judges' and prosecutors' desks and in their drinks, making them forget the thread of their arguments. McTeer fastened his line of enquiry on local conjure men or wise people. They were flouting the law in return for payment, he argued, and must be stopped. Reputedly having some of their "art" himself, he resolved to find out more about them and by doing so rigorously enforce the law against them. He singled out Dr. Buzzard as the most famous conjure man in the area and set his sights on him. If someone of Dr. Buzzard's stature could be brought to book, McTeer said, the others would soon be cowed. He began to gather information to bring Dr. Buzzard to trial on a charge of illegally practicing medicine. The "doctor" evaded him at every turn. McTeer recruited local cab drivers who ferried people out to Dr. Buzzard's house for consultations but soon after he began, the men whom he paid suddenly began to forget what had transpired and the sheriff's line of enquiry dried up. Some cab drivers noted, "They useta come back ravin' about how great Dr. Buzzard is, now they ain't sayin' nothin'." Obviously, Dr. Buzzard had placed a stricture of silence on all his clients and had made an impression on some cab drivers as well. McTeer, however, refused to give up. He was convinced that the doctor was using his second sight and spells to thwart him. He decided to play Dr. Buzzard at his own game and began to immerse himself in magic, both Celtic and African. The struggle between the two men would probably have been quickly resolved if it had not been for one significant event—World War II.

With the advent of the conflict the feud took a new turn. To prevent any form of aid from reaching the Allies in Europe, German U-boats lay off the American coast covering the ports of Charleston and Savannah, torpedoing ships as they set sail. There was even talk of German spies coming ashore to make contact with local sympathizers. McTeer was placed at the head of the coastal guard to watch for German landings. With these concerns, his struggle with Dr. Buzzard assumed a relatively minor role. However, Dr. Buzzard had also entered the war.

Unsure as to whether the officially neutral United States would take up arms against the Nazis, the South Carolina Draft Board began to send busloads of young men, both black and white, to Fort Jackson for weapons training and induction into the American forces. Of course, many resisted; they did not see why either they or their country should become involved in what was essentially a European war. The Gullahs, especially, opposed the draft and they were prepared to do something about it. Soon, Fort Jackson was sending the majority of its intake—both black and white—back home as being "unfit for service." Stomach pains, diarrhea, palpitations, suspected heart murmurs—all were cited as reasons. However, once they returned to Beaufort, the rejects seemed to be in the best of health. McTeer suspected that the local root doctors, especially Dr. Buzzard, were at the bottom of it all. He wrote a long and angry letter to the Department of War denouncing the South Carolina root doctors and Dr. Buzzard in particular. With administrative skepticism, the department tossed the letter aside and took no action, but a little later they were to change their minds.

On October 26, 1943, a number of young men, all draftees under the South Carolina scheme, set out by bus from Hampton, South Carolina, for Fort Jackson. One of these was a rather outspoken Gullah man named Crispus Green who made his feelings about the draft widely known. In fact, he had assured his family that he would be spending practically no time at all in Fort Jackson but would soon be home. "I ain't goin' t' no war," he declared. "Dr. Buzzard'll see that I don't." His words were tragically prophetic. He was not alone because a number of other young men had received various potions and powders from local practitioners which would ensure that they would fail the medical at Fort Jackson. However, as the journey progressed, Crispus Green became more and more ill, and by the time the bus reached Columbia, he and another young man were dead. Half the others on the bus, a mixture of whites and Gullah, had to be taken to the local hospital. Suddenly the War Department was very interested and notified the FBI. Federal officers arrived in Beaufort and Ed McTeer was ordered to leave his coastal patrol and assist them. Here, fortune aided him for, using his new-found authority, he was able to obtain a bottle of the mysterious potion and send it for analysis. It proved to be little more than homemade moonshine whiskey to which a small amount of lead arsenate had been added, turning it into a poison. McTeer made further enquiries at local stores as to who had bought that lead arsenate and soon came up with a result: not Dr. Buzzard as everyone had suspected but a certain Dr. Bug who lived out on Laurel Bay Plantation.

Although nowhere near as famous locally as Dr. Buzzard, Dr. Bug was arrested with great pomp and formality and was brought to trial at the Beaufort County seat. He faced a grave-looking judge, solemn FBI agents, and a triumphant McTeer; nevertheless, Dr. Bug was described as a feeble-looking, disheveled, and shambling old man, very timorous and dull-eyed. The purpose of the court was to enter a plea and have a bond set, and Dr. Bug pleaded guilty. In fact, he made no attempt to excuse or defend himself, stating that nobody should go to war "if'n they didn't wanna." He further claimed that he himself drank the same potion every day "t' keep my pecker up" and offered to drink some in front of the court to prove it. He tried to take the exhibit from the judge's bench but was restrained by the sheriff. Obviously, the court was frightened that he would poison himself and so deprive the assembled of a trial. The guilty plea was accepted and the court moved to set the bond if Dr. Bug could pay one. If not, he could spend the time in the county prison.

"Bring me my box!" demanded Dr. Bug, and bailiffs brought in a good-size trunk. Opening it, the root doctor revealed that it was absolutely crammed with dollar bills—tens, twenties, even fifties. The bond was set at just over a thousand dollars, which Dr. Bug paid with ease. He was now ready to take his leave, but the law still had one last nasty surprise in store for him. As he left the courtroom, a stranger stepped forward—an officer of the Internal Revenue Service, an organization about which the good doctor knew nothing. The official demanded another three thousand dollars in back taxes, which Dr. Bug was forced to pay out of his box. Convinced that some of his rivals—maybe even Dr. Buzzard—had put a curse on him, Dr. Bug returned to Laurel Bay Plantation a broken man. He gave up his conjure practice and simply pined away. Within a year, according to legend, he was dead.

Dr. Buzzard, however, continued to practice and prosper. Despite Ed McTeer's best efforts, he also remained a free man. Certainly he was brought in for questioning by the FBI on the draft-dodging matter, but there was no real evidence to link him with it and no one could be found to testify against him, so the whole issue was quietly dropped. After the war, however, McTeer resumed their feud.

Less than a year later, a burglary suspect was brought in to Ed McTeer's office. He had been found in possession of a strange white powder and a piece of "conjure root." McTeer immediately suspected Dr. Buzzard's hand in the robbery. Knowing enough about the complicated nature of the superstitions round about, the sheriff donned "haint blue" sunglasses before he interrogated the suspect. With these sunglasses, the color of ghosts in Gullah folklore, McTeer fixed him with the evil eye, drawing upon the man's fear of spirits to see into his soul. The man was terrified, broke down, and confessed everything. The root was supposed to make him invisible while the powder was to protect him from arrest. He had received both from Dr. Buzzard. McTeer immediately sent for the "wise man." Dr. Buzzard showed up with all the authority and self-assurance of his status in the community. McTeer brought the suspect in and began to interrogate him in front of the doctor. Dr. Buzzard simply slipped on a pair of blue sunglasses and the witness began to stumble and falter in his evidence. He began to scratch as if an army of stinging ants were walking over him. After half an hour, McTeer knew that he would never get reliable evidence from his witness as the man was paralyzed with fear. He had the deputies take the man back to his cell. The doctor, assuming that the interrogation was finished, promptly excused himself and left the police station. "You do your job an' I'll do mine," he told McTeer as he departed. History does not record McTeer's reply.

Immediately behind the Beaufort County Courthouse stood the city water tower, an ancient and rusting spire amid a hinterland of roofs. Here a flock of buzzards had made their roost. Sometimes when the court was in session the birds, obviously alarmed by all the activity below, would rise up out of their nests and soar high above the town, circling the old courthouse itself. It was a sign, said locals, that Dr. Buzzard was at his work, and McTeer firmly believed that through the eyes of the circling buzzards, the doctor could see what was going on in the city. When Dr. Buzzard walked free from the police station, McTeer drew his pistol and walked over to the courthouse. The buzzards were wheeling above the building and, pausing only to take aim, McTeer fired. One of the birds dropped like a stone. However, recent winds had blown the roof off the old water tank and the dead buzzard fell into Beaufort's water supply. Before officials could retrieve the body, it had begun to pollute the water. Another victory for Dr. Buzzard! And yet, Ed McTeer's luck was soon to change.

Shortly after, Dr. Buzzard's eldest son—who was forever crashing the expensive cars his father bought him—was driving home across one of Beaufort County's tidal marshes during a blinding rainstorm. Not noted as a careful driver, he missed a turn, drove off a narrow causeway, and was drowned in one of the saltwater creeks which ran through the county. Believing that Ed McTeer had hexed his son, Dr. Buzzard finally agreed to call a truce. He arrived on the sheriff's front porch one night bearing two live chickens as a peace offering. A compromise was hammered out between the two men: Dr. Buzzard would stop prescribing his "witchy" potions and powders but he would not stop casting his spells and curses. However, McTeer was free to lift the spell or curse if he could. By this Dr. Buzzard acknowledged that the sheriff was just as potent a conjure man as himself. McTeer, believing in his own Celtic supernatural prowess, agreed. And so the deal was struck.

But it did not last. Soon Dr. Buzzard was again practicing medicine without a licence and once more he found himself in court, courtesy of Ed McTeer. By now he was old and he was convinced his powers were starting to fail. He debated whether he should bring in another conjure man to hex the judge or hire himself a slick white lawyer. In the end, he opted for the latter and hired himself a former state senator who had retained his legal practice. It did him no good. He had lost his touch and, for the first time, the case went against him. The charges against him were, as his lawyer argued, "trumped up," but the state had not forgotten Dr. Buzzard's involvement in the draft avoidance during the war and was determined to make an example of him. The court found the doctor guilty and fined him three hundred dollars, a trifling sum which he paid on the spot from a roll of bills which he pulled out of a back pocket. But the conviction had humiliated him and he more or less withdrew from the world. He lived out on Oaks Plantation and saw very few people. Even his former clients drifted away. By the end of his life, he was bedridden. A proper medical doctor was called and diagnosed cancer of the stomach. Several months afterwards, the famous Dr. Buzzard was dead.

His supernatural nemesis, Ed McTeer, lived on. He remained in law enforcement for another twenty years and, during that time, is known to have practised as a wise man or white conjure doctor. He was convinced that his ancient Celtic roots had given him occult powers, much in the vein of Dr. Buzzard himself. In the 1960s, he was challenged at the polls for the position of Lowcountry sheriff by a South Carolina Highway Patrol sergeant. The campaign was a long and bitter one. Rumor and innuendo appeared on both sides, the most prominent being that McTeer was some kind of "witchy" person who consorted with conjure men and was therefore unfit to hold office. Both men agreed to appear on television, reading a prepared half-hour long statement. McTeer cited his forty years in the job and his respect in the community. The following night, as his challenger began to speak, all television sets over the Carolina Lowcountry began to flutter and buzz so badly that nothing could be heard or seen—evidence, in many minds, that McTeer had put a hex on his opponent. To this day, no one can explain the peculiar interference. However, the situation worked against Ed McTeer, and at the polls he found himself removed from office. Some people had started to fear him and his "witchy powers." The vote unseated him by the narrowest of margins, but the former sheriff took it as a sign and left public life. He began to write his memoirs, *Fifty Years as a Low Country Witch Doctor,* and though hunted by the media, he refused to discuss any aspect of his alleged supernatural powers. In his latter days, he became something of a recluse. His opponent and new Lowcountry sheriff had a stormy tenure in office and eventually descended into drunkenness and insanity, proof positive in the minds of the people of the area that the old spells and curses still work.

Ed McTeer died in 1976, leaving behind a daughter to handle his affairs and the sale of his books, which are still widely read. His youngest son dabbles in the wise craft, no doubt drawing upon ancient Celtic and African traditions, just as his father did before him. Dr. Buzzard's son also took on the mantle of conjure man. Widely respected, he was known by the nickname "Buzzy" until his death in 1997. No one is sure who has taken over his practice and the mantle of Dr. Buzzard.

Nobody knows exactly where Dr. Buzzard is buried. There is an alleged gravesite on the south side of a Beaufort cemetery, but it is not known if this is truly his final resting place. The reason for such secrecy is that the grave dirt—goofer dust—from the burial site of such a great conjure man has mystical properties and may lead to its desecration. And of course, if there is more than one person using the name "Dr. Buzzard" then there are bound to be a number of gravesites. Maybe the doctor is having the final laugh.

The Roan Mountain Shapeshifters

Writing in his book *The History and Topography of Ireland*, the Welsh scholar Geraldus Cambrensis (Gerald of Wales) in 1185 confidently asserted that certain old Irish women had the ability to change themselves into the guise of hares. Gerald had come to Ireland in the retinue of Prince (later king) John, then Lord of Ireland, and he took a scholar's interest in everything he saw and heard. The problem was that he believed it all. The notion of shapeshifters—people who could exchange their human guise for that of an animal—was an old Celtic belief which had been prevalent in Ireland long before Gerald arrived. In other Celtic countries, too, there were stories of men who could adopt the guise of wolves or fierce boars and of women who could take on the shape of stoats, cats, or birds. All such changes were firmly associated with magic and wonder-working.

The origins of such a belief may lie with the early Celts, who were primarily a hunting people. Their existence depended on the great herds of creatures—elk, wild pig, deer, etc.—which roamed the lands where they dwelt. They also competed with predators such as the wolf and bear for meat. In order to ensure good hunting or that their hunters would be successful against the competitive carnivores, local shamans and early Druids went through elaborate rituals to invoke the aid of the gods, many of whom had animal aspects. Often dressed in the skins of the animal spirits whom they wished to contact, the shaman or early Druid capered and danced within his sacred enclosure in an attempt to draw down magical forces and bend them to his will. Only in this way could the hunting be successful and predators be driven off. This must have been a terrifying sight: the man (or woman)

169

dressed in the skin of a beast, gyrating and making eerie noises and motions as he cried to the spirits. The proceedings surely seemed almost unnatural.

That was the view the Christian church took when in the late fourth and early fifth centuries it came to consider some of these ancient rituals to be pagan. The church held that they must not be tolerated. The dancing man in animal skins with his stag's antlers and hairy mane became the Devil with black and bumpy skin, horns, and a long beast-like tail. The staff, which had been the symbol of the shaman's power, became the pitchfork which the Infernal One used to roast captured souls in the fires of hell. Those who donned the animal skins and who called down the spirits were now, according to the church, agents of dark and evil forces and were counted as sorcerers and witches who worked dark spells against their neighbors.

With the shaman now considered to be an incarnation of the Devil, it was only a small step to claim that the sorcerer had the power to change himself into the very animal whose skin he wore. Odd people, lonely people, people who were strange in their ways were all suspect. All of them, believed the Christian holy men, went about in the guise of animals to spy upon those around them and work mischief against them. So common did the belief become in the Christianized Western Celtic lands that it was widely considered to be an essential part of the rural magician's stock of powers. Almost every rural witch or warlock could transform into some sort of (usually unobtrusive) animal for the purposes of effecting his or her evil.

In Ireland and in parts of Scotland, for instance, it was said that old and antisocial women went about in the guise of stoats or cats. This feat of magic was performed usually in the morning so that the dark creature could suck the milk from the udders of grazing cattle before the farmer or dairymaid got to them. In the guise of stoats, especially, they invaded the hen-roost and carried away eggs. This, of course, explained why cows were dry and why hens did not lay. It was all due to the work of local sorcerers, perhaps some person with a grudge against the farmer concerned. But there was worse. In the guise of cats, witches could sometimes steal the breath of infants sleeping in their cribs by leaping on the end of the cot and smothering the child. There is no doubt that this sometimes happened, but the tale may also have served as an explanation for what we would term today as Sudden Infant Death Syndrome. This was as inexplicable then as it is today, but in these former times such deaths were attributed to the work of supernatural agents.

In order to effect this transformation, the witch usually had to have some kind of magical artifact or potion which could turn her into the guise of the desired animal. Certain unguents could be prepared or talismans used to transform the old woman into a ghastly form in which she could roam about the countryside committing mischief and evil as she saw fit. The most common method of transformation was a portion of the skin of the animal which the witch could place inside a shawl or cloak and so wear it close to her own skin. This, combined with certain incantations, would allow the witch to take on both the attributes and form of the animal in question. The belief was widespread and was not simply confined to Celtic countries. In 1589, the notorious warlock Peter Stubb (or Stubbe or Stumpf), who was executed near Cologne for his evil ways, was reputed to transform himself into a wolf by the aid of a wolf-skin belt or girdle which he had received from the Devil himself. In this guise, he attacked several people.

Stories of transforming rituals were also widespread. In the Isles of Carnmoon, near Bushmills in North Antrim, Ireland, an old legend tells of a traveling tailor who witnessed a local woman, the widow of a wealthy farmer in the area, change into a hare by taking an enchanted, ritualistic bath in the early morning. The tailor, who was staying at the house, decided to try the same ritual and he climbed into the bath when the woman had gone abroad in her hare form. He, too, was transformed and traveled across country to a gathering of hare-witches in an abandoned cemetery. There, all the sorcerers of the countryside had gathered in the form of either hares or cats to plot mischief against the Christian people of the land. Unfortunately the tailor was recognized as being not one of them and had to dash back to the magic bath in order to transform himself back to his human form. He had a narrow escape for the local witch was close behind and he was only just able to empty the water out of the bath in order to prevent her from changing back. Nevertheless, the tailor was left with a ruff of fur around his neck where the bath water had not touched him.

The notion of women who could transform themselves into

animals or birds crossed the Atlantic from Celtic lands with the first immigrants to America. Amongst the earliest stories of the pioneer immigrants, tales of ancient crones who could turn themselves into creatures can be found. For example, the Massachusetts writer Samuel Adams Drake in 1883 records the legend of Margaret Wesson, known as "Old Meg," who dwelt near Cape Ann prior to the Revolutionary War. Following the successful siege of Louisburg by colonial troops in 1745, he states, two Gloucester soldiers of the Massachusetts line became rather alarmed by the movements of a large crow which kept hovering over them in a mysterious manner as they made their way home. They threw stones and fired their muskets at it but to no avail. Instead the bird cawed at them in a most threatening manner and made dives at their heads. At last it occurred to one of them that it might be Old Meg, who had long been suspected in Gloucester of being a witch. He communicated his suspicion to his comrade, who told him that neither missile nor bullet could harm the supernatural creature; only something made of silver could drive it away. The only silver which the soldiers had about their person were the silver buttons on their uniforms. These they cut off and, leading them into their muskets, discharged them at the crow. The experiment succeeded for with his first shot, one of them hit the bird on the leg, breaking it. With the second shot, they killed the crow stone dead. Upon returning to Gloucester, they found that Old Meg had endured a strange and ultimately fatal accident. While walking to a nearby fort, she had mysteriously fallen and broken her leg at roughly the same time the crow had been hit with the silver button under the walls at Louisburg. The break had caused a fever from which the old woman had eventually died in some agony. A silver button cut from a uniform was inexplicably found amongst her bed linen shortly after her death. The legend of Meg Wesson lingered on and became part of the folklore of Gloucester and was recorded as history as late as 1832 by the Reverend Charles W. Upham.

Old Meg was, of course, not the only colonial witch able to change into animal form. There are legends concerning many others all across America. Dr. Buzzard from South Carolina, in addition to being a great conjure man, had alleged powers of transformation. He was said to be able to transform himself into a cat or a bird, particularly his namesake buzzard. This was one reason why McTeer, in the previous chapter, tried to shoot the buzzards around the city water tower in Beaufort. In the following tale transcribed by the great South Carolina folklorist Genevieve Wilcox Chandler, whose collected stories of old regional tales—both black and white—were compiled by the WPA Federal Writers' Project between 1936 and 1938, Dr. Buzzard's ability is featured.

Dr. Buzzard lived out on the Oaks Plantation and everyone knew that he was the greatest conjure man in the whole of South Carolina. The High Sheriff in Beaufort was always trying to arrest him on some trumped up charge and it's said that the Sheriff was no mean conjure man himself and that he had "witchy ways" about him which his folks had brought from the Old Country. But he could never catch Dr. Buzzard. . . .

Anyhow the sheriff was getting mighty tired of the Doctor's tricks and he challenged him to prove his magic in front of the people of Beaufort. He arranged for a big gathering in the town hall where everybody could see what a sham he was. He challenged the Doctor to attend, saying that if he didn't he would be exposed as a fraud and a liar. He had a special challenge for Dr. Buzzard, he said.

Dr. Buzzard thought long and hard about this but in the end, he turned up. A big crowd had also turned out to see him for the feud between himself and the Low Country Sheriff was well known. The sheriff brought out a big old trunk about the height of a grown man and a set of chains.

"Now Dr. Buzzard," said the sheriff. "If you get into this box an' let my deputies chain you in. An' if you can escape from this trunk in under four minutes, then I'll say that you have real magic powers an' I'll leave you alone in future." The sheriff had seen a trick like this done in a traveling fair and he believed that it couldn't be done in under six or seven minutes. "But if you're one minute over the four, then you'll have to give up all your practices and tell everybody that you're a fraud. Do you agree?" Dr. Buzzard thought for a moment but then he stiffly nodded his head.

"Put me in the trunk," he demanded. "An' I'll sure give you a surprise." So the sheriff's deputies put him in the old trunk and closed the lid, fastening it with chains and padlocks so's not even a fly could get out. The sheriff brought out an old fob-watch that's belonged to his grandfather and checked it.

"Are you ready Dr. Buzzard?" he called. "You have four minutes tops to get yourself outa there."

"I'm ready," said a voice from inside the trunk but somehow it didn't sound exactly like Dr. Buzzard. It was a deep, echoey voice, like Dr. Buzzard was speaking from somewhere far away or from deep inside a well or something like that. It frightened everybody a little bit to hear it.

"Then off you go," said the sheriff. "I'm timin' you Dr. Buzzard." For a long minute there was only silence from the big old trunk. Nor was there any movement.

"You still there Dr. Buzzard?" called the sheriff.

"I'm still here," came the funny voice again. But there was no other sound or movement from the trunk. The minutes crawled by.

"You still there Dr. Buzzard?" called the sheriff again. This time there was no answer. The sheriff was worried now for the trunk was closed so tightly that he thought Dr. Buzzard mighta suffocated and he'd find himself facing a murder charge. But still he waited as the minutes passed.

Finally, as the fourth minute went by, he could stand it no longer. There'd been no sound and no movement from the trunk and he was sure that Dr. Buzzard was dead. Bringing the deputies back in again, he ordered them to open the trunk, which they did with a rattle of chains and locks. Everybody in the audience held their breath. Fearfully the sheriff lifted the lid of the box and threw it wide. He expected to see Dr. Buzzard's still body lying in the bottom of the trunk but what he saw was—nothing. The box seemed empty—at least at first. Then, suddenly something jumped out and past the sheriff's ear with a loud hiss and scream. A great black cat landed on the floor and stood there spitting. It looked directly at the sheriff with sulphurous yellow eyes before turning and vanishing into the crowd. Everybody was stunned. A few minutes later, Dr. Buzzard was seen walking down the main street in Beaufort and bidding the ladies "good day" as if nothing at all had happened. There wasn't a mark of the bizarre experience about him and he never mentioned it again. But it was a talking point in Beaufort for a long time afterwards—the day Dr. Buzzard got the better of the Low Country sheriff. He was a great magician' all right.

There seems little doubt that Dr. Buzzard was considered to be a shapeshifter in the style of the rural Celtic magicians and cunning men and that like them, he was held in both awe and esteem throughout the Lowcountry community. In other parts of the South, however, a different sort of shapeshifter can be found and it too contains echoes of earlier Celtic legend. The following story, which in many ways parallels the County Antrim legend above, comes from the Roan Mountain area of East Tennessee. According to the tale, a chilling wind was blowing across the mountains from the North Carolina border as John Riley tried to find a trail that would take him home. It was late October, around Halloween, and the year was 1801. Riley was anxious to leave East Tennessee as quickly as he could. He was badly in debt and while it was not a hanging offence (as armed robbery and horse thievery were), the law was still harsh against debtors who could not pay their bills. Riley had gotten into debt in Jonesborough, a settlement not noted for its tolerance against ne'er-do-wells. Records state that not even the pettiest crime went unpunished in that place. A woman found guilty of simple larceny, for example, was sentenced to publicly receive ten lashes in the hot August sun in 1788. A gossip had one of her ears cut off in 1790 while another minor criminal had both his ears nailed to a post by the town blacksmith. Sometimes more serious criminals were hanged in a spot known as Hangman's Hollow, just outside the town, and while debt was not considered to be a major crime, Riley was taking no chances. He had struck out for his home in North Carolina. To get there, he would have to face the wintry Roan Mountain country, but his fear of being arrested and charged with debt in Jonesborough outweighed the cold of the mountains.

Up on the high trails, well away from the town, he wondered if he had done the right thing. The cold of the mountains was numbing and Riley had not eaten for quite some time. Finding a warm barn on one of the lower trails, he had stuffed straw into his boots as insulation and rubbed his hands against the warm body of a calf to keep his fingers from getting frostbite. He knew of a trail which might get him home: it would take him around the lower end of Roan Mountain and to a gap into Carolina by a large outcropping known as Sunset Rock. This had been a trail used by the patriot backwoodsmen militias during the American Revolution on their way to fight the British at the Battle of Kings Mountain. The drawback was that the gap channeled a shaft of cold wind and slowed him as he struggled against it. An edge of snow was coming down with the wind and it formed against his coat and beard as he tried to make his way to Sunset Rock.

This was a sorry estate that he had come to. Originally from a poor but honest family who owned a small farm in North Carolina,

John Riley had made his way to East Tennessee to find fame and fortune and make his name. But no fortune had materialized, and he was almost penniless and up to his ears in debt. He had hoped that a prospective marriage might solve his problems and had borrowed heavily against that dream. The girl, however, had found someone else and left him in a worse predicament than when he had first met her. With creditors closing in, there was nothing to do but flee from Jonesborough and try to make it home.

From time to time he would walk backwards to keep the biting wind from his face, but he knew that this was only a temporary measure. As soon as night fell, the temperature in the mountains would drop below freezing and that would mean his end. He would never make the gap before darkness came across the mountains. He had condemned himself to death in the snowy waste.

Suddenly, he smelled something on the wind. It was the smell of wood smoke. Somewhere nearby a fire was burning. That meant safety and warmth—and maybe food as well. He hurried along the trail, following his nose as the smell of burning wood grew stronger. Then, in the fading sunlight, he saw something in which he was almost afraid to believe. A small cabin protected from the freezing wind by a large overhang sent plumes of sweet-smelling smoke high into the cold air. And, as the day darkened, he saw a light burning in the window like a welcoming beacon, guiding the traveler to its door. As he struggled towards it, the wind coming down through the gap farther up the trail seemed to increase. Riley had been this way several times on his way to Jonesborough, but he could not recall a wind this violent or one with so keen an edge. Almost dropping with cold, he made the door of the tiny cabin at last, falling against it in his weakness. It opened inwards and he stumbled forward and into the warmth. Almost immediately, the wind outside stopped and a great calm descended upon Roan Mountain.

The old woman who had opened the door helped him to a chair by the fireplace where another ancient crone was attending a hearty blaze. Lifting him up, they propped him on cushions by the fire and forced hot owl soup between his lips to revive him. Slowly, sensation returned to John Riley's body and he became aware of his surroundings. He was in a narrow mountain cabin cluttered with all sorts of things. In large stoppered jars he saw roots and powders of indeterminate origin. Set in a corner there were boxes of varying sizes, some covered by queerly marked cloths, and to his right was a large mirror in front of which certain black-colored candles had been placed. Riley remembered a mountain tradition that a lighted candle placed in front of a mirror at certain times of the year could reveal one's future. If a young girl was to marry, she would sometimes see the face of her future husband in the glass; if a man was to be murdered, he would see the face of his killer looking back at him. There were also bowls and basins containing indefinable elements on stools and sideboards. Those who had saved him from the cold were two old women, perhaps in their late sixties, who looked just like friendly grandmothers and who were now staring down at him with the utmost concern. "I'm all right," he managed to blurt out before falling unconscious from his ordeal on the mountainside.

For the next couple of days, the old sisters (for such he supposed them to be) looked after him and slowly nursed him back to health. Their names, he discovered, were Alice and Abigail although he never did find out their surname. They had lived way up on Roan Mountain for years and had very few visitors. Occasionally some of the mountain people would visit them but these instances were few and far between. He reckoned they both were extremely lonely. They took off his wet clothes and wrapped him in a warm blanket; they fed him more hot owl soup and some roasted squirrel and gradually the exhaustion from his battle against the fierce mountain winds wore off. Most of the time, though, he slept. As he regained his strength, the sisters suggested that he make his quarters in the loft above the tiny kitchen, where he could stay until he was ready to travel again. With typical old woman's curiosity, they quizzed him about his background: where did he come from, who were his parents, did he have a sweetheart? And his answers, such as they were, seemed to please the old ladies. They let him sleep once more. It was good to be in the warmth, away from the coarse mountain wind, and the cabin certainly seemed snug and secure. The only thing about it which disturbed John Riley were the dreams. He could not remember them clearly, but he knew that they had started as soon as he fell asleep within the cabin and that they were absolutely terrifying. Still, the old women were good to him, even if they were as ugly as a mud hole. They let him sleep on the floor of their loft and carried him up more soup and warm cornbread, hot with melting butter. At first he was very content.

On the second evening of his stay, Riley awoke with a start from one of his dreams. He was lying on the floor of the loft and right beside him was a knothole which looked straight down into the kitchen below. As he rolled over to wrap himself in his blanket, a shaft of moonlight caught him in the eyes. It came up between the floorboards from the kitchen and he knew that somebody had opened the curtains below him onto a large, full moon. Wondering what was going on—for he assumed that the old sisters would be asleep—he crept over to the knothole and peered down. A startling sight greeted him.

Alice and Abigail were both standing in front of the kitchen fireplace. He could see them in the moonlight which streamed in through the now-uncurtained window. They were both entirely naked. The braids of their hair were undone, allowing their locks to fall down about their shoulders like a shawl. They were both cackling and laughing and passing what looked like a lard can between them. They rubbed their wrinkled bodies with the contents of the can, coating every inch of themselves with it. They even rubbed it on their faces and on their pointed chins. As he watched, John Riley became more and more sure that they were changing slightly. Their noses were growing longer and more hooked, like the beaks of two predatory birds; their hair splayed out more until it looked like large gray wings on either side of their scrawny bodies. When their bodies were fully coated, the women took down two hemp sacks from nearby pegs. Then, returning to the fireplace, they stood in front of the open grate and recited a rhyme. Instantly, they became two great owl-like birds and, drawing out their wings, flew into the smoke of the chimney and were gone.

John Riley was astonished and could not believe the evidence of his own eyes. Throwing off the blanket, he came down from the loft and went over to the fireplace to investigate. As he did so, his foot hit something. It was the can that the old ladies had used. Lifting it up he looked inside at the queer, black-looking mess with which Alice and Abigail had greased their bodies. He could not make out what sort of substance it was. Better leave it alone, he thought. However, he did remember the words which they had used before they had turned into birds, and he repeated them himself now, like a chant:

Willie Waddie, I have spoke;
Willie Waddie, take this yoke,
Let me rise like chimney smoke.

If he thought that he, too, was going to turn into a bird then John Riley was much mistaken for nothing happened at all. He repeated the words again without any transformation. Who Willie Waddie was, he had no idea but he assumed it to be some sort of mountain spirit. Then, Riley had an idea. Dipping his fingers into the strange substance of the lard can he took out a portion. It was cold and greasy and had a queer texture to it. He rubbed it on his legs, his arms, and his elbows. He even rubbed it on his face. Then he said the words again. This time the transformation was almost instantaneous. He felt his skin prickle and sprout feathers; he was lifted from the ground and almost dragged up the chimney and into the night sky.

Just outside the cabin was a small tree and it was here John Riley sat in his bird shape, to catch his breath. It was certainly cold but his new feathers and the grease kept him warm. On another tree, farther down the slope, he saw two other birds which he assumed were the sisters, Alice and Abigail. Even as he watched them, they rose up into the air and flew away across the frosty face of the winter moon. He heard their voices drift back to him.

Willie Waddie, I do cry;
Willie Waddie, let me fly,
Like a blackbird through the sky.

Riley repeated the rhyme and suddenly he was whisked from his perch and found himself following the sisters across the cloudless mountain sky. He was moving faster than a galloping horse, and the sensation of the wind through his feathers was exhilarating. Slowly Roan Mountain fell behind them and the lights of a town sparkled underneath from out of the darkness. Swooping down, Riley recognized the gables of the houses; the old town clock; the narrow, muddy main street. He was back in Jonesborough and he had traveled the same distance in a matter of minutes as it had taken him to walk in more than two days.

In front of him, the two old ladies, still in their bird guise, lit on a chimney cap then seemed to revert to almost human shape as they vanished like smoke down the chimney itself. Soon, however, they returned with their sacks brimming with stolen items. They reverted to large birds once more and flew off again, each carrying a laden sack in its beak. Riley, however, landed on the edge of a nearby chimney to rest and suddenly was yanked down the chimney as though by magic. He landed on his hands and knees—he was now back in his human form—in a darkened room. As his eyes focused on his surroundings, he saw that he was in a storeroom, perhaps that of the local grocery store. He found he could see as well as if a light had been lit although none was. Soon, he was no longer alone, for the old ladies were appearing in the fireplace in their human guise and were proceeding to fill their sacks from the shelves round about. They called on Riley to help them and when they spoke it sounded to him like the chirping of birds. Still, he followed them into a small back room where a number of casks and barrels were stored. Each of these contained over forty gallons of aged whiskey and the old women magically placed a tap on the nearest one and started to draw off the liquor, which they decanted into a jug supernaturally produced from the sack.

The grease must have made them thirsty for they began to gulp down some of the whiskey as they worked. They also poured the liquid down John Riley's throat, and as he consumed more and more the room slowly began to spin around him. At length he sat down in the shelter of a barrel while the sisters made him drink. Soon he forgot that he was naked and he could not even remember the old women's names. They asked him again if he had a sweetheart. Riley said that he had some unfortunate experiences with women and the sisters cackled like hens. "I seen the face o' my future husband by the light o' a candle in the mirror," one of them said. "Looked over my left shoulder at the time o' th' new moon and I seen him in the glass as clear as day. An' he looked a lot like you." And she handed him the whiskey jug again. Riley took another swallow. "It wasn't me that you saw," he said with some bravado. "I'd never marry, 'less it was t' get outa jail." And he laughed at the joke, but the two old women looked at him queerly. "Then I'd take a look at yerself, my fine bucko!" said one, lifting a metal can from a nearby shelf. Its bottom was smooth and polished and acted like a mirror. Riley stared at what he thought was his own reflection. Only it was not his reflection but something hazy, strange, and inhuman. It was something that, in his drunken state, he could not quite make out. For a moment, he thought it was something birdlike or even bestial. It was not the face of a man at all, but something far more primitive. From somewhere, one of the crones produced a tin cup and filled it almost to the brim with more whiskey. She handed it to Riley, who gulped it down readily.

Suddenly, the old ladies told him it was time to go. Morning was not far away and they would have to move quickly. Now very drunk, Riley told them that he would come in a minute, just let him finish the drink. The sisters were gone, leaving him behind. Awkwardly, he put down his cup and staggered over to the fireplace. He tried to remember the rhyme but his mind was fogged and blurred. He mumbled some things but nothing worked. Desperately he tried to remember. Eventually, the words came to him and he recited them, slurring a little over every one. Nothing happened. He recited them again, and again nothing happened. He rubbed his hands and his legs, feeling the grease on them, together with a kind of downy fur, but still he stayed in human shape. He tried again but his tongue now felt as if it had furred and the words would scarcely come. In order to "grease his throat," Riley went back into the storeroom and tapped another barrel. Distilled liquor spilled out in a puddle on the floor and he went down on all fours trying to lap it up like a dog. Once he had drunk his fill, he staggered back to the fireplace again. By now, he was nearly too drunk to walk. He mumbled the words but as before, nothing happened. He tried to hop like a bird but fell over and crashed to the floor. Soon his mumbles turned to snores and he was still snoring when the storeroom owner opened up in the morning. On his floor was John Riley, completely naked and fast asleep. They had to wake him up to arrest him.

The judge listened to Riley's bizarre story with an expression on his face which told the accused that he did not believe a word of the tale. The sheriff of Washington County tried not to laugh at the young man's defence. "Roan Mountain people can be mighty queer," he acknowledged, "but even they would be pushed to come up with a tale as tall as that!" Even so, against all advice, Riley stuck to his story about Willie Waddie, the witches, and flying through the night on the wind to venture down chimneys. The barrel of whiskey cost Riley more than he could afford for under the judge's ruling the shopkeeper was allowed to charge him twice the price of the consumed goods. In East Tennessee, the courts strictly controlled the price of goods and of all liquors. And once he had been brought to court, other creditors showed up with small bills made out against him. These were the creditors he had originally been trying to flee. As he could not pay, he was sentenced to be held in the public pillory for one hour, to have his ears nailed back, and then to have both ears removed as a thief. He was also sentenced to be branded with the letter "T" on his right cheek so that everyone who met him would know him as a thief. And, as a matter of routine, Riley would be barred from entering Washington County for the rest of his natural life.

This sentence was to be carried out the next day, and that night, Riley was to remain in the jailhouse and be restrained with leg irons. The jail was a long, low log house directly behind the Jonesborough courthouse and it was there that John Riley was taken. As sentenced, the leg iron was clamped round his left ankle and was attached to the wooden wall of the jail, hammered tightly in by the town blacksmith. For supper he received a cold stew of cooked corn and greasy beans. The sheriff was stationed outside the cell in an old iron cot with a rifle by his side in case the prisoner tried to escape. Riley was regarded as "a tricky customer."

The lawman lit a large fire in the fireplace and began to doze in front of it, his rifle across his lap. A little later he stirred as a burning log fell in the fireplace for he thought he heard voices somewhere close by, female voices. Maybe it was the ladies from the church at a service outside in the street praying for the sinner inside the jailhouse walls. He listened more carefully. It seemed to be some sort of chant. Maybe, he thought, some female had got into the jailhouse. Then he noticed that the front door was not properly closed. He had closed it himself and no one else could have opened it unless the prisoner had gotten out of his cell. He jumped to his feet and ran into the back to check that all was still in order. John Riley was still in his cell but, as the astonished Washington County lawman looked on, some sort of glistening sheen appeared to be spreading over the prisoner's body, even his face. And there seemed to be odd shadows in the cell with him—shadows which came and went and flowed into each other but somehow appeared to be those of two women. The stunned sheriff watched in disbelief as Riley seemed to waver and change in front of his eyes into a small birdlike creature which easily stepped out of the leg irons and moved towards the tiny window of the place, high up in the wall. In a desperate attempt to stop him, the sheriff lunged, but it was too late. The bird-thing dissolved into smoke and was gone. The law officer rushed to the jailhouse door, his rifle at the ready, but the night outside was still except for a couple of stray dogs moving in the street and some birds flying against the moon. In an instant, they were gone, even before the startled sheriff could raise his shotgun and take aim.

Returning to the cell, he examined it, if only to make sure that he had not dreamt the whole thing. The only thing he found was a greasy footprint—human, all right, for it had five toes—roughly about the size of a man's naked foot. He took a sample of the greasy substance with him over to the doctor's surgery; maybe the medical man could tell him what it was. But the doctor could not and to this day, the grease has defied analysis. And, as for the footprint, it stayed where it was. No amount of washing or scrubbing could remove it. In the late 1820s, the old log jailhouse mysteriously burned to the ground, leaving only ash behind. Otherwise the eerie footprint might still be visible today.

John Riley was never seen around Jonesborough again, nor are there any records of him appearing anywhere else. However, old-timers are certain that he still lives up on Roan Mountain, long years after he should have died, and that he is sometimes seen circling through the clouds over the bald mountaintops. But that is just old superstition. Or is it? Shortly after his strange disappearance, the storekeepers in Jonesborough put heavy screens across their chimneys and even today, when the wind blows down from the Roan Mountain country, they look nervously up into the hills and go and check their storerooms. Some say that they can sometimes hear the sound of church bells carried down on the breeze, and there certainly is a little church up in the mountains, but it has been long abandoned. Nevertheless, its bells would have rung during a wedding. Maybe the old woman did not lie when she said she saw the face of her future husband in the candlelit mirror and that he looked a lot like John Riley.

Part 4
Ghosts, Spirits, and the Unquiet Dead

Ohio

The Daylight Wraith

One of the central features of prognostication in the Celtic world was the ability to foresee death. Druids and Celtic auguries cast individual horoscopes for both leaders and common people, often giving predictions of the date when and the manner in which they were to die. In the ancient world, the necessity of such information is obvious. For the head of a household, it was important to know the date of his death so that he could make provisions for his family and dependants. This need affected all strata of society. In the charged and bloody atmosphere of the Scottish Highlands and islands, where the clan system was still extant and local families often ferociously feuded amongst themselves, it was vitally important to know the outcomes of such disagreements and who would live and who would not. Clan territory could be acquired, for example, through the murder of an important chieftain and it was not unknown for a clan to be utterly exterminated in a murderous conflict. In this respect, the prophesies of the seers took on a highly political aspect and seers were much sought after.

Predicting such doom could be accomplished in various ways, sometimes depending upon the social status of the consultant (since Celtic society was incredibly status conscious). For a king the Druids might employ, amid great ritual, the *coelbreni,* or omen sticks. When cast upon the ground omen sticks that landed crossed, for instance, could mean death or disaster for a ruler or military leader. For persons of lesser status, the wise men might read the entrails of chickens or other birds or divine the future from the movement of clouds. But perhaps the most favored method chosen by these ancient Celtic augurs was that of the *taghairm.* It involved a sleeper entering what might be considered an altered state by ritualistic means and then "seeing" the future, particularly disaster or death.

Certain individuals, it was thought, gave out clear supernatural signals as death approached which could only be read by occult means.

Gradually this supernatural ability evolved into what became known as the "second sight." In some cases, the seer went through elaborate ritual in order to achieve his or her vision, but in most cases, the "sight" was simply an ability or gift which the individual possessed. There were many such seers scattered across the Western Isles, but the most famous Highland seer was the Brahan Seer, Kenneth MacKenzie, who earned much awe and respect in his local area of Seaforth in Ross-shire. Most of the prognostications of the Brahan Seer were gloomy and concerned death and destruction but they were highly valued amongst the Scots of the day. Although people such as Kenneth and the Reverend John Morrison, the Petty Seer, were justly famed for their prophesies, many others experienced visions of the future, especially where death was concerned.

In some cases, futuristic visions would come upon ordinary people unawares. For instance, a man working in a field might see a peculiar halo about one of his companions and would instinctively know that he or she was not long for this world. In 1842, while staying in County Clare in Ireland, the German travel writer Johann Kohl was introduced to a venerable Irish seer named Cosideen, an ancient woman crouched by a smoky peat fire, who claimed to be able to see Death "leaning on two crutches" at "the end of the meadow" and to know who it had come for. This "sight" was something over which she had no control and which came upon her when she least expected it.

There were still other types of visions experienced by the Celts. In parts of rural Wales, phantom funerals abounded and could be witnessed by anyone unfortunate enough to be in the proximity. These ghostly processions would follow the route of an actual funeral destined to take place in the near future. It was sometimes even possible to tell who the dead person might be if one was able to discern the mourners present. In Cornwall and in some parts of Wales it was possible to "communicate" this sight from one person to another simply by standing on the foot of another or by gripping his or her arm during the morbid parade. However, it was an evil thing to see because there was always a chance that a person might see his or her own funeral.

In Ireland, too, prognostication or foreseeing one's own death or the death of a friend could be quite common. This type of vision was known in many parts of the Irish countryside, particularly in the north, as the daylight wraith. Such visions did not appear at night but during the day when the light was at its best. The seer would witness himself, a friend, or an acquaintance who was known to be in some other place as a kind of phantom. This was considered to be an infallible sign of the approaching death of the person concerned.

An example of the daylight wraith comes from Rathlin Island, off the North Antrim coast. It was originally told by the great island storyteller Rose McCurdy but relates to another Island man, Frank Craig, who often told the tale himself. Frank Craig and Robert Black were working in a field on the southern end of the island when they witnessed what appeared to be a serious fight on the side of a nearby road. A small man was being pinned to the ground by a larger man who seemed to have a long knife in one hand. This was around midday and Frank Craig noted that the sun was glinting on a large gold ring in the larger man's left ear. Looking at the pair, Frank thought he recognized the smaller of the two. "Isn't that Lochy Veg [Lochlin McCurdy]?" he asked, straining to get a clearer look. "It looks like him," agreed Robert Black. "But it can't be. Didn't he go to Australia years ago? I never heard that he was back." The two men looked at each other in great astonishment and when they looked towards the fight again, the road was empty. There was no sign that there had been any sort of brawl there at all. It was all very puzzling. They asked around amongst their island neighbors but nobody had heard that Lochy Veg had returned to Rathlin. Several months later, word reached the island that Lochy Veg had been killed by a seaman in a brawl in New South Wales, over half a world away. Although he did not know for fact, Frank Craig suspected that Veg had been killed by a man with a great gold ring in his ear and that he and Robert Black had witnessed the murder before it had happened.

Similarly, from the Clogher Valley in County Tyrone comes a tale of the daylight wraith besetting a farming family. The family consisted of four members—a mother, two sons, and a daughter. Their father was long dead and the sons looked after the place while the mother and daughter kept house. The younger of the brothers, John, was a hard-working individual who put every effort into maintaining the farm, even through difficult times. The other brother, Richard, however, was something of a wastrel who hated work and spent most of his time trying to avoid it. He had little love for the farm, his family, or the people round about. He treated his mother shabbily and when the old lady died, he simply quit the farm rather than help his brother about the place. He was rumored to have gone to either America or New Zealand. He did not bother to keep in contact with his family and neither Mary nor John were worried too much about him. Neither of them married; John continued to work the farm and Mary looked after him. Their life settled into an uneventful routine on that isolated farm.

One evening many years later, Mary was making breakfast as John had gone out to milk cows in the barn when she heard a sound coming from the room next to the kitchen. It was a small living room not much in use, but it was where their mother had kept her best things. Fearing that they were being robbed, she lifted a heavy poker and crept to the door of the room. Turning the handle, she peered inside. A man was crouching over a small cabinet in which Mary's mother had kept some good chinaware and cutlery and appeared to be helping himself to them. "What do you think you're doing?" Mary threw wide the door and stepped into the room, poker in hand. The man paid her no heed but seemed to go on rifling through the cabinet. Mary repeated her question and stepped farther into the room. Only then did the other turn and, for the first time, she saw his face. It was her brother Richard. However, it was not the Richard she remembered for the haughty face was now twisted into a mask of hate and was streaked with dirt. The stubble of a beard covered his chin and his clothes were torn and filthy. With an audible snarl, he turned on her like a wild animal and she felt his hands slide around her throat. Taken aback she could only scream his name: "Richard! Richard! For God's sake, let me go!" And, as she uttered the holy name, she was suddenly alone in the room and the vicious pressure about her neck was gone. All the same, the red marks of fingers remained. Breathless, she went out into the yard to tell John what had happened. At first, he did not believe her but then he saw the finger marks on her neck and he wondered. For a few days there was an almost palpable atmosphere of fear in the house, but then things gradually started to return to normal.

Several weeks later, John was sitting at his breakfast by the kitchen window when he was sure that he saw somebody moving outside. He did not hear anyone but he thought he glimpsed a shadow on the floor out of the corner of his eye and felt a presence pass by the house. Rising from the table, he walked outside into the yard to see who it was. There, standing in the open doorway of the barn, his hand on a pitchfork, was his brother, Richard. Assuming that Richard had somehow returned unannounced, John went forward to greet him, but with a snarl of anger, the other leaped forward and attempted to run him through with the pitchfork. Leaping out of the way to avoid the threatening prongs, John attempted to defend himself, grabbing the fork from his brother's hands as he made yet another lunge. The two fell to the ground, locked in struggle, as Mary ran out of the house. Just as his sister had, John felt Richard's hands around his throat. These were not the insubstantial fingers of a phantom but what seemed to be the real hands of a solid man. Richard, the older and clearly the stronger of the two, struck his brother across the face and then turned to squeeze the life from him. "In the name of God let him be!" Mary screamed in terror as John rolled clear. Her eyes lifted for a moment to check his fate and when the two looked again, they were alone in the farmyard. There was no trace of their brother although the pitchfork lay on the ground where Richard had thrown it. Neither of them knew what to make of it, but they were badly frightened. John decided to make enquiries as to his elder brother's whereabouts.

After much investigation, John finally learned the truth. His brother had gone to America and had traveled west into developing territory. There, he had gotten into a fight over a gambling wager in a small Midwest town and had been stabbed to death. Nobody had been able to trace his family to inform them of his demise. The time of death was thought to have occurred around the time that Mary found him rifling through the cupboard. It was his ghost that his sister and brother had seen back in the Clogher Valley.

That should have been the end of it, but it wasn't. Following the appearance of the daylight wraith, the farm never prospered. It was thought the phantom had somehow blighted the place. Crops failed, animals died, and both John and Mary suffered a series of illnesses which kept them from working. The wraith appeared to have laid a curse on the property. At last they could stand it no longer. They sold up and they too went to America and disappear from our story and from the pages of history. The farm was sold to a local businessman who never put it to use. It was considered to be bad land and was simply allowed to deteriorate. The buildings all fell in on themselves—including the house itself—and the unused land became badly overgrown. The place also acquired something of a dubious reputation in the surrounding countryside. It was said to be haunted. Some people claimed to have seen a figure standing alone in the weed-grown yard or at the door of the now-falling house, a figure which they thought might be the "evil" brother Richard. But this was always seen at a distance or in a poor light and no one could be sure. Others thought the figure was of somebody they knew and some even imagined that the figure closely resembled themselves. It was a dangerous thing to see this figure as it always preceded some misfortune: a death or a local or family disaster. The farmhouse is now gone—it was pulled down long ago—but the legends still haunt the Clogher Valley.

Other relatively similar stories are to be found all across the North of Ireland and even into Scotland. In parts of County Down, for example, it was believed that small children were exceptionally good seers, and tales of infants seeing the wraiths of grandparents prior to the death of the individual concerned are extremely widespread. Often such visitations also heralded misfortune, as it did in the Clogher Valley tale. It was probably from the North of Ireland and from Scotland that the belief transferred itself to the shores of America. Although not all that widespread on the new continent, the notion of the daylight wraith appears in at least some communities, particularly within areas which are primarily farming based. As such, the notion was usually confined to certain states, usually in the Midwest. Generally speaking, the American belief followed or was close to its Celtic counterpart: the wraith was either the appearance of somebody well known to the viewer or else resembled the viewer himself, was seen in a place where the person could not possibly be at the time, and usually presaged death or some terrible misfortune. The following story, known locally as "Aunt Rosie," comes from Ohio and bears a startlingly resemblance to tales told in Ireland and Scotland.

In the 1920s, Mose Edison and his family took over a small farm in Fairfield County, which at that time was a very rural part of the world. Time passed slowly in parts of Fairfield and the folks there were deeply superstitious. An old train trestle which spanned a shallow ravine was believed to be a cry-baby bridge where on moonlit nights the screams of some unknown infant could be heard. (At one time cry-baby bridges were relatively common all over Ohio. One is still counted to exist in Rogue's Hollow in Wayne County, while another was said to exist along the Wilberforce-Clifton road at "the Devil's Backbone" near Wilberforce University. It was believed that the ghosts of small children who had been in some way taken before their time hung around such bridges and wept as travelers passed over them.) Mose Edison, however, was a hard-nosed farming man with little time for superstitious tales. He had a large family to keep. Besides his wife, Nancy, and six children ranging in ages from five to seventeen, he also took care of his late mother's younger unmarried sister, Rose, who lived with the family as a dependent.

Despite relying on Mose and his family, Aunt Rosie, as she was known, was a pretty stubborn old woman and was well used to getting her own way. If denied anything, she would sulk for long periods or else would show a temper for which she became justly famed all over Fairfield County. She was the only one in the family who could stand up to the hard-edged Mose. In her day, Rosie had been a keen horsewoman and, as an old lady, still took an interest in horses. At most of the local horse fairs, she was to be found examining horses with the meticulous eye of a dealer, and many of the local farmers asked her opinion on their animals. It was said that old Nate Burrows, who had once bought and sold horses, was kind of "sweet" on Rosie, even though the two of them were well advanced in years. It was even said that Nate, who was a widower, had asked Rosie to marry him and to live with him in his big frame house in the woods and that Mose had tried to encourage the union but that Rosie would have none of it. All the same, Nate had not given up hope and took to calling at the Edison house rather more than was necessary in the expectation of seeing her.

One day, Rosie received an invitation to attend a barn raising at Paul Sweeny's place. Normally, she would not have gone near those noisy, drunken celebrations; however, Paul had a new bay mare that she wanted to have a look at and judge for herself if the animal was as fine as everybody said. However, Mose was not keen on her going. He did not like Paul—he thought Paul had ideas above his station—and he knew that Rosie would be saddled with chores for the barn raisers such as making tea and doling out bread and cakes and he did not want her put upon. Besides, one of the children was not feeling well and Rosie was needed about her own house. Despite the old woman's protestations that she would be gone for only a short time, Mose flatly forbade her to go. He could be just as stubborn as she when he put his mind to it. Rosie fumed and sulked, not because of any wish to party with Paul Sweeny and his "uppity" wife, but because she would not get to see the new horse. She fretted and scolded but it made no impression at all on Mose. Nevertheless, she had her own plans.

On the day of the barn raising, Rosie stole away from the house. She reckoned that she could be over at Sweeny's place for a couple of hours and be back before anybody missed her. Mose's child was feeling a good deal better and there was little need for her at the moment. She just wanted to have a look at the horse.

On that same day Nate Burrows came calling. "Suzy," Nancy Edison called to her youngest child, "run out into the barn t' fetch Aunt Rosie. She's sulkin' in there somewheres but likely she'll come out when she knows Mr. Burrows is here." The child ran off to the barn to fetch the old woman. She returned soon after, looking extremely puzzled. "Aunt Rosie seems in a mighty big sulk, Mama," she told Nancy. "She wouldn't say anythin' to me but just kep' sittin' there in the barn, starin' at the wall. She didn't even let on that I was there." Nancy was puzzled. She was used to Rosie's sulks, but Suzy was her favorite and she would not deliberately ignore the little girl. In fact that was why Suzy had been sent. Angered by the woman's coldness, Nancy stormed out to the barn to speak sharply to Rosie but, to her surprise, she found the building completely empty. Rosie was nowhere to be found. Imagining the old woman had gone somewhere else to sulk, Nancy came back to the house and scolded about her loudly and in no uncertain terms.

"Let me go out and look for her," said Nate Burrows kindly. "I'll see if I can bring her home. She's just an ornery old woman that needs a little sweet talkin'." And he went out into the yard to see if he could smooth Aunt Rosie's ruffled feathers. Although he looked around the place, not a trace of Rosie did he see. Then, near an old barn on the far corner of the yard, he saw a figure moving out of the corner of his eye. It was going around the side of the building and in a moment had vanished from view, but he was sure that it was Rosie slipping out of his line of vision. He had known her long enough to recognize her walk and the way she carried herself. "Rosie!" he called after her, but the figure paid him no heed. Nate ran to catch up to her but when he rounded the corner himself there was nobody there. The yard was empty and the fields stretched away on either side. There was nowhere for Rosie to go, nowhere for her to hide. Nate was baffled. He went back into the house, shaking his head, hoping that the old lady had somehow made it into the kitchen, but found only Nancy and Suzy there.

There were no further sightings of Rosie for more than an hour until Mose Edison came in. Mose had been working out in the field, was tired, and was in no mood for the old lady's sulks and tantrums. When he heard about how Rosie was behaving, he got up from his chair and went out into the yard to have strong words with her and make her see some sense. Sure enough, as he stepped out of the house, he saw Aunt Rosie going into a barn ahead of him. She was waiting for him in a far corner as he stepped into the dark building. Mose opened his mouth to speak—to berate Rosie for her odd and frightening behavior—when the old woman launched herself at him with all the ferocity of a wildcat. She had lifted a piece of broken wood with which she struck him about the shoulders as she passed. Then she turned to attack him again. Mose was dumbfounded. In all the years Rosie had lived with them, she had never harmed anyone. Now she was like some wild creature, looking as if she would kill him. Running to the door of the barn, he lifted a broom handle with which to defend himself and for a moment he lifted his eyes off his attacker. When he turned back, he was alone in the barn once more. He searched all around for Rosie but there was no sign of her. It was as though she had never been there. Badly shaken, he returned to the kitchen and told everyone what had happened.

He was still recovering when another caller arrived at the Edison home. Aunt Betty Miller was renowned as an "uncanny woman" in the local community, a kind of healer who knew all about "boogers" and "haints." On her way to the Edison house, she had stopped over at Paul Sweeny's barn raising where she had briefly seen Aunt Rosie although she had not been able to talk to the old lady. She assumed that Rosie had come home and, as she wanted to speak with her on some matter, she had stopped by to see if she had returned. Mose told her about the strange encounters—the whole family was badly frightened by now—and how he himself had been attacked by the old lady and of how she had mysteriously vanished. On hearing the strange tale, the blood left Aunt Betty's face and she made a curious sign in the air with her right hand. "You've bin visited by a daylight wraith," she told them. "Nothing good can come from one o' them things a-comin' about the place. It means death and misfortune, you mark my words." Mose, hard-headed man that he was, refused to believe any such thing. There were no such things as wraiths, he declared, whether in the dark or in broad daylight. He would not have any more of that sort of talk in his house. Rosie had been real enough; she was just old and confused—that was all.

Within the hour, Aunt Rosie returned from Paul Sweeny's place. If she thought that she had not been missed, she was very much mistaken. The place was in an uproar and she was required to give an account of herself: where she had been and what she had been doing. She did so very reluctantly. She had just gone over to Paul Sweeny's and taken a look at the new mare, then she had served a couple of party-goers with strong drink and come home. Nate told her about the queer goings on and, like Betty Miller, Aunt Rosie paled. She recognized that the home had been visited by a daylight wraith and it would mean the end of her or one of the family. She fretted and worried for the rest of the day.

Weeks went by and nothing seemed to happen. Aunt Rosie remained hale and hearty and although a couple of the children had worrying colds, they did not sicken. The only one who seemed affected by the visitation was Mose Edison himself. He became sullen and intolerant, picking on Nancy or Aunt Rosie as the mood took him. One evening, he was riding home from a neighbor's house when he saw a man at a distance working in the fields. The stranger seemed to have his back to him, but even so, Mose thought he looked a little bit like himself. However, the light was poor and the man was too far away to clearly make out. A bird called from a nearby tree branch and instinctively, Mose turned his head. When he looked back, the field was empty. Then he remembered the stories of the daylight wraith and how he had confronted "Rosie" in the barn. There were bizarre things afoot and they frightened Mose deeply, but he still could not admit what was happening, even to himself. He just rode on home and said nothing. About a week later, he mentioned the incident in passing but quickly dismissed it out of hand. However, it certainly was a sign of doom and unhappiness to come.

A few days later, Aunt Rosie was working in the kitchen. It was just after the meal and Nancy had left a heated pot to cool in the shadows, near the door. Rosie did not notice it and banged her leg against its rim, breaking the skin and cutting herself badly. The cut began to swell and she was laid up for a couple of days. She then seemed to recover well enough to get up and hobble around the kitchen doing small chores. However, the swelling did not go down; in fact it got worse and it was not long until she was laid up again. These were times when there were few rural doctors and even those who practiced did not come all the way out to remote Fairfield County. Aunt Betty Miller was summoned but she was baffled by the swelling. She guessed it might be blood poisoning, but she could not be sure. She put a poultice over the cut and gave Rosie an herb posset to drink in order to counteract the infection, but it did no good. Within days, Rosie took sick and went to her bed. She never rose again.

As she lay, growing steadily worse with the poison, she got the news that finished her. Mose had been on his way home from a neighbor's house when his horse had shied at something in the road and thrown him. He had fallen awkwardly and broken his neck, dying almost instantly. Less than a week later, Aunt Rosie followed him to the grave. From then on, there was nothing but misfortune for the Edison family. Without Mose to act as breadwinner, the family soon got into financial difficulties. Nancy did what she could to manage the farm but she was not experienced enough, nor were any of the children old enough to help her. Nate Burrows tried to help them by lending some money, but even he found himself in trouble with the bank as several of his investments which had seemed rock solid suddenly collapsed. Illness plagued the Edison family, resulting in high medical bills which they could barely afford to pay. A barn inexplicably burned down and livestock unaccountably took sick. In the end, the bills mounted and creditors began to close in. Money the family had been expecting failed to materialize and to keep the bank at bay, Nancy and her family were forced to sell and move from Ohio. They relocated to upstate New York and were never heard from again. Their former farm fell into neglect and was shunned by many local people. It was said that the daylight wraith of Aunt Rosie hovered about the falling house and that to see it was to invite ill luck. However, nobody was ever brave enough to find out and the building, together with its barns, is long gone. Even so, some people still claim to have glimpsed a figure at a distance around midday on the place where it stood. The appearance of such a figure usually precedes some misfortune in the community. At least that is what the old folks say.

And there may be something in the tale for more Ohio people have seen wraiths than Mose Edison and his family. One of the state's most famous sons, James A. Garfield, the twentieth president of the United States, thought he saw himself walking down a street in Washington on a hot day in June 1881. The figure seemed to have removed his coat and was in his shirt-sleeves but when Garfield looked again, it had disappeared into the crowd. About three weeks late, on July 2, 1881, at a Washington railroad station, an embittered attorney who had sought a consular post shot the president. Mortally wounded, Garfield lay ill in the White House for weeks. Alexander Graham Bell, inventor of the telephone, tried unsuccessfully to find the bullet with a new induction-balance electrical device he had invented. The iron springs of the president's bed gave conflicting readings and no one thought to move him. In September, Garfield was taken to the New Jersey seaside in the hope that he might recuperate. While he was there, he thought he glimpsed the same man he had seen in Washington walking at a distance along the beach near midday. On September 19, 1881, Pres. James A. Garfield died from an infection and an internal hemorrhage. The question remains, had the daylight wraith followed him from Ohio? Not even presidents, it seems, are immune from its attentions.

Sarah Tillinghast

Arguably, the world's oldest recorded vampire story comes not from Transylvania but from Ireland. The legend of Abhartach, a fifth-century vampiric warlord whose grave can still be seen in Glenullin, North Derry, was first written between 1629 and 1631 in *Foras Feasa ar Eireann* by the Irish scholar Dr. Geoffrey Keating and has resurfaced in works by Dermod O'Connor (1725) and Patrick Weston Joyce (1880). It may even be possible to argue that Joyce's work influenced Bram Stoker, himself an Irishman, in his famous vampire creation *Dracula*. Some commentators have argued that the novel owes more to rural Ireland than it does to Transylvania, a part of the world Stoker never visited.

However, in the matter of vampires neither the Celts nor the Transylvanians are unique. Almost every ancient civilization has recognized the significance of blood. Blood was a restorer; blood was a revitalizer; without blood there could be no existence, either human or animal. Blood, therefore, was the essence of life itself. The ancient Celts, of course, were no exception to this belief. In fact, from what we can gather about their earliest religious perceptions, blood played a central role in many of their forms of worship. It is highly probable that, in common with many other early peoples, the Celts practiced human sacrifice. As a primarily agricultural community, their belief systems coalesced around fertility, rebirth, and resurrection. Everything which lived and grew followed a great cycle: the crops were harvested but grew again; animals died and their meat was eaten but new life blossomed; even members of the human community passed away but others were born to replace them. During the dark winter days, the sun hung low in the sky and the ground was hardened like iron by frost and was unsuitable for planting. To the ancient Celtic mind, it seemed that the very world was either dead or dying and in need of drastic revitalization. The only element which could competently achieve such a task was blood. Thus, through the medium of human sacrifice, they offered blood to the ground at the beginning of the year in the hope of good weather and abundant harvests. Blood would restore the dead soil and breathe new life into the desolate, frost-hardened landscape. And, with the coming of spring, when the earth burst into verdant life once more, it seemed to the Celts as though their bloody sacrifice had worked. Gradually, the notion of blood and sacrifice found its way into ritualized Celtic religion. The early peoples gathered at specific sites—at remote standing stones and lone trees—to perform their bloody ceremonies. Blood, both human and animal, continually seeped into the earth, always denoting resurrection and renewal.

It was but a small step from the concept of a reanimated nature to the idea of the reawakened dead. Like the land, the dead had always played a central part in the Celtic psyche and religion. We do know that there were ancestor cults and cults of the dead amongst many ancient cultures, including the Celts. Amongst some antique peoples, the dead were especially venerated, their mouldering skeletons placed on open display so that they could watch over and protect their descendants. Other cultures summoned the spirits of ancestors in times of community crisis to drive away demons, stamp out illnesses, or protect their people from some catastrophe. These forces usually came as gusts of wind, monstrous shadows, or else took over the bodies of specified people—for example, of a shaman—through whom they could take decisive action or make their wishes known.

With the rise of ancestor cults in Western Europe came veneration and worship of the dead. Those who had gone before did not protect their descendants without some form of recompense. Offerings of food and clothing were sometimes left in return for favors and supernatural protection. And at certain times of the year, the dead returned to visit those who were descended from them in order to receive a reward for watching over them. After a long period in the grave without the comforts of the mortal world, such returning spirits expected to be fed or at least to have a drink of whiskey awaiting them. This belief was widely held in Ireland until at least the early twentieth century. The author, who was born and raised in a rural area of County Down, remembers as a youth seeing a glass of whiskey and an oatcake being placed by the hearthside on Halloween night for the returning dead. In some cases, the dead were invited to partake in a family meal. A number of tales exist all over the Celtic world regarding the prodigious appetites of these corpses, which would not have eaten for a very long time. In one story from the North of Ireland, a family dreads the return of an elderly female relative who eats her descendants "out of house and home" upon her return each year, and they are eventually forced to bring in a priest to exorcise her in order to avoid inordinate debt. Of course, some families simply refused to feed these returning ancestors, but they did so at their peril for the dead did not like to be ignored and could, if so inclined, exact a terrible supernatural revenge upon those who had crossed them

It is at this juncture that the notions of the vengeful dead and the idea of blood as a restorative may come together. If refused ordinary food upon their return, the dead would sometimes imbibe blood— mostly animal but sometimes human—to nourish themselves for another period in the grave. The warmth and vitality of the fluid would sustain them when they returned to the cold, damp clay and would reinvigorate them for the coming year in the ground. Farmers might find their cattle drained of blood or, in a much more sinister turn of events, some family member greatly debilitated for the same reason. It was thought that the animated corpse would first attack members of its own family but, if not fully satisfied, might venture into the wider community as well. Thus the notion of the vampire, the blood-drinking corpse which never fully dies, was born in the Celtic mind. Such creatures enjoyed a quasi-existence in the tomb during the hours of daylight but traveled abroad at night, drinking the blood of sleepers in order to continue its weird lifespan. This was the ultimate example of the vengeful, unquiet dead.

When we speak of vampires, images of ruined Eastern European castles and lonely Transylvanian forests spring immediately to mind. And yet, these images are relatively modern and misleading. Vampires exist almost everywhere in the world. Not all of them, admittedly, drink only blood and not all of them take on human form. Ancient Rome had its strix, ghastly beings with the bodies of vultures and the heads of old women who drank the blood of sleeping infants as well as the old and the sick, who were powerless to drive them away. In ancient Israel, it was believed that if an old and wasted Semite magician slept with a young girl, he could draw the vitality from her into his own body. This magic was used to revitalize the decrepit King David of Israel when he slept with Abishag and she "warmed his body." A more modern vampire, the aswang of the Philippines, a green, scaled, dragon-like being, drinks the "essential fluids," mainly sperm, from young, sleeping Filipino men. It does this through a long and hollow tongue which it lowers through the leaf-covered roof of the victim's house. The penangal of Malaysia is little more than the bloodied, disembodied head of a woman who has died in childbirth which feeds on the energies of the sleeper (usually male), leaving him weak and torpid the following morning. The jaracinda of Brazil, a small, monkey-like entity, devours what flesh it can from the limbs of sleeping warriors, creating frightful sores and disfigurements. But it is the lust for blood which characterizes the Western vampire. This impression has been strengthened by strong cultural images of a blood-drinking undead fiend which emerges from its grave after dark to imbibe from the throats of the living and can only be driven away by the power of the Christian cross.

Written stories concerning blood drinkers first appeared, as has already been noted, around 1629 with Geoffrey Keating's work. The *Foras Feasa ar Eireann* concerns an early tyrant named Abhartach who was killed twice by another local ruler but who returned each time and sustained himself with a bowl of blood taken from the veins of his subjects. In the end, he was pronounced as one of the *marbh bheo,* the walking dead, by the Druids and was eventually "killed" using a sword of yew wood. It is thought that this tale may have been one of the sources used by Bram Stoker for the development of his famous vampire count.

But this is not the only Irish story concerning blood-drinking creatures that may have led to the evolution of Dracula. During a lecture in 1963, for example, the Kerry-born archivist of the Irish Folklore Commission, Sean O'Sullivan, mentioned a notorious fairy fortress high in the Magillicuddy Reeks mountains of Kerry which was known as Dun Dreach-fhoula (pronounced "drak'ola"). According to Kerry tradition, this was the habitation of blood-drinking beings who preyed on travelers through the mountain passes. Unfortunately, the location of this fortress—apparently known as "the Castle of the Blood Visage"—was not given and all attempts to locate it have proved fruitless. Other tales of blood-drinking fairies are to be found in Scotland and the Western Isles.

Another influence on the Irish vampire myth may have been the impact of the Great Potato Famine of 1845-1852, which touched the West of Scotland as well. With their staple diet of potatoes gone, the starving Irish turned to other forms of sustenance, and one of these was blood. Cattle were taken to remote sites and bled, usually little more than half a pint. This nourishing liquid was then mixed with whatever oatmeal and turnip tops the community had in order to form "relish cakes," which were then cooked in the manner of black pudding. Sometimes, though, the blood was drunk raw in order to restore vitality to bodies emaciated by the effects of the famine. The notion of the returning dead, perhaps transformed into vampires by the consumption of animal blood, sometimes found its way into rural folklore. Here and there, eerie tales of creatures which drank blood or consumed flesh were to be found in the darker corners of the country mind, evoking memories of the deprivation and hardship of the famine. For instance, as late as 1937, tales of ghoul women who dug up dead bodies and ate their flesh were being recorded for the Irish Folklore Commission in Sneem Parish, County Kerry, by Tadhg O'Murchadha; earlier, Jeremiah Curtin was hearing similar stories of blood-drinking corpses in County Limerick. Such stories existed in the Western Isles and in the most westerly parts of Scotland, which had also been hit by severe food shortages in the mid-1800s. Here the notion of blood drinkers combined with the tales of supernatural sprites and ancient gods to create a race of vampiric fairies which lived in the vicinity of lonely standing stones, remote cairns, and desolate raths that dotted the landscape. Such beings preyed upon travelers, shepherds, and the incautious person who ventured too close to their harsh abodes.

These were the basic traditions which the Scots-Irish immigrants brought with them to America and which would be modified both by the conditions which they found there and by the people themselves as they adapted to their new home. The land in which they settled was often harsh and relatively alien to them. Early America was a wilderness of desolate mountains and plains, deep and near-impenetrable forests, and dark and dismal swamps. It was already inhabited by wild Indians and fierce creatures which the early colonists had to subdue. In such conditions, the notions of dark, cruel, and malignant spirits must have seemed very real. The Indians with whom they established contact had their own rather dubious (from the colonists' perspective) supernatural beings and practices and also spoke of strange monsters deep in the forests and dwelling in caves in the high mountains. Black slaves from Africa and the West Indies also brought legends with them, including stories of the walking dead reanimated by malignant magic or of dark creatures which haunted the gravesites of their own countries. Slave tales fascinated many of the early settlers because they sometimes bore a tenuous connection to familiar stories. Gradually, the legends which the settlers had brought with them from Ireland and Scotland fused with the myths of the remote lands in which they settled. Amongst them must have been the tales of blood-drinking ghouls. It is not hard to imagine some ghastly creature roaming around the dark hollows and isolated forest clearings where the pioneers built their cabins with the sole purpose of drinking human blood.

Other concepts colored this belief. The first of these was disease for the early colonists suffered from fierce epidemics which all but destroyed their settlements. Typhoid, poxes of various kinds, and the dread cholera carried away old and young alike and reduced the immigrant population. Today, scientific answers to the problem would be sought, but in an age when medical knowledge was in its infancy and conditions were rudimentary, other explanations were looked for. Devils that dwelt in the landscape, supernatural creatures from the forests, dark and inimical beings from the swamps were conjured up to account for the deaths of loved ones, very much as the fairy folk had been used to explain similar deaths in Ireland and Scotland. The intervention of diabolic forces accounted for the sudden debilitation of formerly healthy settlers as the disease took hold, and the notion of vampiric beings was used to explain the weakness, loss of appetite, ghastly pallor, and general malaise which were the symptoms of sicknesses such as cholera. And, as epidemics swept the isolated communities, such ideas gave the settlers added commitment and purpose. Rather than remain powerless as their kinsfolk were carried away by some nebulous and untreatable illness, they could do something about it: they could find and destroy the fiend that was ravaging their numbers. Once that was done, things would return to normal, and in this respect, the notion of the vampire provided some measure of comfort to the frightened settlers.

Other factors which probably shaped American vampire beliefs were the unusual religious practices of some of the sects which settled there, particularly in New England. A significant proportion of the late-seventeenth/early-eighteenth-century settlers were from strict Calvinist-based groupings who had come to the New World to escape persecution and intolerance of worship in their own countries. Their beliefs permeated the communities in which they lived and their influence continued until the early twentieth century, albeit in modified forms. Some of these beliefs were rather unorthodox and a few of them concerned death. The Brownists, for instance, took the view that no female might enter heaven since Eve, the first woman, had given herself to the Devil and had led Adam into sin. Especially saintly women were supernaturally transformed into men at the point of death so that they might ascend directly to paradise. Another sect were the followers of Shadrack Ireland, who styled themselves "the New-Light Brethren," flourishing mainly on the East Coast during the late eighteenth and early nineteenth centuries. This austere group held that the bodies of the elect, chosen by God to sit with him in heaven (and amongst whom they counted themselves), were incorruptible and would be restored to full vigor upon the imminent day of judgement. Consequently, deceased members of the Brethren, sound in wind and limb, could walk out to meet God and were to be unencumbered by coffin, shroud, or grave earth. To this end, Ireland and his followers constructed chambers and crypts deep in the remote hills of Massachusetts, Vermont, and Rhode Island in which the bodies of all their members could lie upon tables made of stone while awaiting the final call to judgement. The practice was uneasily tolerated by their non-sect neighbors, and there is little record of how many decaying bodies were hidden away in desolate hillsides and valleys by the Brethren. Certainly the idea of uncoffined bodies ready to rise at a specific command had some sort of effect on the communal psyche. No further reference is made to the Brethren after 1790 although it could be assumed that they continued into the early 1800s. By modifying their teachings, they may have been absorbed into other sects of the time such as Mother Anne Lee's Shakers or some of the strains of

New Light Presbyterianism which were to move into the southern hills before the advance of Anglicanism in New England during the early nineteenth century. Their legacy, however, was to create the legend of incorruptible bodies lying in carefully constructed tombs somewhere beneath the earth, the very meat of the vampire tale.

Another factor which in all probability further molded the vampire ideal in America is what we might term "the stranger syndrome." Early settlement on the American continent was usually centered on small, tightly knit communities where everyone knew and helped each other. In fact, faced with a harsh and unyielding wilderness, such communities could take no other form if they were to survive. Any stranger who arrived in such localities was often treated with suspicion and mistrust. This latent communal hostility was also a feature of Celtic society. The Celts, who were a fiercely territorial people, considered themselves the very embodiment of the land upon which they dwelt and viewed outsiders as unwelcome interlopers bringing, as they did, unusual ways and practices. The members of many early American communities often shared a common religious and social perspective and so incoming strangers may have brought new forms of worship and different viewpoints which were not wholly welcomed by their neighbors. An example of this mistrust can be examined in the treatment of the Quakers in Puritan-dominated Salem Village, Massachusetts, before and during the witch persecutions there in 1692.

It was a fusion of many influences—the underlying Celtic beliefs coupled with Indian and African tales and those of other incoming cultures, together with the problems and the psychological nightmares of a developing society—which encouraged the growth of the vampire tale in America. As we shall see, these beliefs covered a fairly wide area of the continent and took many forms. Today, through the influence of Hollywood, it is fashionable to think of vampires inhabiting San Francisco, rainy Washington state, or thriving New Orleans, but perhaps the idea more properly belongs to the settlements of the East Coast where small, isolated rural communities closely resembled those in both Scotland and Ireland. Here, in the birthplace of the American Revolution, where the air is still thick with the smell of wood smoke and apples, lie the abandoned, weed-choked graveyards of ancient colonial families and unfortunate Revolutionary soldiers. Here, crooked, vegetation-strewn roads and lanes lead to some long-forgotten hamlet or to some empty clapboard farmhouse tucked away in a remote hollow. Decaying mansions, too, lie hidden amongst thick copses of dark trees. This is true ghost and vampire country—just as eerie as anywhere in wild Transylvania.

In 1896, the noted American anthropologist George R. Stetson drew attention to a recent vampire case near Newport, Rhode Island ("The Animistic Vampire in New England, "*American Anthropologist*). A local mason whose two brothers had died found himself the focus of vampire attacks. Although skeptical, he agreed that the bodies of his brothers should be exhumed and destroyed and, following this, the nightly attacks ceased. Stetson also found the vampire belief still rife in the hamlets and towns of Exeter, Kingstown, Foster, and East Greenwich, scattered across what is known as the South County of Rhode Island. He should not have been surprised by his findings. In Jewett City, Connecticut, in 1853 the vampiric figure of Horace Ray reputedly drank blood and "life essences" from his two surviving sons, turning them into vampires themselves. The bodies were dug up and destroyed lest they attack the surrounding community. Woodstock and Manchester (both in Vermont) suffered the attentions of vampire creatures from as early as 1790, the most famous instance being that of the Curwen family of Woodstock in 1834.

Even when the vampire belief came to the city, it held echoes of its rural origins. During the late 1890s, a terror of the undead spread through outlying parts of New York. The unease centered on a house on Green Street, Schenectady, where a peculiar man-shaped silhouette had appeared on the floor of the cellar. This was, at first, taken to be mold, but no amount of sweeping or cleansing could remove the shape. On consulting old records, it was found that the house in question had been built over the site of an old Dutch burial ground. One of the interpretations offered was that the shape on the floor was the outline of one of the restless dead or of a vampire which had been imprisoned there by a "virtuous" spell. Several people within the building complained of an inexplicable lethargy and this was, of course, attributed to the silhouette on the cellar floor. Eventually the house was destroyed, obliterating the malignant outline. The incident, however, inspired the horror writer H.P. Lovecraft to pen one of his most macabre tales, "The

Shunned House," which paralleled many aspects of the New York occurrence. Similarly, in Newark, New Jersey, streetwalkers of the 1920s were required by order of the city police department to be photographed as "vampires" or "vamps" when arrested. The idea was to indelibly mark them with the social stigma of vampirism. This would not have been effective unless there was already a widespread belief in vampires throughout the city, as Charles S. Poots pointed out in his presidential address to the Philadelphia Psychiatric Society in 1920.

And in the southern states, where Celtic folklore fused with African legend, slaves had their own tales of vampires, werewolves, and other night creatures which partly echoed those brought from Ireland, England, and Scotland. These traditions, however, also held hints of black magic and voodoo. One such tale recorded in Missouri in 1893 was told by an old black servant, Aunt Mymee, to a sick white child left in her charge. This concerned a blood-drinking, goat-footed creature—the spawn of a witch and the Devil—which crept into plantation houses to gorge itself upon the blood of those sleeping within. The being was a shapeshifter which could take on the appearance of any person it chose. Oddly, this story from the American swamplands resembles a story from the Highland uplands of Kintail, in the West of Scotland, where goat-footed fairy women drank the blood of shepherds and lonely tenant farmers by pretending to be those whom they knew.

In the South Carolina Lowcountry, below Charleston, an old black woman called Old Sue was actually tried as a vampire. A field hand no longer able to work, Sue was over one hundred years of age and was accused of sucking the blood of white children as they slept. The woman was greatly feared as a witch and enchantress, and servants concealed red peppers in their shoes to protect themselves against her sorcery. Many of them also described how they had seen the old woman traveling "faster than a bird can fly" or standing at the door of her shack with her raised arms slowly turning into batlike wings that lifted her into the air and beyond their sight. One morning after Old Sue had been seen in this condition, several small white children on a neighboring plantation were found dead. The outcome of the old woman's trial does not appear to have been recorded but there is little doubt that she would have been found guilty.

Other strange tales from the South Carolina region—many

concerning eerie, undead beings—were collected at the end of the last century by the South Carolina folklorist Genevieve Wilcox Chandler. A daughter of the plantation and fascinated by the tales of the black servants and poor "white trash" who inhabited the region, she left behind a rich treasury of folklore concerning the "boo-daddies," "haints," and "plat-eyes" which inhabited the South Carolina woods, inlets, and cemeteries. Much of her work has never been fully catalogued or collated and may yield further vampire tales.

This heady mix has fueled the American vampire belief to the present day. As late as 1981, American soldiers stationed in West Germany were put on "vampire watch." According to several newspaper reports, soldiers from the Third Infantry Division, billeted in Kitzingen, Germany, were attracted by a nineteenth-century family grave in the local cemetery. They gathered each night in the graveyard fully expecting a vampire to appear at the tomb, which was elaborately decorated with skulls, crossbones, bats, and scenes from the Old Testament. Even though the site was between seven and eight hundred miles from the Transylvanian border and there was no tradition of vampirism in the area, the soldiers were firmly convinced that a vampiric entity in the style of Count Dracula would appear. A spokesperson for the army described the location as "scary, mysterious and old—like a shrine." Its reputation spread through the U.S. Army and it was usually the first thing soldiers asked about on arriving in Kitzingen. The mayor of the town commented, "You can't stop these young fellows from believing what they want." All the men involved in this "watch" were young, sober, healthy American GIs, proof that although there is a temptation to consign it to earlier, less sophisticated times, the notion of the vampire is alive and well in America, even today.

Without a doubt, the most famous American vampire stories come from the East Coast and from one state in particular: Rhode Island. It is here that we find the celebrated Mercy Brown case. In 1892, after the mysterious deaths of her mother and sister, and the sickening of her brother, Mercy Brown died. Because the ground was frozen, she remained unburied and rumors began to circulate that Mercy was a vampire. Her father had the bodies of his three recently deceased loved ones exhumed. While the bodies of the mother and sister were badly decomposed, Mercy, dead now for several weeks, was found to be in a state of preservation when her coffin was opened. Her father had her organs removed and burned and fed to her ill brother, who died shortly after. This incident was probably another primary source of inspiration for Bram Stoker. Indeed, newspaper cuttings from *The Providence Journal* relating to the case were found amongst his papers after his death. He had collected these while on an American tour with the actor Sir Henry Irvine, for whom he acted as manager. Yet, Mercy Brown was not the first of the Rhode Island "vampire ladies"; there were earlier incarnations of the undead, one of whom was Sarah Tillinghast.

The southern region of Rhode Island, the area known as the South County, is apple-growing country. The rich fragrances of applewood smoke and cider fill the rural lanes which wind across this particular locality, adding to the pleasant, sleepy dusk which steals softly over the countryside. However, South County, Rhode Island, has not always been so idyllic.

Around the late 1770s, just following the Revolutionary War, a farmer and orchard owner named Stuckley Tillinghast was scratching out a living near the settlement of Exeter. He was not a wealthy man but he was not overly poor either; in fact, he was one of a new breed of entrepreneur who was starting to emerge in the newly independent America. His neighbors nicknamed him "Snuffy" on account of the drab, homespun coat which he always wore, the color of tobacco snuff. He was widely known and respected throughout the Exeter community as a stolid working man, level headed and not easily given to flights of fancy.

The land he owned had been one of the centers of Revolutionary fervor. From behind the low stone walls which circled his orchard, Revolutionary volunteers had fired on English soldiers as they marched into Rhode Island, and the cemeteries around were filled with volunteer dead. Nevertheless, with those dark days behind him, Snuffy Tillinghast set to work to build up his farm and his apple business. His wife, Honor, and their growing family helped, maintaining the house, working in the orchards, or tending livestock. By the end of 1787, Snuffy had built up a thriving business and Honor had presented him with eight daughters and six sons, the last child having arrived that year.

The year of 1796 promised to be a bumper apple crop. Lush fruit hung in the orchard and the trees were bowing down with the weight. The air was softly scented with the smell of apples and around the Tillinghast farm it was like breathing in cider with the suggestion of good and prosperous times ahead. All seemed well in Snuffy's world, except for the dreams. Each night during autumn, Snuffy experienced the same nightmare which caused him to toss and turn in his narrow bed and shout out in his sleep. As he told an anxious Honor: "I am walking among the trees in my orchard and it is late evening. From somewhere close by, I hear the voice of our daughter Sarah calling me. I turn and there she is, standing in the shade of a tree, but as I walk towards her, a cold wind springs up, blowing leaves and dirt before it, and it almost blinds me with its fury. I put up my hands to cover my eyes and when I bring them down again, Sarah has gone. But I can still hear her voice, calling to me, though now it seems very far away. And looking 'round me, I see that the fruit on the trees has rotted and the leaves have turned brown and are falling. I call out to Sarah but can't see her. Only her voice . . . calling, calling. A great smell of decay, like graveyard mold, rises up around me and I am nearly sick from it. I turn to see that half my orchard is dead. And all the while Sarah calls to me."

Honor reassured him that there was nothing to worry about. Sarah had just turned nineteen and was a quiet, pleasant girl, preferring stitching, sewing, and embroidery to the rough games of the other children. She would harm no one. Nevertheless, the nightmares persisted and Snuffy's fear of them grew. They terrified him so much that he went to see his local minister, the Reverend Benjamin Northup, and told the clergyman of his fears. No help was forthcoming. The Reverend Northup simply told him that he was worrying over his crops and that as soon as they were in he would enjoy proper rest again. Snuffy returned home still ill at ease. The dreams became worse. Each night, he saw and heard Sarah much more clearly, and his slumber was continually invaded by the keen stench of death and decay.

The harvest passed and, as promised, it was the best year so far. With wealth piling up in his barns, the nightmare receded to the back of Snuffy Tillinghast's mind. Maybe the Reverend Northup had been right. Besides, Snuffy had other matters concerning his daughter Sarah on his mind. She had always been a dreamy and withdrawn girl, and her father secretly wished she would take up with some beau from Exeter Village. Now almost twenty years of age, Sarah Tillinghast had become even stranger. She had taken to wandering alone in cemeteries where the Revolutionary dead lay beneath their funeral markers and where the mausoleums of local military families broke the autumnal skyline. Some of these overgrown places were said to be haunted and it was rumored that the ghosts of dead soldiers appeared there as soon as the sun began to go down. However, these tales did not seem to bother Sarah, who continued to visit the old places with an unhealthy frequency. Not that these walks did her any good for she always seemed pale and drawn upon her return and went straight to her room, closing herself in. Indeed, she had become something of a recluse, remaining in her room for long periods and refusing to join the family even for meals. Alarmed, Honor went to sit with her and it soon became apparent that Sarah was very ill. As the autumn days turned into weeks, her condition worsened. The doctor from Exeter was sent for, but he could do nothing. It was now clear that Sarah was not long for this world and before there was snow on the orchard, she was dead. Snuffy and Honor laid her in the family plot on the edge of the Exeter cemetery. The doctor's diagnosis was consumption.

Several weeks after, as Honor was making breakfast, James, the youngest of the Tillinghast boys, came down into the kitchen looking very pale. Honor offered him some fresh-brewed coffee but he refused it, complaining of a pain in his chest. His mother joked with him that he had been secretly stealing his father's unripe apples from the barn, but the boy was adamant. "It hurts just here," he told her, lifting his shirt and pointing to a spot on his chest. "Just where Sarah touched me." The name of her dead daughter prompted a mixture of emotions in Honor—alarm, uncertainty, and anguish. She grabbed the boy and held him close to her, feeling the unhealthy rattle in his thin body. "Sarah's dead," she whispered. "She's gone. It was all a dream." But James shook his head. "No, mother. She stood by my bed and hugged me, just like you are hugging me now. Only there was a pain—she was very, very cold." Imagining the boy to be delirious with some sort of fever, Honor put him to be with hot broths, balsams, and vinegar. She piled him high with blankets and shut all the windows against night chills. But, in spite of all her precautions, James continued to grow worse. And for Snuffy there was an added terror. The dreams had returned clearer than ever. Each night, his dead daughter called to him from amongst the misty apple trees and the persistent stench of decay almost made his stomach turn in his sleep. Less than a month later, he followed James's coffin to the local cemetery.

A week later, fourteen-year-old Adris took ill, as did her sister Ruth. Ruth was the eldest still living at home and was one upon whom her sister's death had made a terrible impact. Both girls told a strange and disturbing story. Adris described, "I was awakened out of my sleep around midnight by a sweet sound which seemed like bells ringing far away. It seemed such a pretty sound that I rose and went over to the window but could see nothing. The bells sounded again and I opened the window to hear them more clearly and when I looked again, Sarah was standing in the yard below. She called to me, throwing wide her arms as if to embrace me, and when I turned, she was in the room with me but I know not how she got there. She enfolded me in her arms and I felt a great coldness and a weight upon my chest." Ruth told a similar story that chilled her mother to the bone: "Sarah came to me last night and leaned over my bed. It was dark and I could not see her face but I knew that it was Sarah by the sound of her voice. She said that she missed me and that she was very cold and lonely and needed warmth. She reached down and hugged me, but she held me so tight I could not quite catch my breath."

Honor was not sure what to do. She spoke of the matter to Snuffy, but the man seemed absorbed in problems of his own. The dreams now tormented him every night and on one occasion, he had awakened out of the nightmare to see Sarah standing at the foot of the bed. She smiled at him, showing blood-flecked lips, and then was gone like a phantom. It might only have been the remnant of his dream, caught in that moment between sleep and waking, but it frightened Snuffy greatly. He was so preoccupied that he had little time to worry about his two daughters and their nighttime visions. Within a matter of months, however, both girls were dead.

A creeping dread now haunted the family, and Snuffy began to think that he and his children were cursed. Once again, he went to see the Reverend Northup and once again, he received little help. The clergyman told him that things would resolve themselves in God's own time and according to his ways and that for the moment, the family should pray together constantly. It was their best hope, he said.

Prayer did little good. Within a month, another of the Tillinghast girls—Mary—showed symptoms of the strange sickness which had carried away her sisters. Snuffy was at his wits' end. Ignoring the local doctor, he sent to West Greenwich for a physician, but it made no difference. The doctor diagnosed Mary as suffering from melancholy and recommended meat broths and fresh air. The girl was bundled out on walks and, like her sister, seemed to spend most of her time outdoors down by the Revolutionary graveyards near her home. When she came back, she went straight to her room and slept. The remedy seemed to be having no effect. She deteriorated further, now confined to her bed. And all the while, Snuffy's awful dreams continued. He slept but found no rest. Soon, Mary was dead and yet another small funeral procession wound its way from the Tillinghast home to the Exeter cemetery.

The blight that was affecting Snuffy's family was beginning to spread. Several neighbors' children were now affected by the wasting sickness, some claiming that they, too, had seen Sarah Tillinghast in their bedrooms. Some recovered but there was now terror and suspicion in the Rhode Island air. Then the strange visitations radiated even farther.

Hannah was the eldest of the Tillinghast girls. Nearly twenty-six, she had married and now lived with her husband several miles away in West Greenwich. However, with all the sickness at home, she traveled back and forth to Exeter, helping her mother about the house. On her way back home on several occasions, and usually late in the evening, Hannah was convinced that something followed her from the farm and though she turned to catch a glimpse of someone, she saw nothing. Late one night as she and her husband slept, Sarah visited her. Hannah told her anxious mother, "I awoke in the dark and there was Sarah standing by my bed just as she was in life. I could not exactly see her face but I was sure that it was she by the way that she stood. She had her arms thrown wide as if inviting me to come to her." Honor was aghast. "You must not come here anymore," she told her daughter. "Not while this evil dwells in our house." Hannah, however, told her not to be so foolish. It had been just a dream, and her mother needed her. The strain of looking after so many sick children and the horror of watching them die was proving too much for them all. Although Honor argued, Hannah would not hear of it. "The strength of our family will overcome any evil of the night," she assured her mother. She was wrong. Hannah succumbed to the "evil" before the end of 1798.

On the night following Hannah's burial, Honor herself was tormented by foul dreams. She dreamed she was in her own bedroom but the air was very heavy and stale. The stench of decay was everywhere and Honor rose and crossed to the window, throwing it open to let in some fresh air. As she did so, she looked down. There, in the yard below, stood Sarah, dressed in her grave clothes and looking up at her. Honor gave a cry and turned to flee back to bed but Sarah was already in the room. The girl opened her arms and turned to her mother with a tear-stained face. "I'm so cold, Mother," she cried in a strange high-pitched voice. "I'm so lonely. Won't you come with me? Won't you hold me as you used to?" Almost against her will, Honor crossed the room and was enfolded in her daughter's arms. She woke with a start, sensing a pain in her chest and the last traces of a foul smell fading from the room. She was terrified, but she could make no sense of the vision.

Two days later, an old friend called at the Tillinghast house. Jeremiah Dandridge, a respected old gentleman, had come to offer his condolences on Hannah's recent death. Although well known and liked in the community, Dandridge was also extremely superstitious and took stories of ghosts and monsters very seriously. Slowly and deliberately, he spoke with authority of a similar tragedy which had befallen a family in nearby Richmond. The circumstances seemed to parallel the misfortune which had stricken Snuffy's own family. According to many traditions, said Dandridge, the dead can sometimes return from the grave to persecute the living. If nothing is done, they can destroy entire families, and this was what had happened to the Richmond family. Snuffy listened to the old man's pronouncements, his face a granite mask. By the time Jeremiah Dandridge had gone, Snuffy Tillinghast had resolved what he would do.

Upstairs, Honor was keeping vigil over the steadily sickening seventeen-year-old Ezra, the youngest of the remaining Tillinghast sons. He told her what Dandridge had said and what he had decided to do. His wife, weakened by grief and lack of sleep, clutched her bosom with the sheer horror of his words and begged him to reconsider, but Snuffy's mind was made up and would not be changed. Besides, in Honor's pale and drawn face, he had glimpsed the first signs of the horror that had blighted his family. He went back downstairs and took a long drink of cider to steel himself for the task to come. Then he went out into the yard and summoned two of his strongest farmhands. Armed with ropes, shovels, mattocks, and a container of oil, they set out for the little burying ground where six of Snuffy's children had been so recently interred. In a long sheath by his side, Snuffy carried a great hunting knife with a broad blade.

On reaching the Exeter cemetery, the men set to work digging up the caskets of all the Tillinghast children who had been buried there over the previous months. As soon as it came out of the earth, each coffin was opened and its contents inspected. Some of the children were long in the ground and their corpses were badly decayed. James, for instance, was decomposed almost beyond recognition. It must have been a heart-rending task for Snuffy, but he handled it with a grim determination, his senses blunted by anguish and pain. The last to be pulled from the earth was Sarah's coffin. Cautiously, Snuffy threw wide the lid and looked down on the remains of his daughter.

Although the casket itself was starting to show signs of decay, Sarah Tillinghast lay in it as if asleep. She had been dead for just over eighteen months and still looked as fresh and uncorrupted as on the day on which she had been laid to rest. Indeed, she actually looked healthier, for a soft blush had stolen into her face and her lips looked red and moist. Her eyes were open but they saw nothing, staring glassily up at the sky and the horrified face of her father bending over her. At the sight of the unblemished cadaver, Caleb Cobb, one of the farmhands who had helped raise the casket, fell to his knees, clasped his hands in front of him, and began to pray for protection. The other hand, Matthew Young, turned away and refused to look at the uncanny vision which lay in the coffin. Both men knew—as did Snuffy himself—that what they gazed upon was not natural. Tillinghast drew the hunting knife. "Fetch the oil from the cart, boy," he instructed Caleb, his voice now a hard, flat monotone. Still mumbling his prayers, Caleb stumbled to the wagon with Matthew at his heels. Grabbing the flask, they came back to the graveside, trying hard not to look at the body within the coffin. With a single movement, Snuffy threw something to the ground at their feet. Matthew drew back, his hand to his mouth to keep himself from retching, then he fled to the cemetery gates and disgorged the contents of his stomach into the long grasses there. Caleb still stood, paralyzed with fear.

Onto a small, reddish lump of flesh, Snuffy poured the contents of the oil container and then reaching into his coat, produced a tinder and flint. Striking a flame to the tinder, he set fire to his daughter's heart, watching impassively as it turned to ashes before his tired eyes. A freshening wind blew through the tiny cemetery.

It was too late to save Ezra; the boy's condition was too far advanced and he died several days after. But the action did save Honor. The disease passed and she went on to bear her husband two more children. All of the remaining children thrived and outlived their parents. But Snuffy's terrible dream had come to pass; out of his fourteen offspring, seven had died, half his "orchard."

The Tillinghast graves can still be seen today in Exeter cemetery although they are badly overgrown and few people tend to visit them. Many of the grave markers have fallen over or have become so weathered that it is all but impossible to read them. In one corner is a small, squat headstone bearing the initials "S.T." which is thought to show Snuffy's final resting place. Another, slightly grander marker bearing the name "Stutely Tillinghast" (another form of Stuckley) is also seen, although it is suggested that this refers to one of Snuffy's descendants. There is no visible indication as to where Sarah was laid or reburied.

In 1994, a television crew, together with prominent Rhode Island folklorist Michael Ball, investigated the cemetery for the program *Encounters*. They were there to test the truth of the story of Sarah Tillinghast. Using the latest scientific equipment—special imaging scanners—the team located several graves which were unmarked and unknown. None of these graves were opened by the crew. One of the bodies, when scanned in its grave, displayed something unusual, a definite "anomaly" in the upper chest area. In the opinion of some medical experts, this could be consistent with the heart having been removed by some form of crude surgery. However, the same experts agree that this is only speculation.

Whatever the truth, the memory of Sarah Tillinghast hangs over South County, Rhode Island, like a musty shadow. It is thought that this regional folktale provided the inspiration for some of the work of H.P. Lovecraft, who set many of his terrifying tales in the

Massachusetts/Rhode Island area. In 1988 playwright David F. Eliet scripted a production based on the eerie episode which was staged at the prestigious Trinity Conservatory in Providence. Although not historically accurate, it was evocative of the period and was very well received, playing to capacity crowds. An interest in vampires, it would appear, is alive and well in Rhode Island.

The case of Sarah Tillinghast was only the first of a number of vampire occurrences in Rhode Island stretching from the late eighteenth century to the beginning of the twentieth. A number of "vampire ladies" have become associated with the state: Juliet Rose, Nancy Young, and Mercy Brown. In each instance, it is thought that these vampires were probably victims of tuberculosis, which raged through the region all through the 1800s. The symptoms of this condition—a gradual wasting away coupled with a ghastly ivory-like pallor of the skin—are suggestive of the commonly held view of the vampire. Furthermore, prolonged bouts of coughing often produced flecks of blood around the edges of the mouth which seemed to suggest that the sufferer had been drinking blood. In rural nineteenth-century Rhode Island, the disease had been barely diagnosed and no cure had been found for it. It was but a small step in the regional mind to associate the tubercular victim with the blood-drinking fiend of mythology, and the attributes of the stories—the draining of blood, the attack on the immediate family, the contact through dreams and visions—all suggest Celtic lore. Further, the impression of the dead world from which Sarah Tillinghast called to her father—the misty landscape and the rotting, wasted trees—may also suggest the Celtic otherworld. Given such immigrant influences, it is little wonder that the early people of Rhode Island used the vampire motif to explain the advance of the terrible diseases which afflicted them.

For many of the more "sophisticated" city-based newspapers and magazines, all this was merely foolishness. "Dead Bodies Dug Up and Their Hearts Burned to Prevent Disease: Strange Superstition of Long Ago," trumpeted the *New York World* in 1896, conveniently forgetting the fact that New York had its own vampire scares. But in the absence of proper medical knowledge and given their immigrant backgrounds, this explanation was as good as any other for a rural populace. Add to this the fact that the full horrors of the Revolutionary War were not all that far behind them. Indeed, they were well within the living memory of many Rhode Islanders. Celtic tradition held that many warriors and those who were associated with them did not actually die but passed beyond into the otherworld. Many local people might have remembered seeing half-dead soldiers covered in blood writhing along the Rhode Island roadsides and this, coupled with the notion of the otherworld, could have exercised a powerful influence on the colonial mind. Sarah Tillinghast spent her days wandering in the old Revolutionary cemeteries, which must surely have strengthened the psychological connection.

As if proof were needed of the continuance of vampire belief in rural Rhode Island itself, we have only to look at a "constructed" vampire, the unfortunate Nelly Vaughn, who died in 1889 at nineteen years old. It was the words on Nelly's tombstone, in a little graveyard in West Greenwich, which inspired the belief. The inscription "I am waiting and watching for you" may have been wholly innocent—a word to a loved one or a message of pious hope and comfort to a grieving family—but many years after her death, her name was connected with Rhode Island vampire tradition. In 1967, a Coventry High School teacher informed his class that there was a vampire buried in the cemetery just off Route 102. One of the pupils may have been familiar with the inscription on Nelly Vaughn's headstone and the connection was made. Similarities were traced between Nelly and the other Rhode Island vampires. Her lingering sickness and an early death fit in with the tradition. Nelly was classed as one of the undead. Suddenly, other "unnatural" facts began to emerge concerning her gravesite. The headstone often leaned in a peculiar fashion as if someone or something were moving about underneath it and, more importantly, no vegetation would grow on the grave itself. Investigators at the site saw things, usually an attractive young woman, or else were subject to pokings and proddings by invisible hands or the disappearance of small and personalized objects. The stone with its mysterious inscription became a focus for vampire hunters and witches and eventually became so vandalized and broken that, in the early 1990s, it had to be removed altogether. Perhaps now, poor Nelly Vaughn can finally disentangle herself from the vampire belief which haunts Rhode Island to this very day.

Virginia

Bouncing Bertha

For the early Celts, spirits were everywhere. They were disembodied and invisible but their impact could be enormous. They could bring disease, misfortune, or even death to those who crossed them or to those whom they disliked. Moreover, they could use physical violence against mortals, sometimes for no apparent reason. Their victims might be women or children working in the kitchen or playing in the yard whom they tormented perhaps simply for sport. More often they were young girls. Initially these "pranks" (nipping, striking, tripping) were put down to the "play" of the fairy people—and this was a popular Celtic explanation. They were simply teasing the mortals they tormented—that was the fairy way. Later, however, a more sinister explanation was invoked. These forces were the spirits of the dead who were taking revenge upon or becoming obsessed with the living. Some even believed that they were demons striking out against God's people and trying to entrap the souls of the righteous. They were viewed with both suspicion and fear and were, in time, sometimes equated with witches and warlocks.

The word "poltergeist" became equated with these disembodied forces, particularly those which displayed violent or aggressive tendencies. The word is a German one, derived out of Teutonic folklore, and means "noisy or boisterous ghost." Poltergeists often threw crockery about the room, pulled burning peat or coal from the fire, and generally disrupted things around the house, just as the Celtic fairies and sprites had done years before. As with the fairies, they fastened attentions on certain members of a family, particularly the females. Small, prepubescent, or adolescent girls were usually their targets. This time, however, they were not mischievous "wee folk" but rather diabolical entities who behaved in such a fashion for some sinister purpose. While no explanation was given for the

222   MYSTERIOUS CELTIC MYTHOLOGY IN AMERICAN FOLKLORE

poltergeist activity, their supernatural motives were clearly dubious. But, unlike many fairies, they could be subject to exorcism and the influence of a priest. Like any other ghost they could be banished back into the afterlife from whence they had come. Yet, in many areas, few priests ventured anywhere near them. Maybe it was out of a genuine fear of the supernatural or maybe it was because such spirits had a fearsome reputation for violence.

In many instances, poltergeist activity seems to have taken place for an extended period and then abruptly ceased. The fear they engendered in the Celtic countryside can be attributed, in part, to the fact that no face could be put to them for they were invisible and they seemed erratic in their ways. Some of them could speak but what they said made little or no sense. Many simply communicated by a system of raps or other noises. Although uncommon, it was even sometimes possible to hold a conversation with one of them. Mostly, however, they made their presence known by violent means and would ignore all attempts at communication.

Throughout the Celtic world, these disembodied spirits tormented ordinary people, despite the efforts of the church to subdue them. They rapped and threw things; they disturbed households with strange noises; they even spoke disconcertingly from the empty air. For the Celtic peoples these were the voices of the otherworld which were trying to do them harm. In the North of Ireland, particularly, there are a number of well-documented instances of their activity around the late nineteenth and early twentieth centuries. These include sites at Larne, County Antrim (1866), Cookstown, County Tyrone (1876), Derrygonnelly, County Fermanagh (1877), and the famous "Cooneen Ghost," also in County Fermanagh (1911). There were also the earlier and celebrated Scottish poltergeists of Glenluce—"the Devil of Glenluce"—in 1654 and Rerrick in Galloway in 1695.

The best documented of all Celtic poltergeists is, arguably, the Articlave poltergeist from the village of the same name in North Derry, Ireland, which commenced its activities in 1934. It is probably so well recorded because of the efforts of a prominent Irish journalist, J.P. Donaghy (or Donnelly) of the *Irish Times* in Dublin, who had been sent by his editor to check out the story. Tales of the poltergeist's activities had become so famous throughout Ireland that they were starting to appear in Dublin magazines, and the

Times editor was intrigued as to whether there was any substance to them. So, Donaghy was dispatched north.

According to the stories, a family in Articlave village had become the center of poltergeist activity. The site upon which their house had been built was that of an ancient Celtic rath, or fairy fort, and the activity was supposedly related to that. In all his reports, Donaghy consistently refused to give the name of the family involved as he had no wish to cause them further distress, but their descendents still live in the Articlave area. The only family member he did name was the daughter of the household since she was the center of the bizarre activity, but he simply calls her by the pseudonym "Laura."

The invisible spirit, it was said, was making life unbearable for a small tenant farmer, his wife, and family of two sons and a daughter. Household articles had moved about the rooms of their own accord and dishware, cloths, and glass lamp globes were tossed about the place with an almost reckless abandon under the very eyes of the family. The girl, then aged ten years, was flung out of bed during the night, injuring herself, and was repeatedly troubled by ghostly knockings and unseen objects like sharp needles being stuck into her, some even leaving painful welts and marks on her skin. The family, good church-going Presbyterians, were at their wits' end. A minister had been summoned to exorcise the phantom but without much success.

The reporter arrived in Articlave just as a storm was gathering over the nearby mountains. The clouds seemed to be lowering in the sky and a strong wind was rising, setting the scene for a ghostly encounter. Donaghy found the farmhouse by following a rutted track on the very edge of the village, and this led him to a solid-looking two-story dwelling standing by itself on a desolate piece of land well away from the main road. A number of people had gathered in the kitchen and it appeared that since the disturbances had begun neighbors had stayed with the family each night in order to keep vigil. Donaghy later admitted that he was surprised by the nature of the people who were gathered in the lonely farmhouse. They were, he said, solid Presbyterian country people, not much given to flights of imagination or fancy. Laura, a shy, intelligent girl no different from any other child her age, was there too. If there was a practical joke being played here, in Donaghy's opinion, she was not the one who was playing it. The kitchen, as he describes it, was lit by a single oil lamp which cast long and menacing shadows all around the room. The talk was very general: crops, the weather, anything but the supernatural.

About midnight, three "substantial men" from the surrounding countryside arrived to take over the vigil and one by one, the neighbors began to drift away to their own homes. Laura had long since gone to bed. As the hours drifted past, the conversation waned. Outside, the wind howled about the chimneys of the farmhouse and rain beat against the windowpanes as the storm which had been threatening all day finally broke. Donaghy and his companions began to doze in the heat of the peats from the fire but were wakened from time to time by the whimpering of a collie dog from under the table which moved and growled in its sleep. The animal seemed to be badly troubled by disturbing dreams. Now and again, it would suddenly start up as if it were expecting the kitchen door to open and somebody to come in. Then it would sink back into its troubled sleep. At one time, Donaghy imagined that the door did, in fact, open slightly as if somebody were peering momentarily into the kitchen, but there was nobody and he admits that he might have been dreaming. More probably, the dog's reactions were due to the storm outside.

Around 5 A.M. the men were awakened by a noise from the stairs, signaling that something was starting to happen in Laura's bedroom. Donaghy followed the others up the narrow staircase and into the room. Laura lay in a small wooden bed pushed tightly against the stone outer wall of the house, just below the room's only window. The bedroom was lit by two candles. Her mother sat at the head of the bed looking anxiously towards the door and for a moment, Donaghy could distinguish nothing unusual in the tableau in front of him. Then he heard the sounds.

There was a low, clear knocking in the candlelit room. It was exactly like knuckles being rapped against woodwork or the sound of a carpenter's hammer tap-tapping against a piece of planking. It seemed to be coming from somewhere close to the bottom of the child's bed—from the very bottom of it, Donaghy thought—and from the stone wall. The sound was a regular one, coming in both single and double taps, sometimes loud but at other times falling away again. Sometimes it maintained a steady, regular rhythm; at other times it increased in speed, becoming an angry and impatient hammering. Donaghy looked around the room for something wooden which could have been used to make the sound but he could see nothing. The tapping continued more rapidly this time, and the nerves of the people in the room were clearly being strained. This was something far beyond the usual experiences of those who were present and it was frightening them badly. The candles flickered and threatened to go out and a very cold sensation was experienced by everybody in the room, including the hard-bitten Dublin reporter. Looking around, Donaghy tried to locate the exact source of the sounds. At one stage he thought they came from a spot about two feet above the floor, then they seemed to come from a place high up in the wall. He put his hand to the stone but could feel no vibration. Nor did the sound appear to stay still but traveled around the room, sometimes seeming to come from behind him, at other times from the wall in front of him. In search of a logical explanation for the occurrence, Donaghy suggested that it might be caused by something either inside or outside the house—a bird on the windowsill or the branch of a tree tapping against the glass of the window. He looked outside. Again there was nothing. No bird flew away at his movement and there was no tree close enough to the house for its branches to reach the window.

One of the church elders who was present began to ask the poltergeist some questions which it answered with a simple rapping code. It was asked personal details regarding those who stood around the bed—things which Laura could not possibly have known—to which it accurately responded. For example, it was asked by Donaghy to pick his birthday from a list of dates. He asked the spirit directly and no one else in the room knew the correct answer as he was a stranger in the district. Once again, the poltergeist answered correctly. It would not, however, answer questions about itself and these were simply greeted with long periods of absolute silence. All the while, the candles in the room guttered and flickered and seemed on the verge of extinction at any moment, even though there was no draft. From time to time, they would flare into an inexplicable brilliance and this was regarded by the church elders as evidence that the spirit was passing them. They gave, reported Donaghy, an unearthly glow to the grim faces of those gathered around the bed.

Sometime just before daylight, the sounds in the room ceased and Laura fell into a deep and seemingly restful sleep. Donaghy, quite shaken by his experience, decided to take his leave. Shortly after that particular night, the weird rappings and other phenomena stopped altogether and peace returned to the farmhouse at the end of the track. No explanation was ever found for the ghostly sounds and movements, and the case remains unsolved. Laura died an elderly lady in Articlave a number of years ago, but her offspring still live in the village and none of them will talk about the strange happenings. The house itself has long been demolished. Donaghy never went back to Articlave but as he said long after, "I have never forgotten the experience." In contrast, in the village today there are only a few who claim to remember the poltergeist and fewer still who will talk about it.

The well-documented case of the Articlave poltergeist raised great interest in the world of supernatural phenomena around the 1940s, but the attraction of the spirit world existed long before that. Indeed, it had traveled to the New World where it had taken root amongst the country people of both America and Canada. The Indians there had their own tales of violent and mischievous invisible spirits, and the tales of poltergeists readily mingled with these. Settler legends, such as the famous and much-written-about Bell Witch of Tennessee (a poltergeist which gave its name as Old Kate Batts and was associated with witchcraft) and the case of Esther Cox in Amherst, Nova Scotia, have greatly added to New World ghost lore. These and other old tales were passed down by word of mouth around the settler campfires and kept the notion of disembodied forces alive in the American mind. Many of these old stories have been passed over by rural history and, like the Articlave poltergeist, are all but forgotten.

One of the best recorded of such legends comes from the Blue Ridge Mountains of Virginia and, as with the Articlave case, concerns a young girl. In this instance, however, we do know her true identity. In an old photograph hung on a schoolhouse wall, the pretty face of nine-year-old Bertha Sybert smiles sweetly from the front row of the class at Sand Springs, Virginia. Although her classmates are looking anxiously around them, waiting for the photography session to end, Bertha is a photographic "natural" and easily the prettiest girl of the group. Her smiling, freckled face and soft features, framed by waves of curling brown hair, must have made her a photographer's dream. And from the photograph, she clearly knew how to pose for the camera. This is unsurprising because two years earlier, in 1938, cameramen from all over America were beating a path to the door of her home high in the Blue Ridge Mountains.

Also in the photograph, Raymond Miner stands with his hands on his hips. A bemused smile plays about his lips as he looks earnestly towards the camera. He and Bertha Sybert would be forever linked when something which "no mortal person had control over" came from the world beyond. Miner, retired from his job as a manager with Powell Valley Electric, still lives in Lee County, Virginia, where, according to reports, he is a steady, down-to-earth soul with a ready wit and a good nature. Related by marriage to the Sybert family, Raymond, his father, and his uncle were among the first to see the mysterious things which affected Bertha at her home up on Wallens Creek.

Bertha Sybert's bedroom was as plain and poor as Laura's had been in Articlave. Her parents were simple mountain folk and the bedroom of the cabin had been covered in newspaper. Close to the wall was the unremarkable bed in which Bertha slept. In fact, to the casual visitor, the whole room was unremarkable. But as winter 1938 drew on something remarkable happened in that room and to that unremarkable bed. In the cold, chilly nights, the bed began to shake. At first it was just a tremor running the length of the bed, but gradually it began to increase as though the whole area were shaking in a kind of earthquake which seemed confined to the bed. So violent did it become that Bertha herself was thrown from side to side and sometimes onto the cabin floor. She appeared to have no control over what became known as "the bouncing bed."

Among the first people to witness the phenomenon were her relatives by marriage, the Miners, who were visiting their kinsfolk shortly after the shaking started. Raymond gave an account of events to one of the local newspapers. It started off, he said, with a low, whispery noise like a rat gnawing at a piece of wood somewhere in the room. Originally, it sounded as if it were coming from where the leg of the headboard sat on the floor, but then it would move. Seemingly, it would move up the cabin wall until it reached Bertha's head as she lay between the covers. Then the noise would increase in volume and ferocity. It was, said Raymond Miner, similar to the sound made when hitting a washboard with a block of wood. You could, he went on, put your hand against the bed and feel the vibration because the noise level was so high. More activity would then begin. Gently and almost imperceptibly at first, the bed would begin to shake, then it would become faster and faster and more and more violent. The bed would almost appear to dance on its wooden legs, and all the while Bertha bounced within it. In fact, so strong was the phantom that four large, strong men sitting on the four corners of the bed could not hold it still. It reared and bucked like an unbroken horse, sometimes throwing Bertha to the ground. She lay perfectly still in bed—doubtless rigid with terror—so that it was impossible for her to contribute to what was happening.

Gradually word leaked out about what was happening in the Sybert house as soon as Bertha went to bed. Besides the shaking of the bed, a number of other terrifying things were taking place. According to local folklore, a withered hand with long and ragged nails appeared in the air just above Bertha's head and seemed to make a grab for the terrified girl before vanishing again. Another story told how the cheap wallpaper began to peel of its own accord from the bedroom walls as the bed shook. A woman who lived with the Syberts told how the interior doors had been thrown wide enough to knock the wooden hinges to the floor, how drawers had flown out of sideboards and dressers, and how windows had rattled as though some unseen force were pushing against them. Doors leading outside, she went on, had rattled so much that they had to be secured with locks, but even so they had mysteriously opened by themselves. One witness told of how the sheets on Bertha's bed had seemed to withdraw from the touch of strangers and formed themselves into an almost human shape, standing up like a blind white thing at the foot of the bed and driving them all from the room. A number of people complained of the intense cold and of being pricked and pinched by some unseen agency as they watched Bertha bounce. Rank and stomach-turning stenches filled the bedroom and several people claimed to have heard many voices crying and wailing in unison but always seemingly far away. Raymond Miner told of how a chair on which Bertha usually sat was propelled around the cabin of its own volition. It appeared to "walk," he said. During the occurrences, Bertha herself never clearly saw her tormentor. At times she would talk of a "white, fizzy thing" which sometimes was in the room and which sometimes came to the end of her bed and rocked it. Every time she tried to sleep, this thing (which looked as if it might have a human shape) pulled her hair in the most alarming manner.

By this time, the press was starting to take an interest in the girl whom they now called "Bouncing Bertha." Reporters made their way into the Blue Ridge Mountains to see if they could track her down or get some sort of explanation for the queer phenomena. Most of them were turned away, but a couple of photographers did get pictures, which appeared in all sorts of American newspapers. This generated interest outside the Blue Ridge, and Grandma Jane Sybert began to allow reporters into the little cabin she had occupied since 1888. However, Bertha's father, Robert Sybert, was not so sure that all this interest in his daughter was completely healthy. After a few months of winter's mud trailed through the cabin by pressmen and general sightseers, he decided to put a stop to it. Bertha moved away from Wallens Creek to live with her distant kinsmen, the Miners.

"We thought that she'd be safe over in our house," said Raymond Miner, "but she wasn't." The "thing" followed her from the cabin and, although she had a new bed, it too began to vibrate. In order to drive away the spirit, Raymond Miner began to play hymns on his guitar as soon as Bertha went to bed. No evil entity, he reasoned, could withstand holy music. However, it made little difference; if anything, it made things worse. As soon as the music started, the bed began to vibrate even faster, terrifying Bertha all the more. Raymond then changed his music to ragtime and, according to Robert Sybert, "Bertha and the bed bounced faster then ever."

Bertha's grandmother, Jane Sybert, added to the speculation and mystery by making suggestions of "witchery." She drew attention to a long-forgotten family dispute in which "conjure folks" up in the mountains had been involved and stated that some kind of "mountainy magic" was to blame. Bertha, she declared, could be the victim of "bad blood" between various branches of the family. There were even references to Indian legends of strange forces that had at one time made their home in the Blue Ridge and, of course, there were tales of spirits and powers which the early settlers had brought with them from the Celtic West. The press were intrigued and the old woman was repeatedly interviewed at the door of her cabin, even though Bertha was no longer there.

Bertha was becoming something of a celebrity. Thanks to the newspaper coverage, her name was well known far beyond Virginia and was a familiar subject of discussion on many radio programs, including religious ones. When she left her home in 1939 in order to see her first movie at the theater in Jonesville, she drew more stares from the crowd than the film itself. In fact, the theater manager, with an eye to business, had her take the stage and recite an eight-line poem. Letters poured in from all over the United States. A promoter named Virgil Wacks escorted Bertha to Pineville, Kentucky, to make an appearance in a vaudeville show where she tried, unsuccessfully, to re-create the bouncing phenomenon. The spirit, it appeared, would not oblige. A skeptical press, which had previously supported her, now grew wary.

As recorded by the *Spartanburg Herald* and the *American Weekly,* two academics from the University of Tennessee decided to investigate. Dr. George Haslerud and Dr. Axel Brett, both leaders in the fields of philosophy and psychology, visited the cabin in the Blue Ridge Mountains to make their own investigations into the alleged bouncing. While they were there, it was said, breakfast sausages jumped around the plates and a tureen of soup inexplicably overturned. At first, Dr. Brett described their findings as "peculiar" but refused to offer any further comment or clarification. Finally, both men bowed to the interests of unyielding science and stated that they had observed "noticeable bodily contractions" during Bertha's bouncing. The phenomenon, they deduced, was caused— either voluntarily or involuntarily—by the girl herself. There was no spirit and certainly no poltergeist—at least that is what science said. Mountain folk described the findings as unrealistic, but they were enough to satisfy the wider world. Press interest in Bertha began to wane.

Tourists and curiosity seekers, however, still continued to visit the Blue Ridge in the hopes of meeting her or of even seeing the poltergeist activity for themselves. Bertha also attracted the attention of promoters and entertainment agents who were prepared to market the bouncing as an acrobatic skill. This suggested that many people now thought the phenomenon had little to do with the supernatural but was quite probably self-manufactured. Everyone was turned away. As Miner puts it, the Syberts were "simple mountain people who wouldn't dream up such a far-fetched story for money!"

Finally, after three or four months, the interest died away and even the tourists ceased to come around the home. Curiously and coincidentally, the bouncing phenomenon gradually stopped and the spirits left Berth alone once more.

Whatever terrors she had experienced, she pushed to the back of her mind and gradually her name died away on everyone's lips. Bertha Sybert grew to womanhood, presumably with no further contact with the spirit world, married, and raised a family. For the latter years of her life, she was plagued with and virtually crippled by arthritis. She died in Surry County, Virginia, in 1986, aged fifty-seven. She had not spoken of the queer incidents of her childhood for many years.

But the legend lingers on in the cabins of Lee County. Folks in the Blue Ridge still speculate about what really affected "Bouncing Bertha" back in 1938. Although many know of the academics' report, most mountain folks dismiss it. Raymond Miner is amongst those who knows what he saw. How, he asks, could a sixty-pound child move both herself and a heavy bed around a bedroom? His only theory was that Bertha had attracted something from the world beyond.

Was Bertha Sybert the victim of some ancient power that had been brought to the Blue Ridge Mountains by settlers from Celtic lands? Had she activated some pre-human power that had lain dormant in the ancient mountains? Was it the spirit of someone long dead? Or was it "witchy magic" from the Celtic homelands, as Grandma Jane Sybert had hinted? Maybe the only one who truly knows is the pretty, chestnut-haired little girl who smiles down so enigmatically from the fading photograph hanging on the schoolhouse wall.

The Tidewater Country Gray Man

To the Celts, the sea was just as mysterious, terrifying, and awe-inspiring as anything they encountered on land. It was endless, eternal, and extremely deadly. The ancient peoples were drawn by its steady motion—the coming and going of its tides; the rise and fall of its waves—and often gave it supernatural attributes. It was the home of primal gods, perhaps the earliest deities mankind knew. Although sea deities did not play a significant role in early Celtic mythology in the same way they did in those of other cultures (the Celts, it must be remembered, were not primarily a sea-faring people), beliefs, customs, and maritime-related entities began to appear in Celtic folklore.

Some of the aquatic deities that inhabited the ocean were little more than extensions of those lake- and river-dwelling spirits the Celts already knew and worshipped. It is possible that, in the Celtic mind, these had grown in both power and fearsome aspect to rule the movements of the ocean. Water, throughout the ancient world, was considered a regenerative force—healing and cleansing were closely related in the ancient mind—and so whatever gods dwelt in the sea were credited with immense supernatural powers extending far beyond the confines of the ocean and often even into the sky above. This gave them power over clouds and winds and other elements of the weather. The sight of storms along the horizon would have been enough reason to link one deity with both the sea and sky. Early Celts left offerings and devotional presents at the edges of lakes and rivers to placate the spirits of the waters there, and the coastal Celts presumably did the same for the mightier deities of the ocean. It is highly probable that large offerings were left on beaches to be washed away by the outgoing tide so that no trace of them would remain.

233

Other Celts might well have been puzzled by the bodies of unknown sea creatures which washed up along their beaches from time to time. Monsters such as giant squids, porpoises, and even whales found their way to the coasts of Celtic countries to be gaped at by the astonished inhabitants there. To the coastal peoples, they must have seemed like creatures from another realm—possibly the kingdom of the gods. Along northern coastlines, too, great colonies of seals had made their home amongst the rocks and there was speculation as to the true nature of these animals and their relationship to the sea from which they came. One answer was that they were the inhabitants of a submerged kingdom who took animal form while on land. In Celtic eyes, then, the sea and those creatures that dwelt in it continued to remain things of mystery and wonder which formed a peripheral but nonetheless important part of their folklore and belief.

The problem when considering Celtic sea and water gods is that they are not always instantly recognizable as aquatic divinities. Often their connection with the ocean is a secondary one and is coupled with another function, such as healing. In Roman and Greek mythology, Neptune, or Poseidon, is undisputedly the lord of the sea, but in Celtic iconography this status may be disguised or sublimated, and this makes identification extremely difficult. There are, however, some generalized sea deities such as Lir, who appears in the twelfth-century Irish *Book of Invasions* and later is coupled with another ocean god Manannan—or Manandan—to form Manannan mac Lir, a Manx sea god (from whom the three-legged symbol of the Isle of Man is derived) and one of the lords of the otherworld. Like many other ocean deities, Manannan took on some of the aspects of the sea itself. This was not unusual since Celtic rulers were supposed to be the very embodiment of the lands over which they presided. Manannan was identified with the wild, turbulent, and stormy sea. His steed was Enbharr—the word for "water foam"—and he was supposed to churn up high swells as he thundered past. For this reason Manannan was known as "the Rider on the Maned Sea."

Another such deity was known simply as Shony. He protected fishermen and ensured good catches when the fleets were out. This entity remains rather mysterious and there are no consistent descriptions concerning him. Accounts vary, stating that he is a great serpent, a kind of sea horse, or a mighty octopus-like being. One thing is known, however: he was extremely fond of whiskey and beer. On certain days of the year, Celtic peoples such as those who lived on the island of Islay, near the Mull of Kintyre in Scotland, would pour kegs of beer into the ocean as a libation to their god. According to Martin Martin in his *Description of the Western Isles* (published in 1716), a cup of ale was offered to the god "at Hallowtide," not for a yield of fish but for enough seaweed to manure the land. There are people still alive who can remember this ceremony being performed on both Islay and Lewis. If such an offering were not given, the fishing would not be good and Shony would ravage the coastline with fearsome and continuous storms. When they came to the West of Scotland and the Isles, the Vikings feared and respected Shony, as did the Normans, who called him Shellicoat. Today, some in the Western Isles still make curious protective signs in the air with their right hands when they mention his name—proof that Shony's influence may stretch beyond the confines of the ocean.

Many other sea-related beings cannot be identified as gods in the conventional sense. In early Brittany, a supernatural being known as Yan-An-Ord, or John of the Dunes, lived in virtually inaccessible places along the Breton coast, usually amongst the sandy dunes. Whether he was a spirit, fairy, or ghost is unknown for he was seldom seen but frequently heard. Sometimes he was described as a giant with a loud and extremely harsh, booming cry; at other times, a dwarf with a high birdlike call. His voice was also reported as being clear and ringing, like a church bell, coming from somewhere amid the dunes. At other times he is seen by those at sea and is represented as an old man dressed in oilskins and leaning on the single oar of a rowboat. Generally beneficent, he was also believed to possess an element of trickery. At intervals, he issues long and piercing calls that could either warn fog-bound sailors they were venturing too close to land or else lure curious mariners landward to dash them on the rocks. His weird cries may have been calculated to frighten fishermen from the rocks nearby and so protect the shoals of fish that sometimes sheltered there. His wails were also said to call home those who had wandered too far along the sands. Most of his eerie shouts were to be heard at twilight, mysterious and chilling in their tone and frequently frightening everyone who heard them. At other times, he was to be seen on the cliff tops, waving a small lantern, trying to warn away sailors from sailing too close in the dark. This may suggest his origins for the old Celtic Amorican (Breton) saints would during the hours of darkness walk along stretches of the coast where they had set up their oratories. They would sometimes shake little bells of wrought iron or else wave lights and call out to sailors venturing too close to the shore.

Yan-An-Ord is usually a help to mariners, but the same cannot be said of another Celtic sea entity, the Marie Morrigan. She is said to have been the offspring of the ruler of the sunken land of Ys (or Ker Ys), off Cornwall. Occasionally, she would appear amid the rocks, waving a lantern (like Yan-An-Ord), her sole ambition to lure sailors onto rocks and sandbars, particularly those around the Lizard, so that she could snatch their souls as they drowned. Her main hunting ground was the Bay of Douarnenez, Finisterre, which reputedly had been one of the greatest centers of learning in France during former times. During the Dark Ages, the university there was engulfed by a fearful but unrecorded cataclysm. The Marie Morrigan was the only survivor, but her wits were gone and she only rejoiced in destruction. Whether she is, in fact, a ghost, a mermaid, or an evil sea being is unclear.

Allied to the above are the stories concerning merfolk, who were counted by the Celts as the offspring of Manannan mac Lir. For the ancient peoples of the Celtic world, these were extensions of the sea deity himself. They resembled mortals in practically every detail and could usually live on land as well as in the ocean, being almost indistinguishable from land dwellers. This allowed them to marry and mate with those on the land who took their fancy. There was, however, an important difference between the land dwellers and the people of the sea. When the merfolk traveled through the freezing ocean currents, they wore sealskin cloaks for protection against the cold. This gave them the appearance of gray seals as they sat on the shore. They had to discard these coverings in order to go about unobserved amongst mortals but could not return to the icy water without them. If a mortal were to find such a cloak then the merperson (usually a mermaid) would be enslaved until the garment was returned. Both Irish and Scottish folklore is filled with tales of fishermen who fell in love with mermaids and who contrived to steal their cloaks so that they could be married. Many

Celtic families—such as the Irish O'Flahertys and O'Sullivans of Kerry and the MacNamaras of County Clare, together with a number of coastal Scottish and Breton families—trace their ancestry back to unions between mortals and merfolk.

However, many of the mermen and -women were motivated by evil intent. Some mermaids deliberately took up with mortal men in order to lure them away to the watery depths and, like the Marie Morrigan, claim their souls as they drowned. The celebrated Cornish story of the mermaid of Zennor, who lured away the handsome young Matthew Trewella into Pendour Cove, is an example of this. It was even considered inadvisable to fall asleep on the beach, unless it was within the sound of church bells, in case one would be carried off and drowned by malignant merfolk.

While demonstrating supernatural qualities and powers, Yan-An-Ord, the Marie Morrigan, and the malevolent merfolk could hardly be described as sea gods but rather as supernatural sea beings. This was a distinction of the Celtic belief system concerning such entities. The same could also be said of the Fir Liath, or Gray Man, who haunted the coasts of Ireland, Scotland, and the Western Isles. In many respects, the Fir Liath was simply the embodiment of a weather aspect—that of thick fog. Fog was especially feared by mariners: it cloaked rocks and shoals and resulted in the deaths of as many sailors as any storm which raged along the coast. It seemed only natural that it should take on a personality which would invoke terror, mystery, and awe. The Gray Man was a voiceless creature who took a perverse delight in human misery and misfortune. He is sometimes described as a grim, bearded giant glimpsed far out to sea or in the sky overhead towards the end of the day—much as he appears in the Bram Stoker tale "Under the Sunset." At other times, he is a shapeless, drifting entity moving lazily from sea to shore. He was always dressed in gray—hence his name—wearing a great cloak which he swirled around him, blanketing the rest of the world. He masked the rocks on which ships were dashed to pieces and, if on the land, the cliff tops or marshes into which people might blunder, either falling or sinking to their deaths, a morbid consequence in which he took delight. His touch could turn stored potatoes black or sour the milk, and he was not slow to visit these misfortunes on a household. All mariners feared his attention and took great pains to avoid him. A holy medal built into the prow of a fishing boat would protect it from being lost under the Gray Man's cloak, as would sprinkling its decks with holy water or having the vessel blessed by a priest. Geographical features such as the Gray Man's Path, a long piece of stone stretching over a deep gully near the town of Ballycastle in North Antrim, have been named after him, and though some locals may say that it was named after an old storm god, the way has more to do with the sinister mists which still plague that particular stretch of coast.

These ancient superstitions were surely in the minds of the American colonists as they settled along the coastal regions of the continent. The areas in which they established their towns must, in some ways, have resembled the places they had left behind, and like those locations, the American coasts were buffeted by storms and heavy seas and suffered from damp and clinging mists. They personified these folkloric elements they remembered from their own countries, but the early settlers did not wish to identify these supernatural entities with actual gods—since that might identify them with the pagan Indians—so the nature of the beings was changed. Rather, they were described as "ghosts," the spirits of the dead, and elaborate tales were concocted to explain them, a few, perhaps, with some basis in reality. On the coasts of Massachusetts, strange lights believed to be the ghost of an ancient mariner who had been shipwrecked there were said to flicker on Shawmut Heights near Boston to warn ships away from danger, while near Oswego, New York, an eerie voice called out in the fashion of the Breton Yan-An-Ord. Another of the former "deities" which traversed the Atlantic was the Gray Man, only now he takes the form of a phantom haunting the Tidewater Country around South Carolina.

Perhaps no area in America is as beautiful and as mysterious as the Tidewater Country along the coasts of the Carolinas. The area is intercut with rivers such as the Great Pee Dee and the Waccamaw and eerie swamps like the Great South Carolina which lie shrouded in mist, seeming to harbor dark secrets. And beyond the shoreline itself lie tiny, shrouded islands, some of which can be approached at low tide. Others, cut off from the land by swamps and tidal races, can be approached only by boat. Sandy Island, Pawleys Island, and Pine Island are perhaps among the best known. Each has its own particular legend because in times past these islands were the haunts of smugglers and pirates, rogues such as Capt. Stede Bonnet, "the gentleman pirate"; Anne Bonney, the notorious woman sea rover; and even, say some, the ferocious Blackbeard. There are tales here, amongst the sandy islands, of pirate ghosts and hidden treasure. Similarly fearful legends exist concerning runaway slaves who fled into the swamps never to been seen again. Some undoubtedly died in the quicksand, but others are said to have mated with strange creatures to produce hideous offspring which might still lurk deep in the marshlands. Here, too, are the renowned plantations, locked away behind tightly closed gates in their creeper-covered posts, many dating from the arrival of great English families in the 1700s. Such places mark the sites of the former rice kingdoms of the Waccamaw and the last of the faded gentry who lived along the Santee River. It is amongst these that ghosts, old ways, and unidentified beings seem to proliferate.

The beautiful Litchfield Plantation, for example, was founded by the Simon family from Litchfield, England, in the early 1700s. The estate was some two thousand acres and the plantation house was built circa 1740. The estate was divided around 1794, one half called Willowbrook and still owned by the Simons and the other taking the name of Litchfield, the property of the Tuckers of Georgetown, newly arrived from Bermuda. The Tuckers were to prosper on their new plantation on Waccamaw Neck. By 1850, the plantation produced almost one million tons of rice per year with freighters sailing up the Waccamaw to the Litchfield landing to take on the cargo bound for Europe. Nowadays, when the river mist wraps itself around the old plantation, the sound of a gate bell continually ringing and demanding admission haunts the Waccamaw night, even though the bell and its clapper have long since been removed. And on the roads which run along the Neck, a spectral horseman gallops in the direction of Litchfield, hurtling through the misty night like a soul in torment. All this is thought to be connected to the ghost of Henry Massingbird Tucker, born in 1831, who served as a doctor both in the Confederate army and in the lands along the Neck. He died in 1904 and his body lies buried in Georgetown Cemetery. However, his restless spirit refuses to leave Litchfield and on foggy evenings seems to return to his former home, demanding admittance by ringing a now ghostly bell, just as he did when alive.

On the swift-flowing Santee stands the elegant Hampton Plantation, founded by the French Huguenot Horry family in the

1730s and haunted by the troubled ghost of John Henry Routledge, a later owner, who committed suicide after being slighted in love. And on the North Santee lie the now overgrown ruins of Peachtree Manor, built by Thomas Lynch in 1762 and burned to the ground in 1840. It is said to be haunted by several ghosts: the daughter of Thomas Lynch, Jr., who died of yellow fever and whose overgrown earthen funeral marker still stands in the ruined grounds, and by the ghost of Lynch himself, who went mad with grief at her demise. There are also tales in the region of a colony of cannibalistic creatures, half-human, half-werewolf, who dwell in the deep, impenetrable South Carolina swamps near Columbia and who are the offspring of runaway slaves and "swamp devils," odd pre-humans who have lived in the swamps since before the Indians arrived. Any one of these ghost or monster stories is deserving of further exploration, but a little way from the coast itself is a connection with the Celtic past and more specifically with the Gray Man.

Pawleys Island has a long and checkered history. Now described as an "arrogantly shabby" holiday resort, its early visitors included colonists, pirates, riverboat traders, British invasion forces, and Civil War blockade runners. It is certainly one of the smallest islands along the coast, being only four miles long and one fourth of a mile wide. It has been shaped by the endless tides and winds which have swept up sand and dirt into a high piece of land just breaking above the ocean. Behind it lie tidal races and marshes, making it a haven for fish and birds of various kinds. The island takes its name from Percival Pawley who, together with his three sons, received a grant of land in colonial America from the English Crown in 1711. The land which they were given was mainly swamp, forest, and coastal flats but there was a fair amount of fertile ground in it as well. It stretched from the Atlantic coast to the Waccamaw River and was close to South Carolina's important King's Highway. Pawley and his sons set to work with a will, clearing, draining, and irrigating the land. Gangs of slaves were brought in to complete the back-breaking work, widening creeks and planting rice which was to become the staple produce of the area. And after Pawley, other planters moved in intent on making their fortunes from the rice crops.

A grand and sophisticated community began to grow along the Waccamaw and Santee Rivers. Much of the entertaining was done during the winter months when lavish balls and celebrations were held in the plantation houses and boats traveled up and down the rivers, calling upon neighbors. The summers, however, were different. Even though it had been drained and irrigated, the land had not lost its essential quality. It was still swampy and during the summer months, stagnant water over the rice fields formed a home for swarms of mosquitoes which carried the dreaded "swamp fever." In order to avoid the sickness, the plantation owners and the well-off left the swampy river lowlands for the mountains or the coast.

Pawleys Island was an ideal retreat. It was close to the plantations but it lay beyond salt marshes, which separated it from the soggy, disease-ridden swamps. Cooling winds from the ocean provided relief during the hot, humid summer months. The first shelters on the island were makeshift lean-tos which had been built by slaves, but as the plantation owners began to stay longer and longer, more permanent and durable buildings were erected. Summer cottages were built close to the sandy beaches and, as families now stayed there for months at a time, furniture was brought down from the plantation houses and slaves were stationed there for the summer. From Pawleys Island, the plantation owners could travel to Georgetown and Charleston, while their wives and children could enjoy the beach. The island was the perfect summer vacation spot. Many of the 1800s structures have long since fallen, but some of the later cottages remain and Pawleys Island retains an air of faded grandeur, harking back to an era which has long since passed. It is also said to retain a ghost. With such a varied history, how could it not?

Since roughly 1822, a solitary figure has strolled along the stretch of beach which counts as the strand on Pawleys Island. It is that of a man, always alone and always dressed in gray. Sometimes he is seen quite clearly, other times as a kind of misty apparition, but there is little doubt amongst South Carolina folk that this is a ghost. This is not a good spectre to see for although he is benign and will not harm any viewer, the Gray Man warns of a coming storm or of an approaching disaster. His presence was recorded just before what the locals call the Great Tidal Wave struck Pawleys Island in 1893. And he has been frequently seen during late September during the hurricane season.

For years, the Gray Man was simply a piece of local folklore, but in 1954, he achieved wider fame when he was seen by a prominent

South Carolina woman who had been coming to Pawleys Island for over twenty years. She had come down with her family (including grandchildren) to take an autumn break on the island and they had rented a small house near the beach. Late on a Thursday afternoon, the whole family were sitting at the front of the building looking towards the sea when the grandmother saw someone moving along the beach. He was, she says, a man of medium height, walking briskly and swinging his arms. She could not see his face, nor did she recognize his walk. As he drew farther and farther away, she found herself wondering who he was. "Look at that man!" she exclaimed. "He seems to be vanishing." And even as she watched him, he dissolved into a kind of shapeless, gray blur and then disappeared altogether. There was only the empty beach where he had been. The others had not seen him at all. Although the weather had been good, the next day was a miserable one. Vicious winds lashed the island and the seas were unbelievably high. The local radio stations predicted possible hurricane damage.

Another visitor to Pawleys Island that year tells a similar story. He and his wife had come to the island in late October to avoid the crowds and were staying at a small beach house his parents had owned for some time. Standing at his window one evening, he saw a man strolling along the beach towards him. He was struck by the solitary walker because there were so few people on Pawleys Island so late in the year. He looked like an ordinary man, says the account, except that he appeared to be dressed completely in gray. He was walking with his head downward, as if against a stiff breeze, so that the man could not see his face. As he drew nearer to the house, he seemed to somehow lose focus, becoming simply a gray smear against the sea, and then he vanished completely. The watcher went down to the beach where the stranger had last been seen but there was no trace of him, not even footprints in the wet sand. The next day, the man and his wife were roused by a frantic hammering on their door. It was a neighbor from the other side of the island telling them that they had better quit for the mainland as a storm was about to hit. Within an hour they were gone and Pawleys Island was hammered by savage seas as Hurricane Hazel passed by. When they returned, they found that their house had been spared the storm and was virtually untouched. Even the television antenna was intact and beach towels left on a front rail were still there. The man believed that no harm comes to anyone who sees the Gray Man although there are many who disagree with him. There are those who consider the phantom (if phantom it is) to be a malignant warning of imminent danger.

So who is this mysterious phantom and why does he prowl the beach at Pawleys Island? Is he really the old sea being of whom the ancient Celts were so terribly afraid or is he something else? As is common with many of the ancient beliefs that arrived on the American shores, there is a ghost story connected with the sighting. In 1822, one of the first recorded calamitous storms hit Pawleys Island. It came during the summer months when many plantation owners from the surrounding region were in residence. A little farther along the coast, at North Inlet, was a pretty young girl who was spending some time on one of the minor plantations with her uncle and cousins. She was in a particularly good mood that summer as she had just received word that her fiancé, who had been overseas for at least two years, was on his way home. He would stop off to pay his respects to his own family, who were on Pawleys Island, before making his way up the Waccamaw to see her. She could hardly wait.

The fiancé arrived on the island, together with a black servant, and began to make his way to his parents' cottage. They both galloped along the strand, in a hurry to complete their visit so that they could make their way to North Inlet where the young man could see his love. Near Middleton Pond, the young man glimpsed a shortcut through a marshy area and wheeled his horse to take it. Something caused the mount to shy and throw its rider. The fall was not a serious one but when he tried to get to his feet he found himself sinking deeper and deeper into the mud. In a matter of moments both he and the horse were floundering in dangerous quicksand. The servant tried to throw the bridle and reins to his master in an attempt to pull him out but to no avail. The reins were too short. Desperately, he searched for the branch of a tree to try to lever the young man out of the sucking sand, but he could find nothing. He could only watch in helpless agony as man and horse sank beneath the surface of the swamp. Then he dashed back to the plantation to relate what had happened.

The young girl was inconsolable. In her grief, she set out for Pawleys Island and spent her time there endlessly walking back and forth along the strand. Gradually, her fragile mind appeared to give way. One evening as she was walking, she saw the figure of a young man farther along the beach standing and looking out over the water. He was dressed completely in gray, but there was something about him that made her hurry towards him. As she drew nearer, although he never turned towards her and she never saw his face, she became more and more certain that this was her dead lover. She had almost reached him when a sudden mist swept in and momentarily obliterated him from her view. When it cleared, she was alone again on the beach.

When she told her father and her uncle, they were immediately concerned. It seemed that her wits, so battered by misfortune, were finally starting to fail. And, that night, she had a fearful and very vivid dream from which she awoke screaming. She dreamed that she was in a little boat just off Pawleys Island and that she was being tossed about by vicious seas. All about her floated wreckage and pieces of furniture—some from her own room. And on a high sand dune on the island, which she was powerless to reach, stood her dead lover, beckoning to her. Try as she might, she could not get to the island. The dream disturbed her greatly and the next morning, her father decided to take her to see a physician in Charleston.

Just hours after they left the inlet, another tragedy struck. Without warning a savage hurricane swept down on them and for two days, terrible winds scoured the Carolina coasts. When the storm had finally passed, news came to the outside world that most of the population in and around North Inlet had perished. Homes had been washed into the sea and, not able to escape, people had drowned. The storm of 1822 was one of the greatest disasters ever to strike Tidewater Country and because they had been on their way to Charleston, the young girl and her father survived. Resigned at last to the loss of her fiancé and convinced that he was watching over her, she recovered her wits and began to lead a normal life once more.

Although this took place almost two centuries ago, local people are convinced that the young suitor's ghost returns as a Gray Man to protect Pawleys Island. Some legends say that to see him assures the watcher that he will be spared in the coming tempest; others say that, like a banshee, the Gray Man always presages the death of the viewer in a storm. Whether these stories are true or not is more problematic for the name of the young girl and her sweetheart are never given and cannot be verified. So is the Gray Man of Pawleys Island a phantom or is he a race memory of the ancient Fir Liath, brought into the region by the Scots-Irish who came in the wake of the planters? Many of them worked alongside the slaves in the rice fields and it is possible that their stories mingled with slave legends and old Indian tales to produce the ghost story above. Perhaps, too, the ghost story is nothing more than an explanation for some older, more basic belief. Perhaps the real answer lies somewhere deep in the misty rivers, dismal swamps, and moldering plantation houses that is the still-mysterious Tidewater Country.

Part 5
Devil Creatures

Kentucky

The Thing on the Road

In Celtic folklore there are a number of beings that defy classification. Although the Irish poet and writer W.B. Yeats described them as "solitary fairies," they do not exactly correspond with recognizable fairy kind. Some have more association with ancient Celtic gods and spirits; others have more in common with the dead. The Irish people called them "sheehogues"; the Cornish, "goblins" or "trolls"; the Welsh, "dark ones"; and the Breton folk, "fees" or "fays." They were closely associated with the dark world and with witchcraft and arcane arts, and they often passed through the countryside at night, doing harm to rural people and/or damaging their property. For the most part they were unseen, but at times they made themselves visible, usually on the night-bound country roads, and they were often truly terrible to behold.

The Irish Dullaghan, for example, was a fearsome headless horseman mounted on a black stallion who carried his phosphorescent turnip-shaped head in front of him like a lantern. He poisoned the crops as he rode through the countryside and turned the milk sour at every house he passed. (One of the most popular ghostly figures of American legend, the headless horseman made famous by Washington Irving's *The Legend of Sleepy Hollow*, may owe more to the Dullaghan than to any American rider.) To meet with him was an evil misfortune for he had the power to hoist the traveler onto his horse and carry him away into the afterlife or to the fairy world. Many disappearances in Irish localities were explained in this way. Although classed as a fairy, the Dullaghan is more closely linked to the realm of ghosts and phantoms than to the fairy kingdom.

Another Irish entity, the Fir Gorta, or Man of Hunger, also traveled the night roads creating uncertainty and terror as he went. This was an emaciated being always dressed in rags and with a gaunt, almost skeletal face who went about as a beggar. He carried only two things: a stout staff and a small tin cup. Late at night, he would turn up at the back door of a house where he would rattle his cup loudly and draw back, unseen, into the gloom. The woman of the house would usually come to the door and look out. Knowing that the Fir Gorta was there, she would leave either a small crust of bread or a cup of milk for him. When she was back inside her home, the Fir Gorta would come and accept his offering. If this tradition was followed, then the house would usually have good luck, but if it was not, then some misfortune would befall the building and its occupants.

The Fir Gorta is a complex being who undoubtedly has at least part of his roots in the Irish Potato Famine of 1846-52. At that time, many starving itinerant Irish laborers walked the roads looking for work and depending on the charity of the places through which they passed. It is interesting to note that a similar being sometimes stalks the roads in the West of Scotland where the famine was also quite severe, resulting in many deaths. The offering left at the back door for him, however, suggests some older, more pagan origin and is similar to votive offerings left to roadside gods and spirits by the early Celts. This gives the Fir Gorta a "fairy" classification—indeed, Yeats classes him as such—but his roots may come from many different sources.

Sometimes these sheehogue creatures were insubstantial entities, little more, for example, than balls or patches of light. A good instance of this is the *canwyll corph,* or corpse candle, stories of which were at one time told around many Welsh fires. This being resembled a ball or pillar of light, like a candle flame, which often appeared before a death in the community and which was said to invariably follow the route that would be taken by the funeral procession. At other times, it was said to hover and flutter about old and sometimes abandoned graveyards, luring travelers and passersby into their depths. The light was believed to be possessed of some malign intelligence and took great delight in leading people astray and into dangerous situations.

It was an ill thing, folklore warned, to joke with a corpse candle. In one old tale, attributed to a Rev. J. Jenkins, vicar of Hirnant, a drunken sailor once approached one of these entities and attempted to light his pipe from it. He was whisked away by an invisible force and when he came to himself, he was drowning in the middle of a nearby bog and had to be rescued. He was lucky, said the Reverend Jenkins, for he could have been killed. According to another clerical authority, the Reverend Edmund Jones, the *canwyll corph* was often seen carried by something which resembled a human skull or else in the hands of a monstrous shape which vaguely resembled a giant man—the light being carried between his finger and thumb or in his cupped hands. Such lights were usually seen on the unlit roads which wound through country areas.

As ever, there are many tales of persons who have met with the corpse candle on their way home, and a corpus of folklore has built up around such encounters. In one, an elderly gentleman struck the phenomenon with his walking stick, causing it to dissolve into a shower of livid sparks which quickly reassembled before his horrified eyes. Less than two days later, this particular old gentleman was dead. He had become so terrified by what he had done that he had taken sick and over the next day grew fatally worse. As his funeral progressed to the churchyard, it passed the spot where the old man had struck the corpse candle. Here the supporting bier broke and the coffin slid to the ground, threatening to spill its contents into the ditch and thus seemingly confirming the dreadful story.

Stories concerning corpse lights and wandering things once abounded around the Welsh village of Felin-y-Wig. They probably owe their continued popularity to a local storyteller and ghost seer, John Roberts, whom the folklorist Elias Owen interviewed in 1896, garnering tales that he later transcribed into his indispensable *Welsh Folk-Lore*. The following is a typical Roberts tale:

> One evening, I was standing at my door, looking along the road when I saw a light that I knew came from no house. Even so it looked as though it came from the window of a building and so I was greatly puzzled. Even as I watched, it seemed to move slowly along the road that led from Bettws-Gwerfil-Goch towards Felin-y-Wig. I stepped out of my door to see where it was going. As I did so, it seemed to draw nearer to my own house, which was quite obviously its destination. And behind it there seemed to be a shadowy figure though I couldn't see whether it was a man or a woman. I could see nothing save the light. It seemed to be moving very quickly now and entered the yard of my house, still advancing towards my door, the light and the dark shape behind it becoming ever more distinct. Suddenly a great fear came upon me and I turned and fled back into the house shutting

the door behind me and keeping the *Canwyll Corph* firmly outside, as I thought. Looking through the window, however, I saw it turn aside and pass through the door of one of the outhouses, wavering and flickering as it did so. Frightened that it was now inside the house I ran here and there looking for it but saw nothing. It had vanished utterly as though it had never been there in the first place. That very night, a serving man who did some work for me died and his bed was right above the place where the Corpse Candle had passed through the door. The experience fairly shook me to the core.

At other times, Roberts went on, all sorts of things would come about the doors of houses in the dusk and scratch and knock to be let in. It was as well not to pay them any heed for nobody knew what they might be admitting. It could be a fairy, the unquiet spirit of someone long dead, or some strange and unearthly creature that had never been alive in the mortal world. For example, in County Down in Ireland, there was a great fear that sheeries, the unborn souls of babies who had died in childbirth or who had come into the world stillborn, would try to enter houses at night. Their purpose was to find a way back into the world and they meant to take over the bodies of sleepers within these buildings, bending them to their will.

In addition to opening the door to strange entities, it was always extremely dangerous to throw away dirty water at night for fear of what might be lurking in the yard close to the house or going past on the road. One might strike a passing shade or one of the "sheehoguey kind" and so bring misfortune or supernatural harm upon the house. In southwest County Fermanagh an old man, the late George Sheridan, told the author how women used to recite a short protective incantation before throwing dirty water out into the dark: *Hugitas, ugitas iskey sollagh* ("Away, away dirty water"). This was supposed to keep any entity—invisible or otherwise—which had been struck by the water from returning to torment the house in future. The writer W.B. Yeats records a tale from County Sligo in which a woman threw out dirty water and hit a ghostly thing passing on the road. This entity returned night after night in the form of a black lamb which came in as the family was gathered around the fire, lay down on the hearthstone, and died with a human sigh. The man of the house carried it out and buried it, but the following night it came in again and died in front of the fire once more.

Again it had to be taken out and buried, but the third night the entire episode was repeated. This was becoming a nuisance for the family concerned and in the end, a priest had to be brought in to exorcise the spirit and they were troubled no further.

Traveling during the hours of darkness could be hazardous too for one never knew what might be met on poorly lit roads. For example, devil dogs, wandering ghosts, and fairies were all about after dark. The worst kind of meeting, usually around Halloween or at the "dark time of the year" (i.e., winter), was with the fairy funerals that traveled the roads at these times. It was widely believed that the fairies were compelled by God to escort the souls of those who had died within an area during the previous year to the gates of heaven. The fairies themselves were not permitted to enter paradise on account that they had no souls. This made them extremely bad tempered and antagonistic towards humankind, and woe betide the mortal who met with such a funeral along the road. The fairies had the power to take mortals with them into the afterlife—something which they never hesitated to do—or to inflict some ghastly penance such as carrying a corpse on one's back, and so bodies of travelers were sometimes found by the side of the road while others were found wandering, paralyzed with fear, having met with the terrible procession.

There were, of course, remedies and protections for avoiding such an awful fate. One could turn one's coat inside out, a common protection against the fairy kind in many parts of rural Ireland, or recite a certain incantation that would render the power of invisibility to fairy eyes. Margaret Gallagher in the village of Belcoo, on the County Fermanagh/County Cavan border, told how her grandfather Pat Gallagher met the fairy funeral on the road between the village and the neighboring hamlet of Garrison. Standing stock still, he said, "My back from you, my face to you," and they passed him by without seeing him. But, said Margaret, he had a very lucky escape and was one of the few who had survived such an encounter. In rural Ireland, Scotland, and Wales, many people lived in terror of meeting a procession of wailing souls guarded by hostile fairies upon local roads.

Such beliefs appear to have been easily transferred to the American continent. Here, in geographic terms, society often reflected the Celtic world. Settlements were small and widely scattered within the established areas of the New World and were connected by "roads" which were little more than cart trails. As night descended such trails became dark and gloomy and common natural features exhibited new and menacing aspects. In the evening gloom, solitary rocks or lone trees took on monstrous shapes and heights, and hollows seemed to subtly alter form. Nor were the trails solely the preserve of the settlers for Indians and unknown animals often went furtively about using these tracks for their own purposes. Moreover, in boggy ground, marsh gasses flickered and flared in a most alarming fashion, no doubt reactivating beliefs concerning corpse candles and death lights. There were also mysterious phenomena that the settlers had never encountered before, some of which still perplex scientific minds. All these ingredients—the bizarre and unfamiliar landscape, the comings and goings of Indians and animals of various kinds, and unexplained phenomena—contributed to the folklore of many regions.

In this way, incredulous country people who were slow in neither telling nor sometimes embellishing their encounters often saw strange beings along lonely trails and in isolated hollows. In the Ozark Mountains in Missouri, for instance, a weird creature described as half-man, half-bat was sometimes seen on an old freight trail that led down to the Kirbyville-Springfield road. The same being was seen, according to one informant, near an old ruined cabin on the upper stretches of Bear Creek and it was thought that this might be the unquiet spirit of some settler or homesteader who had died there and taken on a ghastly animalistic shape. There were other stories about old Indian worship in the area and it was even considered that the thing might be one of the ancient gods which had been previously worshipped in that region and which lingered long after the white man had settled there. There were also in that area stories of a half-human, half-owl figure which lived in the woods along the White River, but these tales remain vague and extremely ill defined.

One of the most famous stories of strange and supernatural beings comes from western North Carolina and concerns a huge insect-like entity which attacked travelers along the Nantahala Gorge in Swain and Macon Counties (along Highway 19 from Nantahala to Wesson). This rugged and thickly wooded area was formed by the Nantahala River, and some will tell you that it has been only partially explored even today. It is here, in the very bottom of the gorge, that the insect-creature known as Ulagu, the giant yellow jacket, has its home. The name "Ulagu" is a Cherokee Indian word meaning "lord," "boss," or "master," and it may hint at some form of very ancient ritual or worship. It is said that Ulagu has developed a taste for small children and that few passing through the area are safe. The creature appears only at dusk, its body as big as a house, and it always seems to be accompanied by a rushing wind, perhaps from the beating of its gigantic wings. In some stories, there is also the sound of persistent thunder as the being appears.

There have been many attempts—including some, it is claimed, by reputable naturalists—to locate Ulagu's nest, which is believed to be somewhere in the dense thicket which covers the bottom of the gorge, but not one of these has been successful. There is an old tale that in a desperate attempt to trap the giant yellow jacket, Cherokee hunters set traps of fresh meat to lure it out of its hiding place. The pieces of meat were carried away, it is related, in the blink of an eye and the strings which had been used to attach them to the ground were scattered as though they had been merely straws. The Cherokee increased the size of the offerings until, at last, a whole deer was offered to the great insect. This time the bait proved heavy enough to make the great yellow jacket fly much lower in the sky and so the hunters were able to track it. They saw the being enter a low cave concealed by bushes, trees, and other growth in the cliff face of the gorge. Memorizing the site of the cavern, the hunters returned in greater numbers to investigate Ulago's lair. A fierce wind seemed to come from the depths of the place, doubtless caused by the motion of the enormous yellow jacket's wings. Nevertheless, the hunters were not to be deterred. As they peered into the gloom, they saw that the top of the cave was covered in a sort of honeycomb of six-sided chambers made from a waxy, papery substance. The cave was also teeming with huge yellow wasplike creatures, some of which made threatening sorties in their direction. These were, they imagined, Ulagu's many children. Afraid that they might be stung to death, the hunters drew back. Later they returned and attempted to smoke some of the insects out. Their efforts did not appear to have much of an effect, but they did manage to drive some of the smaller wasplike creatures out of the cave to become the ancestors of all stinging things in the wider world. The monster

Ulagu, however, still lurks in the depths of the cave—the location of which has now been forgotten—and although it ventures out only sporadically, it can still be seen late in the evening in the vicinity of Nantahala Gorge. Travelers in the region frequently go in terror of it as it is said to be big enough to carry away a family car. The locality is a spooky one and it is not surprising that it has become the home of folkloric monsters.

Other bizarre and mysterious beings also travel the roads of the American South as soon as darkness has fallen. A typical entity is Old Walleyes, which follows the remote trails of the Ozarks and is said to dwell in an isolated limestone cave somewhere among the high hills. Although descriptions of it vary, the being is said to be monstrous with four short legs and claws on each foot. Its head is as big as a wagon and its mouth is as big as a washtub. It is covered in dark, shaggy hair which frames long, razor-sharp teeth that will eat anything: man, beast, and everything in-between. However, it is the creature's eyes which are most frightening and which give it its name. These are huge, white, and vacant and seem to "see" without really seeing, emerging from the dark to scare travelers out of their wits. The thing may be blind but it seems to be able to hunt down its prey without much trouble. Although Old Walleyes is thought to stay close to its lair, it frequents many roads in the Ozarks in search of prey. The only way to escape it is to cross a stream or river because like many other supernatural creatures, Old Walleyes cannot cross running water.

A similar being, the Mo Mo, is to be found in southern New Jersey. It dwells in deep thickets known as "pineys" as it is truly a devil creature. No accurate description of it exists, except that it may resemble a human, is completely covered in coarse, filthy hair, and has a twisted human-like face with huge and pointed teeth. Its hands are rending claws, capable of tearing an animal (or a human) apart. Its eyes are large, orange-colored, and glow in the poor light. The Mo Mo steals chickens, guts dogs, and carries off the occasional infant to its woodland lair. The last and scariest Mo Mo was sighted near Mount Vernon in 1959 when a traveler saw what he took to be an old farmer sitting in an unfenced field beside the road one evening. The "farmer" seemed to be sitting on its haunches with his head in his hands and the traveler approached him, intent on asking for directions. The other suddenly reared up, rising to a height of almost nine feet. It was completely covered in dark fur and featured two abnormally large and glowing orange eyes. The traveler took to his heels.

The New Jersey Mo Mo has parallels in many other states. Countless booger, or boogie, men, usually associated with the Devil, stalk Southern roads ready to carry away the unwary or those who have neglected their religious duties. There are, for instance, several variants of the "Ol' Black Booger" in both North Carolina and Tennessee as well as a being known as the "Sally-Bally" in Georgia, the "Smokey Joe" in northern Arkansas, and the "Gowerow," which is said to live deep in the Marble Cave, Stone County, Missouri. The "Pennywinkle," a bizarre and invisible entity said to be something between a monster and a ghost, roams the mountain roads through the Ozarks and the Smokies and is known by its eerie call in a high female voice: "Pennywinkle! Pennywinkle!" If anyone should answer the call—for example, to cry out, "Who's there?" or "Be quiet!"—then he or she will surely bring some sort of supernatural harm or doom upon themselves.

These entities always appear around nightfall as the light begins to falter and things become more uncertain in the dusk. An old tale from Edmonson County, Kentucky, tells of an encounter with one of these shapeless, monstrous, and partially glimpsed sheehogues just as evening was starting to fall.

During the 1920s and '30s, people were often warned about supernatural creatures which lurked along county roads, work roads, and old trails through the woods. These dark entities might do good people harm and carry away young children. There was a particular road that ran through Edmonson County which was badly haunted by a "booger." Road crews would very seldom work there for any length of time and travelers passed along it as quickly as they could, especially when it was starting to get dark. An old man, Philip Pitchford, was told that he and several others were required to work along a section of that road near Poplar Springs as part of a road-widening scheme. Pitchford was to say later that they worked all day, toiling through their dinner breaks, and late into the evening. By this time they were so hungry that the only thing they could think of was sitting down to eat by the roadside—a dangerous thing to do in Edmonson County. In order to keep their spirits up, they began to tell jokes and one of them who was very religious—a Brother Booker—made sure that the tales did not get too "salty."

Brother Booker was in the process of telling them all how he had been a mean and rough fellow when a much younger man—"as mean as the ole Devil hisself"—when there was a noise close to a nearby stand of trees. At once, the crew grew alarmed and excited, remembering the bad reputation of the road, but Brother Booker told them the Lord would look after them. Besides, he went on, it was probably only the wind in the bushes or some birds flying home for the night. Even so, the sound came again, making the men more and more nervous, and this time it seemed as if it were settling on the road close by. Still, Brother Booker told them that there was nothing to be afraid of. One of the men went a little way down the road to investigate. At last he came back and told them that he had seen something that was large, red and white, and that looked like a "big ol' boy" sitting on the road and gathering black wings around it. Then it commenced to walk very quickly along the road towards where they were sitting. The rest of the men, said Pitchford, were ready to run but Brother Booker told them to stand their ground. No evil thing, he said, could touch a person whose faith was strong and pure. Some of the road crew, however, were not so sure about the purity of their faith and ran away in the direction of Poplar Springs as fast as they could.

Pitchford, Brother Booker, and one other man stood and waited for the thing, but it only came as far as the next hill and stopped. Philip Pitchford said that he could not see it properly in the late evening light, but it looked like a very tall, naked, red-skinned man with black wings like a bat. Brother Booker said that they now should stand aside and "give it the road" so that it could pass by without touching them. They drew back to the side of the road, but the thing just stood there and watched them. There was a big straw stack close by and the three men decided to watch the creature from behind the stack. Pitchford was sure that it had a knife—"a big old clumsy thing, like the old Ayrabs used to have"—but it did not use it. Finally Brother Booker walked out from behind the stack and proceeded to curse the creature "usin' words outa the Bible." This had an effect, for the thing emitted an ear-piercing shriek and waved its knife or sword in their direction. Then it launched itself from the top of the hill and came flapping towards them, still screaming. Their nerve—even that of Brother Booker—finally broke, and they turned and ran. The thing seemed to settle on the top of the straw stack but the men never quit running. Only once did Pitchford look back, and he saw the thing change into the shape of a great white horse, which raised its forelegs after them menacingly.

They did not stop until they reached the house of an old man who lived just beyond the next hill. He had been dozing in his bed, but their frightened hammering soon woke him. Brother Booker told him to come quick and to bring his gun as there was a booger thing coming along the road after them. The old man did so and they began to walk back along the road with a rifle at the ready. Pitchford thought that he saw strange lights coming and going over the countryside but he was not sure what they might be. There were odd shadows, too, which seemed to come and go of their own volition. They saw no sign of the creature but when they reached the straw stack, they found it scattered all around the field as if by a terrible wind. Of the thing that had chased them there was no sign. They went back to the old man's house and stayed there that night, and in the morning they returned to the field hoping to see something of their unearthly visitor, but once again there was nothing. Pitchford neither saw anything like it again, nor did he ever find anyone who could explain what it might have been. "It was," he said, "just a booger."

Philip Pitchford's booger story was collected in 1967 by researchers from the University of Kentucky. No one was sure whether or not the story was true—Pitchford was renowned as a teller of tall tales—but it certainly reflected the mountaineer's fear of lonely roads and isolated places. It was a fear which probably stemmed from their Celtic roots. And perhaps there really are supernatural "booger critters" somewhere out there in the half-light. Best not to travel alone.

The Black Booger Dog

In the unstructured belief system that formed ancient Celtic religion, animals loomed large. The religion of the Celts was not a unified theology in the way that we would understand the term; rather, it was a system of largely localized cults under the control of local spiritual leaders, the Druids. For the Celts, spirits lurked everywhere—primarily in the landscape around them, but also in the sky and in the living world—and the cults they followed reflected this. Thus there were cults centered on the sun, stones, fire, and water. There were also cults of the dead, of rivers, and of various animals. Serpents, for example, were venerated and it is possible that the famous story of St. Patrick casting the snakes out of Ireland may more properly relate to snake cults being driven out by the holy man. Horses, too, were worshipped for their litheness and speed; bulls and wild pigs for their strength and ferocity. Amongst certain of the Celts, wolf cults flourished as well.

The rivalry between man and wolf was an old one. At one time the forests of Western Europe teemed with predatory wolves which often competed with humans for available food and game. Wolves were cunning, wolves were swift, wolves were strong, and wolves certainly were worthy adversaries. It seemed only natural that wolves, in the style of the boar and the bull, should eventually become an object of worship amongst the hunting Celtic peoples. There seems little doubt that wolf cults existed in early Celtic society and that they might have been one of the more established and powerful cults within the panoply of Celtic religion.

However, it was the spread of formal Christianity that transformed the wily wolf into a thing of evil and darkness. Amongst the hunting society of the Celts, the wolf had been the "enemy" whom the hunters had challenged for food. As the Celtic tribes became more settled and turned to agriculture and livestock rearing, the wolf remained an adversary. It was the creature which attacked the flocks and carried off newborn lambs and calves. Why, it was even known to abduct newborn human infants from their cribs and eat them! What better embodiment of the forces of evil loose in the Western world? In addition, with the motif of Christ himself as the good shepherd gathering his flock around him, what more suitable image for the Devil than that of a ravening wolf? The image stirred up ancient memories amongst the Celts: the Devil and his minions turned into a pack of savage wolves, ready to carry off the souls of the just and the righteous.

Among the Devil's own were sorcerers and magicians, who were often believed to have the power to transform themselves into the guise of animals. Their supernatural ability was symbolic of the savage beast which lay within every man and woman and which only Satan could fully set free. Records show that many of the early European sorcerers and black magicians were said to possess some artifact—a belt or an amulet reputedly given to them by the father of evil himself—which could transform them into the likeness of an animal, usually a wolf. In this guise they carried away small children and devoured their flesh. Perhaps these are the origins of the idea of the werewolf, the man who takes on bestial form with the rising of the moon.

The church was especially fierce in its denunciation of such sorcerers. They were beyond redemption, it thundered. Even when the body was dead, the unclean spirits might return in animal form, perhaps even in the form of a wolf. This introduced a new element into the mythology and folklore of the time, that of the spectral wolf which intended God's people harm. Once again, it clung close to ancient memories and fears. Somewhere deep in the Celtic psyche, the predatory wolf lurked beyond the glow of the fire, translating itself into the lycanthropy of the medieval and early modern world. Now in the darkness, the ghost-hound waited to attack Godly men and women or to damn their souls.

The notion of the wolf was later transferred to a related animal, the feral dog. During the medieval period, there must have been many feral dogs wandering the European countryside. These were canines which had never been domesticated, had been born in the wild, or had been turned out from homesteads to fend for themselves. They were normally more ferocious than wolves, which were generally shy creatures and rather fearful of men, and may have proved more of a menace to the community. Moreover, some dogs may even have belonged to people within society and become feral once their former master or mistress—perhaps an old and largely antisocial person—died. In the popular mind, such animals often became identified with their deceased owners, and if the person concerned had been feared by the community, then so was the dog. In a sense, the animal became the embodiment of the person, even after he or she was long dead, and so was considered something akin to a ghost. To meet such lone dogs wandering the roads—particularly in the evening—was regarded as a bad supernatural sign, in addition to imperiling the traveler's physical safety. They immediately became suspect as agents of the Devil or, indeed, the Devil himself abroad in the world. The devil dog now entered Celtic folklore.

Stories concerning spectral hounds—some the embodiment of evil people, some the concrete form of the Devil himself—are to be found in tales from all over the Celtic world: Ireland, Scotland, Wales, and Cornwall. In the Cornish tales, they accompany the demonic magistrate Tregagle as he travels through the skies snatching away souls; in Lancashire, England, they are the Gabriel hounds who travel with Old Brockie (the Devil) in his revels across the upper airs. In Yorkshire, they are the sky yelpers, running behind the Devil to catch unwary souls that he may miss. In every instance, they are evil and are to be greatly feared by all good Christian people.

On Rathlin Island, off the North Antrim coast in Ireland, the storyteller Rose McCurdy told of a spectral hound which wandered the island roads at night terrorizing many of the Rathlin community. She had never seen it herself, she admitted, but she knew plenty who had and every description of it was the same. It was as big as a small calf and was completely black and shaggy like a bear. Its eyes were luminous and burned red, and sparks fell from the corners of its mouth as it moved. There was a continual reek of sulfur about it. The creature padded about the island quite silently but, as the light failed, it began to glow with a terrible yellow putrescence. In Rose's mind (and in the minds of many islanders), the hound was undoubtedly the Devil. The impression was strengthened by the fact that the creature was usually only seen at twilight or at night, a time when evil was abroad. In the end, according to the tale, the local priest had to be called upon to banish the thing from the island, which he did with much prayer and fasting. The Devil is reputedly exiled from Rathlin for 999 years although he is always seeking ways to return. Similar stories are to be found all over Ireland from Donegal to Kerry, and the legends extend into Scotland as well.

In Cornwall, great dogs such as Old Shuck or Old Blackie, synonyms for the Devil himself, prowl the moonlit roads sometimes peering in at windows in an attempt to spy out bad or willful children to carry off. At least that is what the children are told in an effort to make them behave. In some cases, these animals are headless—a sure sign of their close connection to the supernatural world—and can often travel faster than the wind. Many of them are the unquiet spirits of evil people or of locals who have dabbled in the black arts. They can only be driven away by the exorcisms of a minister.

There are also traces of the belief in the American southern states, where many Scots-Irish and other Celtic peoples settled. In the rugged American continent, of course, wolf packs were to be found in large numbers, as were coyotes and wild dogs, and these may have fed the lycanthropic mythology, just as it did in early Western Europe. Howls, heard far away in the darkness of an American night, may have been suggestive of a monstrous hound (or hounds) dwelling in the fastness of the remote forests or deep in the dismal swamps of the new country. Amongst the colonists, the presence of the Devil was extremely imminent, lurking along the tree lines of the forests or at the edges of the swamps that could be seen from their settlements. One of the things which sustained the colonists, many of whom had come to America seeking religious tolerance, was their faith and their dependence on God. Only divine goodness could protect them in the wilderness of mountain, forest, and swamp. And, of course, the Devil was always trying to subvert this relationship and seize their souls for his own. He came in many forms to do this, or so the settlers thought, one of which was that of a great black hound. The wolf packs, therefore, that hung around the edges of the colonial villages and towns were thought to be no more than agents of the Devil.

In the rural south, dogs were very strongly associated with sorcerers. In remote areas, many people relied heavily on their canine companions, and these animals were said to take on whatever characteristics their owners displayed. Hermits' dogs, for example, were supposed to be antisocial, reflecting separateness from the world; witches' dogs were thought to harbor supernatural powers and act as a conduit for evil spirits. These animal counterparts were also believed to carry the ghosts of their owners with them long after the individual was dead, giving rise to tales concerning ghost dogs and spectral hounds.

In Alabama, for example, an unseen dog haunts an old bridge in the southwest part of the state. Just outside the town of Silas, a dirt road veers right down a steep incline, and a good way along this trail lies an ancient iron bridge covered in rust that crosses a swift-flowing stream. This is known as Hannah's Bridge or the Hannah Bridge, reputedly because of a terrible incident that occurred there long ago. According to legend, a young girl known only as Hannah became very depressed after the man to whom she was engaged left her for someone else. She made her way to the old bridge, which even then was in a dilapidated state, and looked into the dark waters below. Without a further thought, she threw herself into the swollen stream, was swept away by the current, and drowned. It was a terrible act and one that was in defiance of God's holy ordinance. Consequently, the poor girl's soul could not be admitted to heaven and haunts the bridge to this day. There are those who will tell you that because of her evil and un-Godly act, Hannah's spirit takes the form of a huge dog which prowls from one end of the old bridge to the other. Sometimes this animal is seen at a distance and other times it remains invisible. It is also said that if a person were to stand on the bridge, look into the waters, and shout, "Hannah!" a soft, padding sound like the steps of an unseen dog will make its way across the ancient bridge and pass them by. This was once a great local dare for youth from nearby Silas. Other wisdom in the locality suggests that these are the footsteps of a demon or dark spirit which was drawn to the site by the act of suicide and which appears on the bridge in the form of a dog. Travelers across the stream are advised to be wary, at the peril of their immortal souls.

In North Carolina, too, "booger dogs" wander the countryside, particularly at night. One of the most famous is Old Black Eyes, which was said to frequent an area known as the Baker Rocks near the top of Black Mountain. The hound is believed locally to be the spirit of one Jim Baker, who lived at the rocks (either in a small cabin or in a cave, depending on the story) and gave his name to them. Baker was widely regarded as a witch by the mountaineers and was believed to have great supernatural powers such as firing a rifle across unnatural distances or cursing huntsmen's weapons so that they would not fire at all. Baker was supposed to have sold his soul to the Devil at an old Indian cemetery near Black Mountain and when the evil one touched him, the pupils of Baker's eyes became unnaturally black, a sure sign he belonged to the forces of hell. This was also supposed to give him power over women, and from time to time he lured away a number of local girls and several married women to live with him at the rocks. He is also known to have kept ferocious dogs—part wolves, more or less—which turned travelers away from his home. When he died up at the rocks, his black soul took on the guise of one of his hounds. Local people knew that this was Jim Baker because of the large black pupils of the creature's eyes. It was best not to approach this devil dog for fear of the dark magic that surrounded it. The only way to avoid the power of the witchy creature was to draw a picture of it, set it against a tree, and fire a gun at it (maybe while repeating some sort of incantation, such as an appropriate verse of scripture). If this were done, the devil thing would have no power over an individual. Incidentally, the shooting of a picture or likeness was a recognized way of dispelling witchcraft in many mountain areas.

In West Virginia, slave ghosts took on the appearance of hounds in order to work mischief against former masters and their descendants. The most famous ghost dog was that of Jim Royal, a slave from Africa who was widely regarded as one of the most powerful sorcerers in Virginia. Many of the slaves were terrified of Jim Royal and often had bits of red pepper hidden in their shoes or strings of red thread about their clothing to protect themselves from his awful magic. His favorite trick was with a fiddle, which he would smash to pieces over the back of a chair then magically reconstruct. When he was sent out to hoe the field, people would claim to see him sitting on the stump of a tree playing his fiddle while the hoe worked alongside him on its own. It was said that he could walk through fire, and some of the slaves claimed he traveled about the countryside in the form of a great black bird or a huge black dog, running through the bushes and valleys at tremendous speed. This seemingly gave him the ability to appear at mountain shindigs no matter how remote they might be. Folks would slog all the way up to an isolated cabin in the high hills for a get-together to find Jim Royal already sitting there, just as if he were sitting at home, playing on his fiddle. When he arrived at these celebrations, he could make whiskey flow like water. Quart pots, which did not look like they could hold much, were filled to overflowing with liquor, which never ran dry, no matter how much of it was drunk.

Of course when Jim Royal died, his spirit continued to visit cabins in the mountains in the shape of a great black booger dog. This hound was seen all across the mountains of West Virginia and into Kentucky at various parties and barn dances, and many people reported that its appearance was accompanied by strains of unearthly fiddle music. There was no doubt in anybody's mind that this was the malignant spirit of Jim Royal come back to earth for some evil purpose. To free the mountain folk of his dark influence, his ghost was apparently laid to rest in a most peculiar fashion. Throughout his life, Jim Royal had said that when he died, he did not want moonshine thrown on a fire in a house he had visited. This was a time when moonshine (illegal whiskey) was distilled all across the mountains of Virginia and Kentucky and was the main feature of any mountain gathering. It was a central part of a mountaineer's life and so the request was a surprising one and not easily forgotten. When the booger dog began to be frequently seen and was starting to terrify Christian mountain people, the strange request was suddenly remembered. In one of the mountain cabins, a large booger dog had frightened a man and his family and so some of the mountaineers made their way up there with a large jar of homemade whiskey. Stoking up the fire, they tipped the contents of the jug onto the blaze. The fire spat and crackled and gave out foul-smelling smoke and from across the mountain came the long drawn-out howl of a dog in pain. Then it fell silent and was heard no more. The black booger dog was never seen again and the mountaineers knew that the unquiet spirit of Jim Royal, the conjure man, had been finally laid to rest and would trouble God's people no further.

But perhaps the place in which these spectral hounds were most often seen was in the hill country of Missouri. Much of this particular lore owes its recording to Vance Randolph, who wrote extensively on the stories and beliefs of the Ozarks. Most of the stories Randolph told were unpleasant and dealt with the hound as the very embodiment of evil. They tormented Christian pioneers with their howling as the people knelt to pray in their cabins; they guarded the treasures of awful misers who had lived in the high mountains; they terrified Godly people on their way to church. Some Missouri war veterans told Randolph of a black dog which appeared to their group before any battle in which one or more of them was to die. Travelers at night were accosted by hellish-looking hounds which seemed to appear from nowhere and barred their way or spooked their horses. Such creatures were invariably linked with mountain witches and booger men who had formerly terrorized the countryside in human guise.

In Taney County, for example, Granny Sibley was greatly feared as a witch. She attended many of the mountain births and had brought a good number of mountaineers into the world, but she also had a darker side. She could curse her neighbors and bring misfortune upon them if the mood took her, and she could prepare dark spells that would bring about an illness or even a death in the community. She was also widely known for her love charms, which were the stuff of black magic and against all Christian principles. It was said that she had received her powers directly from the Devil himself, to whom she had sold her soul in an abandoned local cemetery or in an old Indian burial ground. Granny Sibley lived alone in a near-ruined shack at the end of a dirt road in a remote area of the county—alone, that is, but for her dog, a great black mastiff. This beast was feared almost as much as the old lady herself and kept visitors away from the cabin with its growling and frantic barking whenever anybody ventured near. The old woman and the big dog seemed especially close, the animal never leaving its mistress's side. One day, a passing traveler saw no smoke coming from Granny Sibley's chimney and noticed that the door of the cabin was lying open with flies swarming in and out. He waited for the dog to appear, barking furiously, but it never did. Mustering all his courage, the man stepped into the ill-lit cabin to find the old woman sitting in her chair by the ruins of a fire that had long since gone out. She had been dead for a good number of days and the flies swarmed around her as they would rotting meat. Of her dog there was no sign. A doctor was brought and then an undertaker and the old woman was buried well away from decent folks.

Although the mastiff could not be found, up in the hills, Lem Carter, a poor farmer, and his wife were continually disturbed at night by the baying of a dog somewhere in the woods. A couple of times, Lem went out with his gun intending to shoot the brute, but he could never find it. At times he thought he saw a great dog resembling Granny Sibley's familiar passing along a forest trail in front of him or between the trees in the deep woods, but he never caught up to it nor did he ever see it clearly. Folks said that after the old woman died, the dog had run away and "gone to the wild." They said that it might be dangerous and should be left alone, but as time went on the dog seemed to become more and more malignant and was seen more frequently. Several times it came close to the church. Just as the minister got up to read the word of God, the dog would commence barking, distracting the congregants from the message that was being preached. It ran round and round the church, barking as it did, and though some folks went outside to chase it away, it always came back again before the service was over. Soon, people began to think that the animal was a bit uncanny. Stories began to circulate that the dog was the spirit of Granny Sibley come back to taunt those who had crossed her in life. This was borne out by Lem Carter, who had not been on particularly good terms with Granny and said that when it was dark and the family had lain down to sleep, he could hear the sound of a dog just outside the door scratching to get in. He knew that it was Granny Sibley trying to enter the cabin and do him and his family harm. Other folks said that they had seen the dog down in a hollow in the hills and that it had turned into a great black crow before their very eyes. This was sure evidence of the supernatural and of blackest witchcraft. Those who saw the dog, even at a distance, began to be very afraid.

Near to where Granny Sibley's cabin had stood—it had collapsed after her death—was a large rock or stone outcropping, and it was thought that it was here that the booger dog had made its home. At least this was where it was most often seen. A few local farmers— Lem Carter among them—took themselves out to this site with guns and hatchets to see if they could drive the creature out of the community. At first, they saw nothing. The place was certainly very eerie and queer broken shadows came and went, but of the dog, there was no trace. The men searched the area, alert for any sudden movement, but there was none at all. They were just on the point of going home when there came a sudden and frantic barking, like the cry of a large mastiff. There was the dog, standing on the rock above them, though how it had gotten there nobody knew. No one had seen it arrive. Slowly, the men raised their guns and took aim but not one of them pulled the trigger. The dog just stood there on the rock, looking at them quizzically, and every man there said that he was sure the fires of hell burned behind its eyes. Then it opened its mouth, gave a deep-throated howl, and was gone. It seemed to vanish, although it may have taken a wild leap into some surrounding scrub. The men took to their heels and did not stop until they reached their homes, each one counting himself lucky to be alive. But the story did not end there.

The great dog became more and more of a pest in the county, especially as far as churchgoing was concerned. It would sit on the church steps and howl mournfully, particularly whenever a service was in progress. Singers would be distracted from their hymns and worshippers from their prayers by the continual sound. And even when the dog was not there, a huge crow would nest in the rafters of the church and sometimes fly down, alarming and upsetting members of the congregation. It grabbed one woman's hair and fouled another worshipper's best Sunday clothes. The minister professed himself at a loss as to how to remedy the matter. Although he prayed night and morning, his powers were not strong enough to remove the supernatural booger dog. Eventually, the people had to send for a woman, Mrs. Josie Forbes, who was well known as a kind of exorcist all over the Ozarks. When she approached the church, a huge crow that had been sitting in the branches of a tree nearby flew into the building. Then from inside came the steady barking of a great hound. Mrs. Forbes did not hesitate for she was strong in her faith and knew that no harm would befall her. She walked in alone and, according to her own report, saw the black dog standing at the other end of the building where the minister himself might stand. She prayed hard, calling on the name of God to expel Granny Sibley's foul demon, and the creature seemed to dissolve in front of her into a large cloud of flies which swarmed out of the church and away into the sun. After that, the booger dog was never seen in Taney County again.

The story of another booger comes from McDonald County, where an elderly lady lived in a small two-roomed cabin and was tormented by a spectral hound. She had been married several times and her second husband had been violent when drinking. She had been glad to see him in the clay. Nevertheless, many years after, when she was a much older woman, a large dog started coming about her cabin. At first she thought it was no more than an ordinary "critter," but there was something in the way it cocked its head and stared at her that made her think of her late husband. She grew dreadfully afraid of the animal. At first, it only came about during the day and then only for brief periods, but later it seemed to circle her cabin all night while she was in bed. It snuffled round the door and the sides of the cabin, growling as it went. Sometimes she feared it might be inside the building and thought she heard the squeak of her former husband's boots as he moved around the kitchen. It sounded like he was opening cupboards as if he were looking for something to eat (he had been accustomed to doing this when alive) and she heard the rattling of the dipper as though he were taking a drink. Then, as she lay quivering with the bedclothes pulled over her head, the sounds turned into the padding of the great dog once more. She was too terrified to investigate but as soon as the sun rose, the sounds stopped and the kitchen was silent and empty. However, the dog steadily watched the place for the greater part of each day from a tree line nearby. The old lady was convinced that she was being visited by the unquiet spirit of her violent husband and went to see a local minister who prayed with her long and hard. From that day forward, she was never again bothered by the strange black dog.

Not all ghostly dogs, however, are undeniably evil. There are several Missouri stories about how these so-called booger dogs have helped people. A doctor in St. Louis, for example, was guided to a sick person by two of them. The report of the occurrence in *Historic Haunted America* claims that Dr. John O'Brien had a sick patient whom he visited fairly regularly. One night in the middle of winter, the weather was particularly nasty, with a blinding snow falling steadily. Dr. O'Brien set out on his usual visit but as he traveled, the weather worsened and the snow fell more thickly. It soon became apparent to the doctor that he had no chance of finding, let alone reaching, his destination. He was caught in a part of town without streetlights and all that he could see was a wall of falling whiteness against almost total darkness. His reliable horse shied and made to turn back, and the rider had to force it onwards against its will. Then, through the swirling snow, the doctor became aware of movement. Out of the storm, two black mastiffs came bounding towards him. They took up positions on either side of the frightened horse and led it through the snow to the very street the doctor needed. Then they vanished into the wind and snow once more.

He meant to tell his patient about the bizarre incident, but she turned out to be quite ill and he had to work with her steadily for most of his visit. It was just as well that he had arrived when he did—much later and the lady would have been dead. By the time he finished, dawn was breaking and the doctor wanted to get home. The snow had ceased and the morning was pleasant. On his way back home, Dr. O'Brien stopped with a member of the patient's family to deliver the news that she was on the mend. He related the story about the two black dogs and asked if they belonged to anyone in the vicinity. The other simply shook his head and said that he had never seen animals such as the doctor described in the neighborhood. Greatly puzzled, Dr. O'Brien returned home but he made several subsequent visits to the same district in the hope of spotting the dogs. His journeys failed to shed any light on the mystery, which remains unsolved.

Nor are all booger dogs black, the color the Christian mind associates with the Devil. An old slave tale collected in 1939 in Augusta, Georgia, recounts how a large white ghost dog was seen under a tree close to a number of slave cabins. The old lady who was telling the story knew that it was a ghost because it had no head although it moved as though it were an ordinary animal. It simply disappeared, melting away into the night and leaving no trace behind. Although it never seemed to appear again, the spot where it had stood was shunned for many years afterwards as booger ground.

Whether black or white, headless or with a snarling muzzle, ghost dogs still haunt the nightmares of many Americans. Their roots probably lie in the ancient wolf worship of the Celts, transformed by European Christian belief into a rampaging agent of the Devil. And who can say that there is not some dark and malignant wolflike spirit waiting somewhere out there in the American night? You have been warned!

Tennessee

The Woman in Black

Perhaps no supernatural phenomenon is as well known in Irish folk-lore as the banshee. Although primarily Irish, she belongs to a larger tradition of spectral messengers who forecast doom and destruction to those who hear them. Such messengers are probably the last remnants of extremely ancient Celtic deities. The word "banshee" means "woman of the fairy" (*bean Sidhe)* and she is said to be exclusively female, belonging to a type of being which the Irish poet and writer W.B. Yeats classified as solitary fairies. Her warning comes in the form of a call, sometimes plaintive, almost eerie, resembling the ancient keening of Irish women at the death of a loved one. At other times she is said to emit a wild and discordant shriek which more resembles a howl of triumph than a mournful dirge. These sounds are usually heard around the dwelling of the person who is likely to die although they can also be heard by members of that person's family as one of the attributes of the banshee and her kind is that they are supposed to follow established Celtic families and warn them as their demise approaches. Those who have allegedly seen the banshee differ greatly in their descriptions of her. In some she is a beautiful young girl; in others, a comely matron; and in others still, a screeching, raddled hag.

The notion of the banshee is particular to the Celtic world and must have sprung from a belief in a generalized goddess or a localized family spirit. Such goddesses may have overseen the family's participation in warfare and slaughter and are reflected in the Macha, the Badb, and the Morrigan, the triple Gaelic war goddess. This would reflect the threefold nature of the banshee: the maid, the matron, and the old woman. She is also usually associated with birds such as the scald crow or royston crow and the hooded crow or gray-backed crow. These birds were closely affiliated with death for they were frequently seen on the field following a battle, strutting around like generals and pecking messily at the bodies of the fallen. In Carlow, Wexford, south Wicklow, and south Kildare, the banshee is simply known as *badhbh*—pronounced "bow"— further emphasizing her link with the ancient Celtic triple goddess, while in Kilkenny and south Laois she is referred to as *badhbh chaointe* (pronounced "boheenta")—keening *badhbh*.

The banshee is not always connected with warnings of death. In some very ancient tales she is described as something of a muse, associating with poets, dreamers, and writers. In this incarnation, she also appears to mourn, in poetic verse and in the style of the great Celtic bards, the passing of any mighty leader. This inextricably linked her to the arts and poetry, particularly funerary poetry, of which the early Celtic peoples seem to have been especially fond. In her original incarnation the banshee may have been a mortal woman inspired by the gods or spirits with the power of both poetry and prophesy. The word "intoxicated" may be of some significance here as Queen Madb of Connaught (mentioned in the epic *Tain Bo Cuailnge*—"The Cattle Raid of Cooley") is described as "she who intoxicates," and this may refer to her being a conduit through which the spirits spoke and dispensed prophetic powers or utterances. Indeed, the name "woman of the fairy" may actually refer to the banshee's being a mortal through whom the fairies speak, akin to an oracle.

One of the earliest references to a banshee names her as a mortal called Aoibheall who was the banshee of the royal house of Munster. She also appears in a tale concerning the Battle of Clontarf in 1014 when she was said to have offered the Irish champion Dunlang O'Hartigan, whom she loved, and his sons two hundred years of life if they would put off fighting in the battle. They refused and were all killed, and Aiobheall retreated to Lough Derg where she continually cried for the Gaelic nobles that had fallen at Clontarf. Some versions of the tale suggest the Aoibheall had supernatural powers and strong connections with the sidhe (the fairy kind).

A banshee appeared in Scotland to warn King James I of his impending murder by the earl of Atholl in 1437. She approached the king as he neared St. John's Town (St. Johnston) and shouted to him that if he entered the town he would not live another year. The king was advised to ignore her, as she was drunk. Later that night, she came to his chamber door and asked for admission. When she was refused she issued her prophecy again and departed. In both cases, she is described as a banshee or Irish prophetess, but almost certainly she was a living, mortal woman. Her prophecy soon came true as several months later the king was murdered at Perth by some of his nobles.

Another living banshee was recorded by the nineteenth-century German travel writer Johann Kohl when he visited Ireland in 1842. While in County Clare he was taken to see a woman who could predict death within her own family and sometimes in the wider community as well. He gives her name as Cosideen, and she told him that she was able to see Death leaning on two crutches at the foot of a meadow below her house when any family member was about to die. She had not yet seen her own death, she told him.

In some cases, the prophets who transmitted such arcane knowledge would have been seen as embodiments of the spirits themselves, and over time the banshee took on the folkloric aspect which she enjoys today as the ghostly, wailing prognosticator of approaching death. This transition was probably an extremely gradual one and may have paralleled the slow emergence of a relatively stable Gaelic aristocracy. Over the years she became associated with many of the great Irish families, perhaps becoming the personification of the patron goddess or protecting spirit. It is difficult to establish exactly when this change took place, but it seems reasonable to suppose that the increasing incursions of the English into Ireland placed great stress upon many of the ancient Gaelic families and that they amended their folklore accordingly. The first full English expeditions into Ireland occurred in the mid-twelfth century, when they were invited into the country by Dermot MacMurrough, king of Leinster, and it is possible that the transition in banshee lore may date from then.

The new aspect of the banshee as a foreteller of death and destruction may have developed in the south Leinster area where the seizure of some of the old Gaelic lands by the English authorities during the sixteenth and seventeenth centuries was particularly severe. It is thought that during the Penal times in Ireland, the idea spread into other areas and gradually the image of the keening banshee—crying for the loss of nobility and of land—gained a much wider acceptance. Slowly, too, the idea that she was a protective spirit or goddess attached only to the old Gaelic families—those with an "O'" or "Mac" as prefix to their names—also became much wider, and her predictions of death extended to all the Irish peoples. The belief in the banshee had arrived and has survived in Ireland, and further beyond, in urban as well as rural areas.

In some regions, a curious tradition has been attached to her. It is said that she uses a golden comb to arrange her tangled locks and that if it is stolen, the banshee will take a dreadful, often supernatural, revenge upon the person who steals it. There are many stories from all over Ireland concerning men who have stolen the comb and who have been forced to return it by various means. Sometimes, the comb is pushed out under the door of a house using a pair of coal tongs while the banshee howls and rages outside. The tongs are invariably twisted beyond recognition when they are pulled back in again. Sometimes, they are even broken by the ferocious, otherworldly strength of the spirit. Other traditions associate the banshee with knocks at the door or window or with an unseen phantom coach which is heard to draw up at the house of a person who is about to die. Largely, however, she is either a keening or a singing spirit signaling approaching death.

Variations of the banshee are found outside Ireland in other parts of the Celtic world. In Scotland, she appears in her goddess form as Clotha, the Washer at the Ford, from whom the River Clyde takes its name. This legend evolved from an extremely ancient tradition that the goddess symbolically washed the body armor or even the bodies of those who were about to die in battle. The myth appears in some parts of Ireland too. In one ancient story the great Irish hero Cu Chulainn, the Hound of Ulster, together with some of his warriors, comes across three old women (suggestive of the triple aspects of the goddess of war and slaughter) washing armor at a ford. The three greet Cu Chulainn, who is on his way to a great conflict, as though he were a long-lost friend and hold up a bloody piece of armor which he recognizes as his own. This was taken as a sign that he would not return alive from the battle—and the prediction proved to be true. Washing also plays a significant part in the Breton variation of the banshee, the Midnight Washerwomen. These, according to folklore, are the souls of women who have died unshriven (without their sins formally forgiven by a priest or minister) and who are condemned by *le Bon Dieu* (God) to endlessly wash the grave clothes of those who are to die within the coming year. This is carried out at an isolated part of a river or at a remote pond. Such spirits, it is said, are extremely malignant and will try to trick any passerby into helping them since if someone winds one of the clothes with them and winds it incorrectly, then the Washerwoman is released from her toil into the afterlife and the unfortunate mortal must take her place by the water. The Washerwomen are often heard pounding clothes in remote areas late at night and locals try to avoid passing in that vicinity.

It is not clear how a belief in the banshee arrived in the United States, but it most likely came with Irish immigrants who flooded into America in the years following the Great Irish Potato Famine of 1845-52. This was probably the main source of the stories, but it may not have been the only one. French, Spanish, German, and even Italian immigrants all had their own versions of a death-warning phantom, and these gradually became assimilated into the general tapestry of American folklore. One of the more famous non-Irish versions of the banshee is the Spanish *La Llorona,* or Wailing Woman, who is seen in the Santa Fe area of New Mexico and the San Antonio region of south Texas. There are many tales as to the origin of this woman but a common one is that she was a widow with two small children. She received an offer of marriage from a wealthy rancher but he would not accept her children. Fearful that he would withdraw the marriage offer, the distraught woman murdered both children and concealed their bodies in an irrigation ditch. When she told the rancher that she was now free of the children, he was horrified and refused to have anything more to do with her. She went back to the ditch but the tiny bodies were gone. Ever since, her unquiet spirit has wandered the countryside looking for her children and weeping and wailing at their loss. She is immediately recognizable as she wears a black shawl, which conceals her face, and she is normally stooped over with grief. To see or hear this phantom means death for the individual, turning *La Llorona* into a kind of banshee. It is thought that this legend, which is extremely old, came to America with the early Spanish and that it can be traced to rural Spain. There may be Celtic connections here, too, as early Celts flooded into the Iberian Peninsula to settle. Like the banshee, *La Llorona* may be one of the last vestiges of an ancient Celtic goddess which has been translated into a more modern setting.

The banshee belief, of course, became established in states where many of the Scots-Irish made their homes. In areas such as Kentucky and Georgia, there are stories of a spirit who wails or cries out before someone in the community is about to die. Sometimes it is simply a disembodied voice calling out the name of the individual concerned, while at other times it is a shriek or a wailing scream. In Edgecombe County along the Tar River near Tarboro, North Carolina, stories concerning the banshee are especially plentiful. The region is a swampy one where the river moves sluggishly between banks of reeds and overhanging trees. There was once a large gristmill in the county although all trace of it has long since disappeared. During the Revolutionary War, the Tar River mill was run by David Warner, a staunch Whig who hated the English. He used his mill for the grinding of wheat, and he furnished supplies to the Revolutionary army free of charge and allowed them free use of the mill to grind their own corn. Late into the night, the mill would work supplying the American volunteers in the surrounding area.

One August evening, David Warner stood at the door of his mill taking in the last of the sunshine when a neighbor hurried past. The British were not far behind him, he shouted, and he warned Warner that the British knew him for a rebel and he would be killed. But David Warner did not scare that easily. "I'd rather stay and see a few of the British soldiers in hell!" he retorted. The neighbor looked at him in alarm, questioning his resolve, but stayed on to help with the operation of the mill.

The mill was working at full capacity when the first British troops arrived at its door. Pretending not to see them, David Warner turned to his neighbor: "We'll need to hurry. General Greene is waiting for these supplies, and I wouldn't like them to fall into the hands of those British scum. It'd make my stomach turn to think of those British hogs eating gruel made from American corn!" This was too much for the listening soldiers. They rushed in, seized the miller, and beat him. Warner took the beating with great fortitude. When they saw that their violence was having no effect, the soldiers threatened to drown the miller in the Tar River. Warner only sneered at them, "Do what you want and drown me, but I warn you if you commit a murder here, the banshee will haunt you for the rest of your lives. She lives along the banks of this river where the trees are thickest and on moonlit nights you can see her down by the water's edge washing her hair which falls about her shoulders, and on very still nights you can hear her wail all along the Tar River." The soldiers—three of them—hesitated, clearly rattled by Warner's threat.

They had decided to wait for their commanding officer before taking any action when a tall soldier with evil eyes spoke up. "Are you men or cowards to be frightened by foolish rebel superstitions?" he taunted. "Why wait? We were sent on ahead to make the way safe for the advancing army. If we hold onto this dog he'll not only hold up our mission, which will displease our commander, but he might escape and make trouble for us. I say that we get rid of him now." His argument won the day. Seizing David Warner, the British soldiers bound his hands and feet and, weighting him with a large stone, they carried him to the water's edge. They threw him in and as the body sank out of sight, an ear-piercing shriek rang out from the clay banks of the river—eerie and blood-chilling in the extreme. The soldiers looked at each other in terror. Amongst the reeds and bushes on the other side of the river, they saw a woman with long flowing hair and a long veil over her face. For a second, she stood on the riverbank and then ducked down and was gone amongst the rushes. The soldier with the evil eyes was now too terrified to speak. He simply turned and fled back to the mill.

As dusk began to fall, the British commander and the rest of his troops arrived to make camp near the mill house. They pitched their tents under the trees and near the water's edge, and soon campfires began to glow along that stretch of the Tar River. The moon rose over the river and night birds called from the rushes. Then, over the sounds of the night, rose a high, wailing cry, building to a terrible shriek—the cry of a woman in the agonies of death. The commander and several of his troops rushed to the river to see what the sound might be and soon many others joined them. But the soldier with the evil eyes and the two comrades who had helped him drown the miller stayed where they were, too frightened to move. The commander and his officers saw only large patches of mist moving along the river, one of which seemed to move with a great deal more purpose than the others. Once again, the cry drifted back to them, chilling their blood. They looked again but there was nothing more to be seen. Wonderingly, they returned to camp.

The three soldiers who had drowned the miller were now so terrified that they made a full confession as to what they had done. For such an act, the furious commander declared that they should stay at the mill until he decreed otherwise, grinding corn and listening to the terrible, haunting wail from the river. His troops then broke camp and marched on, leaving the three behind.

During the day, the three soldiers ground grain for the British troops in the region, but at night they were tormented by the banshee's eerie cry drifting up around the mill. Then, one, evening, she came closer, appearing in the doorway as they were finishing work, her flimsy garments billowing around her like a mist and the veil still covering her face. With a fluid motion, she threw back the veil to reveal a face of death to the frightened men. The soldier with the evil eyes cowered in a corner, but the other two rose and, lured by the misty apparition, followed it out into the night. The banshee floated just beyond reach with the two men moving after her, down to the river's edge. There, they stumbled into the water and were never seen again. After that, their evil-eyed comrade lived alone at the mill, but his wits were utterly gone. On many nights, he was to be found wandering in the woods calling the miller's name, but only the cry of the banshee answered him. After several weeks, his body was found floating face downward in the Tar River, at the very place he had drowned the miller.

Many years have passed since those terrible events but the cry of the banshee can still be heard all along the Tar River—an agonizing wail which grows higher and higher and inevitably precedes a death in the area. And it is always accompanied by a mist floating on the surface of the water, gradually taking on the shape of a woman, drifting lazily through the reeds and low-hanging trees that mark the river's edge. It is best not to hear or see it for the death it announces might very well be your own.

The above story concentrates on the typical Irish banshee but since arriving in America, the spirit has undergone many changes. A tale concerning a different type of banshee comes from the very edge of the Smoky Mountains. Will Lyons and his wife, Nell, settled in a small farm in the mountains just inside the Tennessee border from Asheville (the nearest town in North Carolina) during one of the final summers of the 1950s. The area in which they lived was rather remote back then and the roads which led up into the Smokies were poor when the weather was good and downright impassable when the weather was not. Bad roads and bad communication only added to the remoteness of the region. The mountain people usually kept to their mountains and the Asheville folks normally stayed in the town. Not that Will minded, for he and Nell were pretty much self-sufficient. He raised livestock and grew a little tobacco on the mountainside. From time to time, he would take a trip into town for supplies but these were no more than once a month and most of the time, he really had no need to be around townspeople. His next neighbor was Andrew Jeffers, who lived on the other side of the valley. If Will kept to himself, Andrew was almost a recluse. Sometimes, Will saw him around the edge of his property and they might exchange a few words but mostly the two neighbors never saw each other. In fact, Will had never even seen Andrew's wife, Ila, as she kept close to the cabin on the other side of the valley.

Life was pretty good for Will and he was well satisfied with the way things were, until Nell got pregnant. The pregnancy was a difficult one, and it was extremely hard for any nurse or doctor to get up to the Lyons cabin, especially as Nell began to grow big in the fall when the roads were at their worst. Days of almost constant rain had flooded the tracks that led into the Smokies and no doctor or medical man could get through from Asheville. That was not to say, of course, that there was no "medical" practitioner to look after Nell. There was Granny Moss. The notion of the granny was well established all across the mountain country. These women were usually mountain midwives who attended births in the isolated cabins but, in many cases, their medical skills were wider than midwifery. It was believed that through their knowledge of herbs and potions, they could cure fevers and "gripe of the guts" as well as stop bleeding and cure the various assorted afflictions that beset the mountaineers. Often the granny women officiated at death as well, washing and laying out the body and seeing that it was "done proper" before being interred. In the mountain region north of Asheville, Granny Moss was something of a legend. It was said that no other granny woman could heal sickness, banish burns, or stop blood like her. It was said that she could cure a severe stomachache with just a pinch of a special powder which could have a mountaineer up and walking about within the hour. There was no medical miracle that she could not perform. And it was she who walked all the way down from her cabin to tend to Nell Lyons. After a preliminary examination, she pronounced the baby healthy but said that she would look in on the Lyons from time to time when she was in the area. And she returned to the area pretty soon for Andrew Jeffers' wife, Ila, took very sick shortly afterwards. No one knew what kind of ailment had overtaken her—a fever of some sort, some people said—but it was serious enough to confine her to bed and compel Granny Moss to come down from the high hills almost every other day. And she often walked across the valley to see Nell as the time of her confinement drew close.

One morning before Granny arrived, Will walked down to the barn to milk the cows. It was shortly after daybreak and the light was still queer and uncertain. Halfway down the yard, he was surprised to see what he took to be a woman in a long black dress standing in the shadowy doorway of an outhouse watching him. Her features were not visible in the semidarkness of the barn door but he recognized nothing about her appearance or the way she stood there. Will had so few neighbors that he knew every one of them even at a distance, and he certainly did not know the stranger. Maybe, he thought, she was a traveler who had gotten lost in the hills and had come down to his yard seeking help. He walked across to her and asked if he could be of any assistance. She did not answer but turned her head into the darkness of the outbuilding so that, even up close, he could not see her features. At the same time she held out a small cup in front of him. Taken aback, he asked her if she would like some milk, and she thrust the tiny vessel even farther out. He filled it almost to brimming and the woman turned on her heel and went around the corner of the barn without a word of thanks. Will walked to the corner to discern where she had gone but he could not see her at all. There were some bushes and trees at the corner of the yard and he presumed he had missed her as she made her way past. He went back to his work but, try as he might, he could not get the stranger out of his mind. Although he was sure he did not know her, there was something vaguely familiar about her that he could not place, even though he wracked his brains.

That day when Granny Moss came to see Nell, Will made a point of asking the old woman if she knew of any strangers in the area. Granny shook her head and Will told her about his strange early-morning encounter. Granny Moss professed herself just as baffled as he. Nell, however, was progressing well. She was a little sick from time to time but Granny said that was to be expected. The child would be healthy. But Granny was concerned about Ila Jeffers on the other side of the valley. Her condition had grown worse and she had slipped into a kind of coma from which nobody could wake her. Andrew had sent down to Asheville for a doctor, but it was a long way and the lower trails were still flooded after the heavy rains. Granny Moss doubted if any medical man would come so far into the Smoky Mountains at this time. She tended Ila as best she could with herb poultices to draw the fever and special teas to restore vigor but nothing seemed to be working. Andrew was beside himself for he knew that Granny Moss was at the limit of her healing powers. A day later, Will saw his neighbor crossing the valley and shouted to him, but Andrew Jeffers was too far away to hear.

The following morning Will met the strange woman again as he was going down to fetch the cows for milking. She was standing where she had before, in the doorway of the barn, keeping so close to the shadows that he could not see her face. But once again, she held out the cup and once more he fetched her some milk for it. This time, he thought he saw her nod gratefully before she hurried away once more. Going back up to the house, he told Nell about it and she suggested that it might be one of the neighbor girls from somewhere on the other side of the valley whose cow had gone dry. Will was not so sure. He thought the woman looked too old to be a neighbor girl or a milkmaid. The thought of the strange lady dressed in black stayed with Will that day and the next.

Across the valley Ila Jeffers' condition grew steadily worse. She slept without waking and Granny Moss had to force-feed her with herbal teas to keep her alive. In spite of everything the old woman did, she knew that poor Ila was not long for this world. Andrew would often go down to the turn of the road to watch for the doctor coming, but none came. The trails farther south were still impassable for either vehicle or animal, and the high mountain valleys were completely cut off. There was little more that Granny Moss could do for Andrew's wife. Nature must now take its course.

Two days after Will had met the strange woman by the barn, Nell began to take very sick. She had not been feeling well—nausea and little shooting pains—but she had put it down to the approaching birth. Now neither she nor Will were so sure. She began vomiting blood and became so weak that she, too, had to take to her bed. In desperation, Will sent for Granny Moss, telling the old lady to come urgently. By the time Granny Moss arrived, Nell was so flushed and feverish that she could barely talk, but the granny was more concerned about the fate of the unborn baby. She had a feeling deep in her bones that the child would enter the world stillborn. Even so, she said nothing to Will so as not to alarm him unduly. Telling him that she would call back the next day, she went across the valley to see Ila Jeffers.

Over the next couple of days, Nell worsened. Although Granny Moss called by the house several times, there seemed to be nothing she could do to reverse the advance of the ailment. She was very worried about the child. At the start it seemed to have been a lively baby, always kicking and moving in the womb, but there had not been any movement for days and the old lady was worried. However, there was more on Granny's mind. Across the valley, Ila Jeffers had died. She had gone quietly in her sleep and Andrew, riven with grief, had asked for a private service. Will, caught up in troubles of his own, had not gone but had sent his condolences with Granny and a promise to come over and see his neighbor when Nell got better. But she never did. She continued to weaken and the baby inside her moved no more. Granny Moss knew that it was dead; she had attended too many mountain births not to recognize the outcome. She might be able save the mother though. Nell was near her time and Granny knew a certain concoction that would bring on the birth and grant the poor girl release.

The evening before Granny was to induce the birth, Will was

in his yard when he met with the strange woman again. She was standing in the door of the barn but this time as she approached, she slid away into the shadows and was lost. He looked around for her but when he did not find her, he went on about his business. Slightly later, he was milking one of the cows when the animal turned its head, its eyes widening, and looked towards the door of the outhouse. Following her gaze, Will saw the woman in black standing there, looking directly at him. But this time she was not alone. Behind her stood a small girl, also dressed in black. This time, the failing sun caught the side of the older woman's face and he could see it quite distinctly. Although he was sure that he did not know her, there seemed to be something familiar about her. The girl, no more than five or six years old, stayed well back and he could not see what she looked like. Again, the tin cup was held out and again it was filled with fresh, warm milk. Then wordlessly and without thanks of any description, the woman and her young companion turned and walked out of the barn. Will turned back into the house to see to Nell, but he already knew it was too late.

The next day, Granny Moss tried all that she knew to save his wife. Using a combination of herbs she had only employed once before, the old lady tried to bring the child on and so save the mother. It worked for neither of them. The birth occurred—it was to have been a baby girl—but it was born dead and the shock on Nell's system was too much. She followed her daughter a couple of hours later. Will was beside himself with grief, but he managed to bear up and only broke down once as he led the funeral procession for his wife and daughter.

A couple of days after the funeral, he saw the strange couple again; this time, they did not approach him. They were standing in the shadow of a barn looking warily towards the house. Once more he could see the woman's face. It looked unaccountably familiar but the child's face still remained in shadow. They then turned and disappeared around the corner of the barn and were gone. Despite his grief, Will was determined to find out who they were and why the strange woman wanted the milk. He decided to follow them. Hurrying from the house, he rounded the barn corner and glimpsed them both crossing a pasture that lay beyond the trees and bushes at the corner of his yard. Keeping a discrete distance behind, he made his way after them, noting that the pair seemed to glide across the broken ground rather than walk. On they went, through the brush and rocks towards the lower slopes of Big Bear Mountain. Will found it hard to keep up with them but as they joined a small trail along the mountainside, he guessed their destination. The track was one which gravediggers used and at the top of a slope on the side of the mountain was a small community cemetery. For the first time, he began to feel uneasy.

He was surprised to see the old graveyard gate standing half-open. The woman and child walked straight through, the woman pausing only to pull it shut after her. Will thought she would now catch sight of him, but she did not appear to be in the least aware of his presence on the hillside. Turning back, the two of them made their way amongst the upright grave markers, disappearing momentarily behind a large tulip poplar. Will continued to follow, staying several yards behind as the figures made their way towards the very center of the mountain cemetery. There, on the edge of a small grave, the two suddenly and inexplicably disappeared before Will's astonished eyes. It was as though they were both made of smoke that faded and broke up in the sun. They were, he thought, most probably ghosts. Shocked, Will left the graveyard. Trembling, he walked back along the track until a man passing in a wagon gave him a lift home.

He recounted his strange experience to Granny Moss when she called later that day. The old woman furrowed her brow and thought for a moment. She had heard of these mountain wraiths before, she said. They were like the ancient Irish banshees, appearing before death to warn and prophesy. And she had a theory as to who the little girl was. "Maybe she's your daughter, Will, all growed up to a child of five. I heerd about such things up among the people in the high mountains." However, she could not explain why the ghost woman had wanted a cup of milk each time she had come. Such specters, she had heard, only came back for a purpose or to complete unfinished business. "The only thing, Will, is to go up to the gravesite and open it up. Maybe there's some answers there," the old woman advised.

Taking her at her word Will contacted one of his brothers and together, the two men went up to the isolated cemetery on Big Bear Mountain. Will had little difficulty in recognizing the grave because of the tall poplar that grew next to it. The men soon broke the grave earth and dug down until their spades struck the wooden lid of a coffin. The sound evoked a response from inside the box—what sounded like the whimper of a small child. Dragging up the coffin and throwing wide the lid, Will looked down on its occupant—or, more correctly, occupants. There, looking as fresh as when he had first seen her, lay the mysterious woman, only this time she was not dressed in black but in a coarse mountain shroud. In the crook of her arm lay a small baby.

"Lord, Will!" cried his brother. "This here child's alive!" And so it was. Will reached into the coffin and lifted out the child—it was a girl—and, as he did so, his fingers touched a metal cup lying in a corner of the casket, the same cup he had continually filled with milk. After reburying the coffin with due reverence, he brought the child home with him and, as he had no idea who she was, he raised the little girl as his own, a replacement for the child he had lost. She grew to adulthood and although Will never married again, his daughter made his old age very happy.

It was several months before Will journeyed across the valley to pay his respects to his neighbor, Andrew Jeffers. Andrew's daughter, Cindy, had come from West Virginia to look after him, but Andrew had become somber and reclusive and a smile rarely touched his lips. Hearing from Granny Moss that his neighbor was "making heavy weather of it," Will thought he should pay him a visit, the first he had ever paid to the Jeffers house. Andrew greeted him quite civilly and led him into the "good room" that was reserved for visitors. It was not lavishly furnished but there were a few pieces of better furniture there. As he stepped into the room, Will's heart suddenly stopped. There, in a gilt frame was a large photograph of the woman he had seen in his own yard—the woman in black. And, although he had never actually met her, he knew he was looking at the likeness of the dead Ila Jeffers.

Was Ila a kind of banshee? As she lay in a deep coma on the other side of the valley and later in the cold clay of the Big Bear Mountain cemetery, did her spirit venture down to Will Lyons' yard? And was the little girl with her Nell Lyons' stillborn daughter? Had the milk Ila taken sustained the tiny child who lay with her in the coffin? Where had she come from? There are many unanswered questions. Perhaps the story is nothing more than an invention of the mountain people of the Smokies, a tale that has roots in the old Celtic beliefs that came with them to the hills.

Ila Jeffers is not the only banshee-ghost which is seen by rural people. In a certain field in the countryside around Augusta, Georgia, a man is seen working at all times of the day and night. He is plowing the earth with two large horses, but neither they nor the plow leave any trace of his passing. This man is said to be the unquiet spirit of a field worker who died there under mysterious circumstances and his appearance invariably signals a death in the community.

Maybe the banshee visits more places than her native Ireland. Who can say?

Bibliography

Abbot, Olyve Hallmark. *Ghosts in the Graveyard*. Plano: Republic of Texas Press, 2002.

Carmichael, Alexander. *Carmina Gadelica*. Edinburgh: Floris Books, 1997.

Chandler, Genevieve W. "WPA Federal Writers' Project, 1936-1938." Partially reprinted as *Coming Through: Voices of a South Carolina Gullah Community from WPA Oral Histories*. Columbia, SC: University of South Carolina Press, 2009.

Cheung, Theresa. *The Element Encyclopedia of Ghosts and Hauntings*. Element, 2006.

Curran, Bob. *An Encyclopaedia of Celtic Mythology*. Belfast: Appletree, 2000.

———. *The Dark Spirit: Sinister Portraits from Celtic Folklore*. London: Cassell, 2001.

Davies, Owen. *Popular Magic: Cunning Folk in English History*. Humbleton Continuum, 2003.

Drake, Samuel Adams. *New England Legends and Folklore*. Reprint, Victoria: B.C., Castle Books, 1993.

Fanthrope, Lionel, and Patricia Fanthrope. *Unsolved Mysteries of the Sea*. Toronto: Hounslow Books, 2004.

Goodman, Keith. *Haunts of Western Oregon*. Atglen, PA: Schiffer Publishing, 2009.

Hartman, Viola. *The Ghost of Gobbler's Knob and Other Tales of the Hill Country*. Privately printed, 1982.

Holland, Richard. *Bye-gones*. Capel Garmon, Llanrwst: Carreg Gwalch, 1992.

Jameson, W.C. *Buried Treasure of the Ozarks*. Atlanta, GA: August House, 1990.

Kane, Hugh. *Portstewart: The Flood Tide*. Privately printed, 1997.

King, John. *Kingdoms of the Celts*. London: Blandford, 1998.

Looney, Ralph. *Haunted Highways*. Albuquerque: University of New Mexico Press, 1968.

Mackenzie, Alexander. *The Prophesies of the Brahan Seer*. Reprint, London: Constable, 1977.

McNeil, W.K., ed. *Ghost Stories from the American South.* Atlanta, GA: August House, 1985.

Miller, E. Hobson. *Myths, Mysteries and Legends of Alabama.* Birmingham, AL: Seacoast Publishing, 1995.

Montell, William E. *Ghosts Along the Cumberland.* Knoxville: University of Tennessee Press, 1995.

Netty. *Chilling Tales from Derbyshire.* Derby, Derbyshire: Breedon Books, 2009.

Philip, Imbrogno, and Marianne Harrigan. *Celtic Mysteries in New England.* St. Paul, MN: Llewellyn Publications, 2000.

Price, Charles E. *Haints, Boogers and Witches.* Winston-Salem, NC: John F. Blair Publisher, 1995.

———. *The Mystery of Ghostly Vera.* Johnson City, TN: Overmountain Press, 1993.

Rhyne, Nancy. *Coastal Ghosts.* Orangeburg, SC: Sandlapper Publishing, 1985.

Roland, Paul. *The Complete Book of Ghosts.* London: Arcturus Publishing, 2000.

Randolph, Vance. *Ozark Magic and Folklore.* New York: Dover, 2003.

———. P*issing in the Snow and Other Ozark Folktales.* Champagne: University of Illinois Press, 1976.

Robinson, Charles T. *True New England Mysteries, Ghosts, Crimes, and Oddities.* North Attleboro, MA: Covered Bridge Press, 1997.

Russell, Randy, and Janet Barnett. *Mountain Ghost Stories and Curious Tales of Western North Carolina.* Winston-Salem, NC: John F. Blair Publisher, 1998.

———. *The Granny Curse and Other Ghosts and Legends from East Tennessee.* Winston-Salem, NC: John F. Blair Publisher, 1999.

Seymour, St. John D. *True Irish Ghost Stories.* New York: Dover Edition, 2005.

St. Clair, Sheila. *Mysterious Ireland.* London: Robert Hale, 1994.

Steiger, Brad. *Real Ghost, Restless Spirits and Haunted Places.* Visible Ink, 2003.

Thompson, Francis. *The Supernatural Highlands.* Edinburgh: Luath Press, 1997.

Williams, Docia S. *Phantoms of the Plains.* Plano: Republic of Texas Press, 1996.

———. *When Darkness Falls.* Plano: Republic of Texas Press, 1997.

Zepke, Terrance. *Ghosts of the Carolina Coasts.* Florida: Pineapple Press, 1999.

Index

Deacon, Richard, 20
Dean, Harry, 116
death light. *See* corpse candle
Deer Creek, Kansas, 93, 96
demons, 75-77, 82, 88, 94-95, 103, 115-16, 128, 157
dercad (ritual meditation), 140
Derry Standard, 45
Description of the Western Isles of Scotland in 1695, A, 142, 235
DeSoto Falls, 17
Devil fever, 95
Devil House, 94
Devil of Glenluce (poltergeist), 222
Devil, 28, 53, 77, 91-92, 94-98, 116-17, 119, 121, 123-24, 128, 133, 144-45, 148-49, 159, 170-71, 253, 256-58, 262-64, 266, 268, 272
Devil's Tramping Ground, 119-24
Diaz, Melchior, 62
Dimond, John, 148-50, 152
Dimond, Molly. *See* Pitcher, Molly
disembodied forces, 221-22, 226
Dog River, 23
dogs, 253, 256, 262-66, 271-72
Dolwyddelan Castle, 17
Donaghy (Donnelly), J.P., 223-26
Dracula (book), 199
Dracula (character), 202, 209
Drake, Francis, 41
Drake, Samuel Adams, 80, 86, 148, 172
dreams, 59, 66
Druids, 48, 75, 89, 101, 115, 139-41, 169, 187, 202, 261
Ducat, James, 47
Duck River, 17
Dullaghan. *See* headless horseman
Dundermot, 90-92, 100
Dungiven, Northern Ireland, 76
dwarf, 235
Dyer, Mary, 146
Early, Biddy, 128, 143, 154-55
earthworks, 89, 115
East Haddam, Connecticut, 80, 82-86
Edmonson County, Kentucky, 257
Edge, Robert, 84-85
Edison, Mose, 192-98
Edison, Nancy, 194-97
Edison, Rose, 192-98
Egwin, Saint, 112
Eilean Mor, 47
El Castillo, 40
Emmanuel Hill, 95-96, 99-100
Enbharr (mythical horse), 234

Ennishowen, Ireland, 45
Entailed Hat, The, 131
Erie, Lake, 49, 56
Evans, John, 25
Evesham, England, 117
Exorcist, The, 95-96
Eynhallow (island), 27
Fabian, Robert, 117
Fairfield County, Ohio, 192-93, 197
fairies (fays or fees), 76, 87-89, 91, 101, 103, 116, 249-53, 273-74
fairy cloud, 154
fairy doctors, 128, 143, 153-54
fairy forts, 89, 223
fairy rings, 89
Fanning, David, 119
Feakle, Ireland, 155
Felin-y-Wig, Wales, 251
Fenian Cycle, 88
Fennel, Enoch, 106
Fifty Years as a Low Country Witch Doctor, 167
Figgy, Madgy (Madge), 128, 159
Fion MacCumhail (Finn McCool), 88
Fiosaiche, Coinneach Odhar. *See* MacKenzie, Kenneth
Fir Gorta (Man of Hunger), 249-50
Fir Liath. *See* Gray Man
Flannery, Tom, 154
flying saucers, 30
fog, 235, 237, 239
Foras Feasa ar Eireann, 199, 202
Forbes, Josie, 270
foretelling, 141-42, 148, 156
Fort Jackson, South Carolina, 162-63
Fort Mountain, 17
fortresses, 102
forts, 89, 116
Francis de Sales, Saint, 105
Gabriel hounds, 263
Gallagher, Margaret, 253
Gallagher, Pat, 253
Gallic Wars, 48
Garfield, James A., 198
Garry Bog, 91
gateways to hell, 89, 93, 100, 102-3
Gaultier, Pierre, Sieur de la Verendrye, 22
Gehenna, 27
General Grant mining claim, 65
Georgetown, Delaware, 134-35
Gerald of Wales, 169
Geronimo, 65
Ghost Trackers' Newsletter, 99